RUSSIAN WORKERS AND THE SOCIALIST-REVOLUTIONARY PARTY THROUGH THE REVOLUTION OF 1905–07

Russian Workers and the Socialist-Revolutionary Party through the Revolution of 1905–07

Christopher Rice

St. Martin's Press　　　New York

© Christopher Rice, 1988

All rights reserved. For information, write:
Scholarly and Reference Division,
St Martin's Press, Inc., 175 Fifth Avenue, New York, NY 10010

First published in the United States of America in 1988

Printed in Hong Kong

ISBN 0-312-01674-3

Library of Congress Cataloging-in-Publication Data
Rice, Christopher.
Russian workers and the Socialist-Revolutionary Party through the
Revolution of 1905-07/by Christopher Rice.
p.   cm.
Bibliography: p.
Includes index.
ISBN 0-312-01674-3 : $40.00 (est.)
1. Partiia sotsialistov-revoliutsionerov—History.   2. Soviet
Union—History—Revolution of 1905.   3. Labor and laboring classes-
-Soviet Union—Political activity—History.   4. Soviet Union-
-Economic conditions—1861-1917.   5. Soviet Union—Politics and
government—1894-1917.   I. Title.
JN6598.S65R5 1988
324.247'074—dc19   87-30760
                                                                CIP

To Melanie

Contents

List of Tables

List of Maps and Figures

MAPS

FIGURE

Glossary and Abbreviations

GLOSSARY

boevaya druzhina	(local) armed detachment
Boevaya organizatsiya (PSR)	Fighting/Combat organisation of the PSR
guberniya	province
oblast'	region
podraion	sub-district
upolnomochennyi	agent, representative
zemstvo	elective district council in pre-revolutionary Russia

ABBREVIATIONS

ARRU	All-Russian Railway Union
CEHE	*Cambridge Economic History of Europe*
PI	*Partiinye Izvestiya*
PKS	*Politicheskaya katorga i ssylka* (see Appendix)
PSR	Partiya Sotsialistov-revolyutsion-erov (Socialist-Revolutionary Party)
RR	*Revolyutsionnaya Rossiya*
RSDRP	Rossiiskaya Sotsial'-demokratich-eskaya Rabochaya Partiya (Russian Social-Democratic Workers' Party)
ZT	*Znamya Truda*

Acknowledgements

I have accumulated many scholarly debts in the course of the last several years. I would, first of all, like to record my gratitude to the Social Science Research Council (now the Economic and Social Research Council) for providing me with the necessary funds to embark on postgraduate work at the Centre for Russian and East European Studies in Birmingham in 1979, and, especially, for the generous travel grant which enabled me to research in Amsterdam during the summer of 1982. My thanks are due to the staffs of various libraries: to the desk staff of the British Library in London; to Liane Kist and the archivists of the International Institute for Social History, Amsterdam; to Barbara Ronchetti of the Inter-library loans department of Birmingham University library and, most of all, to Jenny Brine, librarian of the Baykov library, CREES, whose patience, kindness and expertise greatly expedited my research. I would like to express my warm appreciation of help received from various quarters in Amsterdam. Leo van Rossum and Marc Jansen greatly facilitated my investigation of the *Narodnicheskoe dvizhenie* archive by offering me every assistance and encouragement. Dr Boris Sapir was kind enough to share some fascinating reminiscences of the Russian revolution with me and also helped me to decipher one or two awkward manuscripts. I am grateful to a number of other scholars for their help and advice. Geoff Swain, of Bristol Polytechnic, provided me with invaluable information on the sources for the Petersburg legal labour movement and kindly made available to me the manuscript of his book on that subject. Manfred Hildermeier, then of the Free University, Berlin, and now of the University of Gottingen, and Bob McKean of Stirling University read parts of the thesis in draft and offered a number of valuable criticisms, comments and suggestions. I owe a special debt of gratitude to Maureen Perrie, who not only suggested the subject of this work but also supervised it throughout. She has been unstintingly generous with her time and expertise and has offered me much encouragement and sound advice. The better parts of the thesis best reflect her contribution. I would also like to thank Bob Davies for initially proposing my thesis for publication and for overseeing its preparation. The greatest debt of all however rests with my own family. My children, Catherine and Alex, have had to put up with a domestic routine increasingly geared to suit my own selfish requirements, while my wife, Melanie, has had to make even greater sacrifices. Since persuading me to resume my studies in the first place, however, she has given me constant encouragement and support. She has been responsible for typing the entire manuscript (twice, under the most difficult circumstances) and has also found time to comment on the style of every draft chapter. She has borne the many stresses and strains of the last few years with great patience. It is no exaggeration to say that without her this work would never have been written; so, with all its imperfections, it is to her that I dedicate it.

CHRISTOPHER RICE

Introduction

For a long time, the Socialist-Revolutionary Party (PSR) appeared destined for the oblivion to which Soviet historiography had consigned it, following the humiliations and defeats of 1917 and the subsequent failure of attempts to reverse the tide of history and remove the Bolsheviks from power. More recently, however, interest in the party has revived, particularly, though not exclusively, among Western scholars. Two major works, Maureen Perrie's investigation into the social composition of the party and its activities among the peasantry[1] and Manfred Hildermeier's definitive history of the pre-war movement,[2] while by no means neglecting the actors at the centre of the stage, have tended to shift the focus back to the party's relationship with the working masses. In the course of their research, both authors independently made the significant discovery that the PSR, the 'party of the peasant interest', drew proportionately more of its active support from workers than from any other segment of the population. This paradox formed the starting point for my own study of the PSR which, drawing extensively on previously unpublished archival material as well as newspapers, journals and biographical data, traces the history of the party's urban wing through the revolution of 1905–7 and beyond.[3] In the process, the validity of a number of assumptions and generalisations about the party are challenged, while support for the PSR is revealed as having been more widespread, occupationally diversified and politically significant than many had previously thought. The evidence also serves to highlight the extent to which the Russian working class continued to retain socio-cultural and often economic links with the countryside in the decade before 1914.

The SRs embarked on their mission at a time when Russia was experiencing the varied tensions and upheavals associated with modernisation;[4] indeed the party was itself, in a sense, both a product of, and a response to the dislocations and challenges inherent in that

1

process. The accelerated industrialisation of the 1890s brought with it
(among other things) a corresponding growth in employment opportunities and a remarkable increase in social mobility, fostered by major
improvements in communications. The slender ranks of the industrial
proletariat were swollen by wave after wave of raw peasant recruits
–many of whom, though employed year-round in the factories,
continued to retain rural ties of one kind or another. This vast
migration aggravated social differentiation in the countryside while at
the same time assisting the transmission of urban values, culture and
expectations far beyond the confines of the cities themselves. Rapid
improvement in the standards of literacy, especially among the
peasant masses, presented the regime with new problems and
challenges. In the years before 1905, the government came under
increasing pressure, from the radical intelligentsia and *zemstvo*
nobility in particular, to bring the political system into line with these
momentous changes and thereby achieve the long-awaited reconcilia-
tion between State and society. However, it took the revolution of that
year finally to compel the autocracy to move part of the way, at least,
in the direction of fundamental reform. Despite subsequent rear-
guard action by the ruling classes to contain the processes of
modernisation, the following decade saw the establishment of
parliamentary institutions, a representative electoral system (albeit on
an extremely narrow franchise), legalised political parties, a growth in
the number of interest groups, the advent of public opinion as a
pressurising instrument and a general increase in social interaction. At
the same time, however, the upheavals generated by modernisation
were exacerbated by the deeply ambiguous and often obstructive State
response to further change; by tensions resulting from the uneven
spread of industrial and economic development and by commitments
in the sphere of foreign policy which led ultimately to the cataclysmic
events of 1914–17 and to the intolerable strains which these events
imposed on the country's social, economic and industrial fabric.
Revolution was at this point the almost inevitable outcome.

Firmly rooted in the populism of the 1860s and 1870s, the PSR had
been formed at the turn of the century with the aim of overthrowing
the existing social and political order in Russia. Of necessity a
conspiratorial organisation, led predominantly by students and
intellectuals, the party was, none the less, fully aware that it could not
achieve its goals without mass support. Unlike the Social Democrats,
the Socialist-Revolutionaries saw the middle and poor peasantry, as
well as the urban proletariat, as the harbingers of a new, socialist

order. Counsels remained divided, however, on the relative weight to be attached to propaganda and agitational activity in the urban and rural sectors. The agrarian disturbances of 1902 aggravated rather than resolved this dilemma. While the party's orientation veered even closer toward the peasantry, its organisational roots were, paradoxically, being laid among the workers of the urban centres. During the revolution of 1905–7, the PSR rapidly expanded its influence and activities among workers and peasants alike, but was still far too weak to co-ordinate successfully the movement in town and countryside. In the course of the Reaction, the urban organisations disintegrated under the pressure of persecution, but it was the viability of the agrarian programme and the docility of the peasantry which caused the party gravest concern in the years leading up to the war.

The considerable popularity enjoyed by the PSR, the party of the peasant interest, in Russia's urban and industrial centres during 1905–7, and its ability to turn at least some of that popularity into organised support, suggests the importance of the peasant-worker as a revolutionary actor in his own right. That subject is a major concern of this study. More broadly, we examine the nature of SR activity in the urban and industrial centres, the social location of the party's support, its organisational structure and overall relationship with the working population. Inevitably, frequent comparisons are made with the Social Democrats in all these respects. The somewhat eccentric lay-out was, to a large extent, dictated by the availability of source material, which also imposed the choice of case studies and organisational profiles. Apart from archival material located in the International Institute for Social History in Amsterdam, greatest reliance was placed on the party press. The term 'working class' is used in its widest sense, to include seasonal migrants, artisans and service-sector employees as well as factory workers – both proletarians and workers with ongoing ties in the countryside. Dates (unless otherwise stated) are in the old style, following the Julian calendar. All names have been transliterated directly from the Russian, except where convention dictates otherwise.

1 The Social and Industrial Context: Post-Reform Russia, c. 1861–1910

THE DRIVE TO INDUSTRIALISE[1]

Russia's humiliating defeat in the Crimean War of 1854–6 conclusively revealed to her leaders the extent of the country's backwardness and the urgent need to introduce at least a measure of innovation into the economic and social structure. Consequently reforms in the judicial system, the military, local government and agriculture (culminating in the abolition of serfdom) followed hard on the heels of that defeat.

Controversy has centred on whether and to what extent peasant emancipation can be considered a 'prerequisite' for the subsequent acceleration of Russian industrialisation. Alexander Gerschenkron argued that the emancipation decree contained negative as well as positive features for industrialisation.[2] On the plus side, redemption payments and other tax burdens compelled the peasant to acquire cash earnings, thereby encouraging an increase in the sale of crops and a readiness to undertake wage work in industry where it was available. At the same time, redistribution in favour of the large estates also tended to promote increases in the share of marketable agricultural produce, contributing both to the feeding of an expanding urban population and to the strengthening of the country's balance of payments. Finally, the decisive blow struck by the decree against 'feudal' relations in the Russian countryside removed a formidable psychological barrier obstructing modernisation along Western lines.

The negative features of the emancipation decree, according to Gerschenkron, stem from the preservation of the communal ordering of the land. The *obschchina*, he argues, continued to militate against technical improvements by rigidly dictating the crop-growing cycle and by being slow to respond to change. The land continued to be subdivided into tiny and widely-dispersed economic units subject to periodic re-allocation, another factor working against innovation. The communal authorities retained responsibility for collecting taxes and were empowered to withhold or withdraw the internal passport essential for working in the city. Finally, the patriarchal family structure tended to act as an additional drag on labour mobility: heads of household could, on their own initiative, demand the confiscation of a passport if a member of the family failed to fulfil his obligations.

Certainly, Russian agricultural relations were not ideally geared to promoting industrialisation, even after 1861. On the other hand, as a number of scholars have pointed out,[3] there has been a tendency to over-emphasise the 'negative' features of the emancipation decree, particularly in the area of the labour market. It has been pointed out, for example, that when measures were introduced to abolish collective responsibility for taxes and make communal land tenure optional in the early years of the present century, these did not result in any wholesale departure to the cities. In any case, periodic land redistribution was no longer universal and even where it was still practised, was often little more than a formality. Furthermore, according to Olga Crisp, even before the Stolypin era the existence of the commune did not necessarily militate against those wishing to sell their allotments and take up industrial or commercial occupations; in cases where the land was of reasonably good quality there was no lack of suitable lessees willing to assume the previous owner's redemption and tax obligations. Indeed, rather than agricultural relations operating against the industrial labour market, there was a more or less permanent labour reserve over and above any cyclical rise in demand (a phenomenon known as 'hidden unemployment of expansion').

Recent research has also highlighted the continuity factor in Russian industrialisation. For over half a century before 1861 for example,[4] industries in the consumer-goods sector, such as cotton-spinning and sugar beet, had made considerable progress by using a hired labour force and an appreciable input of modern machinery. Even in heavy industry there were important, if regionally restricted, developments – production for the defence ministry in Petersburg or mining and machine-building in Poland. Of all factories in existence in 1903, fully one-seventh had been founded prior to emancipation, creating small but valuable cadres of skilled workers and contributing to the accumulation of industrial know-how and experience.

A much less ambiguous factor than the emancipation in promoting Russian industrialisation was the remarkable expansion of the railway network, again primarily in response to inadequacies revealed by the Crimean War. Between 1862 and 1878 the length of track increased from a mere 3516 kms to over 22 371 kms.[5] Railway building boosted the construction industry, opened up new markets for the export of grain and sugar crops, provided a lucrative and reliable source of contracts for nascent heavy industry and encouraged urbanisation. Last but not least, the railway quickly became one of Russia's major employers, providing jobs for over 800 000 workers by 1913.[6]

Despite significant progress in the two decades immediately following emancipation, Russian industry remained something of a fragile flower, partly because the government was not yet committed to extending its whole-hearted support. Developments prior to 1885 are therefore perhaps best summarised in the tempered language of Olga Crisp:

> What was happening in Russia in particular up to the mid-1880s was a gradual erosion of the subsistence economy, which took the form of increased marketability of agriculture, of land becoming a commodity (though peasant allotment land was not in this category until 1906), of an increasing variety of cash earning activities in construction, carting, hawking, river transport, domestic and other services, and finally increasing industrial work as kustars or factory labourers.[7]

The 'take-off' phase of Russian industrialisation is customarily associated with the name of Sergei Witte, minister of finance from 1892–1903, though many elements of the Witte strategy are already apparent in the policies of his predecessor, Vishnegradskii (1887–92).[8]

At the heart of the Witte 'system' was an attempt to create favourable trade balances by forcing increases in grain exports. By the time of his dismissal 15 per cent of Russia's grain crop was exported, three times the amount under Reutern, minister of finance under Alexander II.[9] While implying real hardship for the mass of the population (as the famine of 1891 forcefully demonstrated) and thereby courting the danger of serious social disorder and unrest, grain exports on the required scale did create the possibility of deficit financing in the form of larger and cheaper loans than previously possible, a development furthur encouraged by the government's stabilising of the currency and adoption of the gold standard. At the same time the weight of the taxation system was shifted away from direct taxes towards taxes on consumption. There has been some debate about the extent to which this development too meant exploitation of the peasantry; certainly it did nothing to ameliorate their lot. From the government's point of view, however, the changes were necessary and beneficial, producing a doubling of revenue in the course of Witte's term of office.[10]

The State played an energetic role in promoting industrialisation. Loans negotiated on domestic as well as foreign markets were used to prime the industrial sector. Between 1893 and 1900 a total of 2800m. roubles was injected into the Russian money market directly by agency of the government. The great majority of this went to finance the huge expansion of the railway network.[11] In addition to the stimulus received from railway constuction, domestic industry was further assisted by the imposition of high tariffs, by reductions in long-haul freight costs and by the channelling of orders towards native industrial concerns. In addition, unprecedented levels of foreign investment in Russian industry were tolerated, indeed encouraged (especially in the new growth regions of the Donbass and the Caucasus). This in turn led to the training of native personnel, helped foster domestic entrepreneurship and improved the wage and skill levels of the home-grown labour force.[12] The rapidly expanding banking system served as an additional support for industrialisation. Finally, an extended period of peace removed a source of serious strain on government expenditure which had proved disastrous in the past. In fact defence, which had claimed somewhere in the region of half the government's income before the Witte era, was reduced to well under 25 per cent in 1895.[13]

In economic terms at least, the results of 'forced industrialisation' were nothing short of spectacular, making for an annual growth rate of around 8 per cent per annum over the decade.[14] The value of the total industrial output increased from 1500m. roubles (1890) to 3400m. in 1900 and the number of factory workers rose from 1.4m. to 2.4m. during the same period.[15] There were impressive increases in production in all major sectors of industry; mining and metallurgy, metal manufacturing, oil, textiles, and so on.[16] The populations of the major industrial centres climbed sharply, as did the overall population (at an average rate of 1.5 per cent annually).[17] By 1900 the prognosis of the sceptics to the effect that Russian capitalism was an artifical bloom doomed to wither seemed to have proved unfounded as markets for industry continued to materialise. According to the Soviet economist Lyashchenko, railway construction alone accounted for almost the entire domestic output of pig-iron and steel in some years, as well as for huge quantities of bricks, cement, lumber and fuel. Capitalist industry itself provided another important market, in the form of new plant and means of production, while domestic consumption (agricultural equipment, roofing iron, household appliances and so on) accounted for much of the ferrous metal surplus. Textiles too relied almost exclusively on the domestic market.[18]

Spectacular though Witte's achievements were, progress of the order and on the scale just described could not be sustained indefinitely. The European financial crash which occured at the turn of the century brought crisis on his system and demonstrated just how closely Russia's fortunes had become bound up with the fate of foreign capital. In any event, there were limits below which peasant consumption levels simply could not be depressed, while adventurist elements in government and administration had further endangered Witte's policies by becoming increasingly insistent on a more vigorous and expansionist foreign policy.[19] In fact, Russia was now to experience all the social dislocations and tensions which represented the reverse side of the coin of rapid modernisation, a process which would culminate in war and revolution.

COMPOSITION AND CHARACTERISTICS OF RUSSIA'S URBAN WORKING CLASS

Size and Distribution

Between 1863 and 1913 Russia's urban population climbed at twice the rate prevailing in the country as a whole, yet even on the eve of the First World War town-dwellers represented only a little over 13 per cent of the total inhabitants.[20] During the same period, the number of factory workers increased fourfold, the number of artisans by nearly the same amount. In 1913 hired workers were distributed as in Table 1.1.[21] The remainder (8 500 000, or 48 per cent of the total) comprised agricultural labourers, unskilled or day-worker/apprentices, domestic servants and minor officials.

The major sectors within factory industry were textile manufacturing, metal processing, mining and extracting, and food, each of which employed between 400 000 and 900 000 workers.[22] The industrial

Table 1.1   Distribution of Russia's hired labour force, 1913

Sector	No. of hired workers	Percentage of the total
Factories and mines	3 350 000	18.8
Non-factory manufacturing	3 000 000	16.8
Construction	1 500 000	8.4
Transport and communications	1 400 000	7.9

labour force was concentrated in half a dozen major regions: Tsarist Poland; the Baltic (including the cities of Petersburg and Riga); the Central Industrial District (the wheel of provinces surrounding Moscow); the Donbass/Southern Ukraine (encompassing Ekaterinoslav, Lugansk, Rostov and Kharkov); the Urals and the Caucasus (centring on the oil city of Baku).

Women comprised about 15 per cent of all industrial workers in 1897 and nearly 27 per cent in 1914. They were most strongly represented in the tobacco (61.3 per cent), textiles (41.4 per cent), chemical (26 per cent) and clothing (21.3 per cent) industries.[23]

Children, and juveniles under seventeen years of age, accounted for 11.2 per cent of the total workforce in 1897 and were employed mainly in the printing, tobacco and wood industries,[24] though a Moscow *guberniya* survey in 1908 revealed 26.8 per cent of metalworkers and 33.6 per cent of cotton-workers to be under sixteen years of age.[25]

Social Composition and Characteristics

By the turn of the century, Russia's rapidly growing industrial centres were spilling over with huge populations of transient or recently settled migrants from the countryside.[26] In Petersburg, as late as 1910 only 24.7 per cent of those classifying themselves as peasants and 32 per cent of the population as a whole had been born in the city, while of those born beyond its confines, 41.5 per cent had lived there five years or less.[27] The annual influx of migrants leapt from an average of 30 000–35 000 in the early years of the century to 75 000 in 1912 and over 96 000 in 1913.[28] The share of migrants in the total population was similar in Moscow,[29] while some urban centres showed in-flow levels little short of astonishing: in Baku, for example, only 32 per cent of workers in 1913 had lived in the city more than five years.[30] Other areas of high migration included the Donbass and Southern Ukraine.[31]

The largest proportion of emigrants originated from the Central Industrial District and the northern provinces. Here there was already a tradition of factory and rural handicraft (*kustar*) work which helped gear the local peasantry for the exacting requirements of urban industry.[32] By contrast, where that tradition was weak, in the primarily agricultural south-west and the central black earth regions, for example, emigration levels also tended to be relatively low. If the 'cadre' proletariat (workers reliant solely on wage work and fully committed to factory life) accounted for only a relatively small proportion of industrial workers on the eve of the First World War – one estimate has suggested that not more than one-third of the factory labour force had severed all connections with agriculture by 1913[33] – the statistical evidence, at least, forcefully suggests that the ties of migrant workers with the rural community were slowly being eroded, thus facilitating their assimilation into the urban and industrial environments.

The increasing tendency for mechanised factories to demand a year-round labour force (in order to maximise cost-effectiveness) was one factor tending to discourage short-stay migration. As early as 1900, approximately 89 per cent of Petersburg metal workers and 83.5 per cent of those in textiles were 'permanent' workers in this sense.[34] In Moscow by 1908 the proportion of year-round workers was even higher.[35] There were, however, considerable regional variations. Evidence collated between 1886 and 1893 revealed that, while permanent workers represented about 80 per cent of industrial employees in the two capitals, Warsaw, Piotrkow (Poland), and Vladimir, they accounted for only 48.7 per cent of the total in Khar'kov province, 42.5 per cent in Kiev and 23.7 per cent in Voronezh.[36]

Other gauges of proletarianisation also revolve around the migrant's continuing connections with the land. Land-ownership statistics display wide variations, as one might expect. A survey conducted in 1901 at the Baltic shipyard in Petersburg, revealed that 47 per cent of workers of the peasant *soslovie* (estate) did not hold a *nadel* (allotment) in the countryside.[37] On the other hand, an investigation into the Petersburg cotton industry during the same period suggested that only 35 per cent of workers had ceased to own

Table 1.2   Workers without land on the eve of the Revolution

Province	Percentage of workers no longer holding land on the eve of the revolution
Yaroslavl'	85.1
Petersburg	83.5*
Saratov	70.4
Ivanovo-Voznesensk	64.3
Moscow City	60.2
Ryazan'	52.8
Average for 31 provinces	68.3*

*Rashin, *Formirovanie*, p. 575, table 143. This survey was conducted in the Autumn of 1918, a time when many peasant workers, especially in Petrograd, had left for the countryside, thus tending to inflate the proportion of workers claiming to own no land.

land.[38] Similar surveys showed a greater propensity for single workers to maintain direct land ties than married workers.[39] A survey of landholding before the revolution, undertaken in 1918 and covering only a third of the total factory labour force, nevertheless makes clear the large regional fluctuations which still existed (Table 1.2).

As far as individual industries were concerned, landholding was confined to 24.1 per cent of workers in machine and instrument production, 29.3 per cent in metal manufacturing, 33.6 per cent in cotton textiles and 44.4 per cent in mining.[40]

Even in cases where workers continued to hold an allotment they did not necessarily engage in farming themselves, but relied on relatives, friends or hired labourers to tend the land for them. The 1918 census, for example, revealed that only 7.9 per cent of the surveyed Petersburg workers either engaged in farm work themselves or with the assistance of their families. The corresponding figure for Moscow city was 22.8 per cent, for Ivanovo 22.6 per cent, for Saratov 19 per cent and for Ryazan' 35.6 per cent.[41] In a survey of mainly skilled Petersburg workers conducted by S. N. Prokopovich in 1908, 50 per cent of single workers and 33 per cent of married workers owned land, but only 33 per cent and 12 per cent respectively farmed it themselves.[42] In return for help with looking after the land (or merely from a sense of filial obligation) workers were expected to send a substantial proportion of their income back home, together with the occasional gift. In some cases money was handed over only to ensure that the vital passport was not withdrawn.[43] Evidence of money sent by workers to relatives in the countryside is not, therefore, the best measurement of a worker's attachment to his place of origin.

By the time of the 1905 revolution a considerable proportion of migrants were already treading in the footsteps of their parents. This does not necessarily mean that all such 'hereditary' workers were born and resided permanently in the city. It does nevertheless suggest a growing familiarity with urban surroundings, culture and work patterns. In Moscow in 1908, 54 per cent of male metalworkers and 43 per cent of textile-workers were second generation;[44] evidence from Petersburg is broadly consistent with these findings.[45] On a more general level, L. M. Ivanov used the 1929 census to show that 58 per cent of workers beginning their industrial experience prior to 1905 came from working-class families and 59 per cent of those of the 1906–13 generation.[46]

Many workers who were not city-born and whose parents may not have been workers nevertheless managed to accumulate many years' experience at the same factory. Data from the giant Prokhorov-Trekh-gornaya mill in Moscow, for example, reveals that the number of workers with at least five years' experience increased from 28 per cent in 1905 to 48 per cent in 1914.[47] At the Tsindel' mill (also in Moscow), the average length of service was 5.4 years in 1904–5; at the Sormovo engineering works (Nizhnii-Novgorod) it was four years; 22 per cent of workers in the Baku oil industry had at least five years' work experience; and in Petersburg, 46 per cent of those employed at the Treugol'nik rubber plant and 25 per cent of workers at the Putilov works had served at least ten years.[48]

All the evidence produced above testifies to the slow but steady growth of a cadre proletariat. Steve Smith has suggested that perhaps 50 per cent of Petersburg's industrial labour force belonged to this category by 1914.[49] The Polish cities of Łódź and Piotrkow and the Russian engineering centre of Riga were also relatively proletaria-nised by the time of the First World War. Notwithstanding the fact that these are exceptional examples, there can be no denying that they reflected a trend. Statistical evidence alone, of course, provides no more than clues about workers' behaviour, aspirations, cultural leanings and political attitudes. However, historical research has confirmed that cadre workers came to share an outlook quite distinct from that of the peasant-worker, let alone the seasonal migrant worker.[50]

The cadre proletarian, like the artisan, lived permanently with his wife and family in the city. Brought up in an urban environment, he had been able to avail himself of opportunities often denied his peasant counterpart. Attendance at a trade school and/or a factory apprenticeship provided specialised training in skills which attracted high wages in industries such as metalworking and printing. Part of the 'labour aristocracy', skilled cadre workers came to look down on less urbanised hands from other factories. It was not only skilled workers: Aleksei Buzinov, employed in the forge of the Nevskii shipbuilding factory in Petersburg reacted disdainfully towards peasant-workers in the neighbouring textile mills and cardboard and stearin factories before realising, to his discomfort, that there was a more exalted hierarchy within his own place of work which divided the skilled elite from middle-of-the-road workers like himself:

> Soon I began to feel … that workers in the mechanical shop – tool workers and fitters – also looked down on me. After this the humble station of workers in the 'hot' shop struck me clearly … I also saw that, alongside an experienced foundryman even a shabby toolworker seemed an educated and thinking person.[51]

Loyalties were first of all directed not to the enterprise as a whole, but to the particular shop (*tsekh*) where the worker was employed. In this sense the social hierarchy of the factory tended to act as an impediment to the development of proletarian consciousness.[52] Nevertheless, to the extent that cadre workers did take a leading part in revolutionary politics their interests were obviously urban-orientated.

If the cadre proleterian represents one end of the working-class spectrum and the seasonal migrant the other, there were infinite gradations in between.[53] As we noted earlier, even in an advanced industrial centre like Petersburg the cadre proletariat accounted for little more than half the industrial workforce in 1914. The bulk of the remainder were what might be termed peasant workers in transition: factory or shop-based, year-round workers who had nevertheless not cast themselves adrift from their rural moorings. As it was to these workers that the PSR primarily addressed its message and among whom it recruited the major portion of its support, it seems appropriate to dwell a little on their experience, within the overall context of the migration process itself.

Recent research on Russian rural–urban migration has revealed striking similarities with the experience of other industrialising societies in nineteenth-century Europe as well as in the contemporary Third World.[54] It has recently been contended that the motor primarily responsible for generating migration of this kind was not so much over-population or crushing poverty, although these were surely pertinent factors, but more the desire for economic and social self-betterment. Observers touring Russia's Central Industrial District towards the end of the last century noted how peasant youths pressured their parents into allowing them to look for work in the city, and how they returned affecting urban manners and style of dress, at pains to emphasise the distinctions between themselves and those 'grey' peasants who had not undergone the experience.[55] In truth, urban life, with all its attendant hardships, compared very favourably with the stifling dullness and lack of opportunity typical of the average village; and even an unskilled worker could command higher wages in a large industrial centre like Petersburg than in the provinces.[56] Not surprisingly, migration was most favoured by the young – youths from Kaluga province were commonplace in the crowded tenements of Petersburg's Narva district, for example;[57] while apprentices at some factories (the Guzhon metalworks in Moscow, for instance) were sometimes taken on even earlier.[58] Women as well as men (though in smaller numbers) responded to the call of the big cities, but they tended to enter different industries and occupations. The majority of migrants were single and travelled alone: married workers generally left their families in the care of relatives in the village.[59]

Early encounters with the city were sometimes disconcerting for the uninitiated or unprepared. Witness the recollections of A. M. Buiko, a migrant worker from Vil'no province:

> For a long time the city overwhelmed me with its size and noise, with its to-ings and fro-ings and its masses of people. In my home village I knew everyone personally; the crowds in the capital were strangers, indifferent people speaking to no-one, each occupied with his own affairs, hurrying somewhere or other.[60]

This sort of evidence has sometimes been produced to attest to the likely political volatility of the migrant worker wrenched, so it is argued, from his preferred surroundings by the demands of grinding poverty and unable to adjust to his new environment.[61] This picture considerably exaggerates the impact of migration however, at least so far as the workers' political behaviour is concerned. On the contrary, employers sometimes testified to the reliability of migrant labour.[62] Pressure to earn enough to keep not only the worker himself, but also to contribute to the income of relatives and dependants in the countryside, was often enough to promote conformity.

Workers from provinces with high emigration levels also benefited from *zemlyachestvo* (the extensive network of ties between fellow-home-landers temporarily resident in the city).[63] *Zemlyachestvo* considerably eased the transition between field and factory and mitigated feelings of alienation. It functioned on any number of levels and its pervasiveness tended to vary from one rural community to the next. At the most basic level, it was common for a worker to be offered accommodation from fellow-*zemlyaki* on his arrival in the city. In exceptional cases this even became a permanent arrangement: Kabo cites the metalworker from the Guzhon factory who arrived in Moscow from Vladimir province at the age of twelve, stayed with relatives and was still living in the same apartment well over twenty years later.[64] Migrants generally resided in the same tenement blocks and neighbourhoods as fellow-homelanders. In the third Narva precinct of Petersburg, for example, 70 per cent of workers in one apartment building were from just two provinces, Pskov and Smolensk.[65] In Moscow, peasants from Kaluga province were concentrated in the Lefortovo district of the city.[66] Similar migrant clustering has been noted in the cases of nineteenth-century Paris and Milan and in modern-day Cairo.

The *zemlyachestvo* system also played an important part in finding jobs for newly-arriving migrants. In some factories, management relied directly on foremen to recommend reliable and trustworthy employees from their native district, while in other cases a fellow *zemlyak* might put in a good word for a prospective recruit who would meanwhile 'tread water' in some other urban occupation.[67]

Inside the factory, *zemlyachestvo* placement tended to result in the concentration of rural neighbours in the same workshop or section. At the Tsindel' cotton mill in Moscow, for example, 22.5 per cent of workers (1891) originated in the same county of Ryazan' province.[68] At the Baltic shipbuilding plant in Petersburg at the turn of the century almost all workers employed in the shipwrights' shop were natives of Staritskii *uezd*, also in Tver' province (Tver' provided the largest number of migrants to the capital).[69] This trend was reinforced by the custom for a particular village or district to specialise in a particular skill – Kimry village in bootmaking, for example. Peasants from Kimry were closely associated with the development of the Petersburg Shoe Factory.

If workers from the same homeland worked together and lived as neighbours, one might also expect them to socialise together. Sure enough, like the modern Cairo coffee shop, the inns of Moscow, Petersburg and elsewhere were often places of association more or less reserved for fellow *zemlyaki*. *Zemlyachestvo* also had a role to play outside factory industry. Building workers, for example, were traditionally organised into teams (*arteli*) by a local contractor (*podryadchik*). As a result, urban construction gangs tended to come from the same rural district and were often friends and relatives. Finally, one might note the tendency for fellow-homelanders to combine in defence of their working interests. Two recent historians of the Moscow labour movement have provided substantial evidence of *zemlyak* ties among strikers, both before and during the 1917 revolution.[70] Clearly then, *zemlyachestvo* was important in influencing workers' attitudes, life-patterns and behaviour. It might also be argued that it encouraged the preservation of ties with the land and partially insulated peasant workers from urban acculturation, hence protracting the process of proletarianisation.[71]

Zemlyachestvo aside, one must also remember that at the turn of the century more than half of Russia's industrial plant and 58 per cent of the labour force was located in the countryside,[72] and that many 'urban' factory-settlements were sited on the fringes of towns and cities and were semi-rural in character. Take the Shlissel'burg suburb of Petersburg, for example. This, the home of one of the city's largest metalworking factories, was situated far from the city centre and was further isolated by the cost and inefficiency of the public transport system. Consequently, local workers rarely ventured outside the settlement or the adjoining Nevskii district. Such circumstances certainly had an impact on the mentality of factory employees, even those with long industrial service:

the Obukhov factory was situated twelve versts from town on the Shlissel'burg Highway. Workers at the Obukhov plant were frequently recruited from among the peasants of the surrounding countryside; they often had their own cottage (*domik*) with kitchen-garden, or hired rooms and apartments in the houses of half-peasant, half-worker 'proprietors'. This left a special impression on the psychology of Obukhov workers.

While this Social Democrat observer drew a distinction between the Obukhov employees, who were often firmly tied to the factory, and the local textile workers who retained the mentality of the 'grey village', he acknowledged that they were 'surrounded by countryside ... lived in close proximity to the suburban peasants and ... had a good understanding of the peasant psychology and of peasant needs'.[73]

2 A New Party and a New Programme

THE FORMATION OF THE PSR, 1891–1901

It is generally accepted that the main stimulus to the revival of populism, which had fallen into abeyance following the assassination of Alexander II, came in the shocking form of the famine of 1891 and the subsequent cholera epidemic.[1] Even before this calamitous event, however, a new generation of *raznochintsy* intellectuals were turning their attention once again to the plight of the Russian peasant. This revival of interest assumed legal and illegal forms. On the one hand there was a second, but more practical, 'going to the people', with young students joining the ranks of the rural *zemstva* and serving as doctors, teachers, lawyers and agronomists;[2] on the other there was a growing proliferation of populist circles in the towns. The movement was strengthened in the mid-1890s with the return from exile of veteran *narodniks* of an earlier generation, including the celebrated 'grandmother of the Russian revolution', E. E. Breshko-Breshkovskaya,[3] P. F. Nikolaev and V. A. Balmashev. These respected figures returned to active service in the movement and were invaluable in stirring up enthusiasm and in co-ordinating the activities of an as yet inchoate assortment of isolated groups.

By about 1895 most populist circles had ceased to refer to themselves officially as *narodniki* or *narodovoltsy* but were instead adopting the title 'Socialist-Revolutionary'. This new nomenclature served to distance them both from the purely terrorist connotations associated with the now defunct People's Will, as well as from the Social Democrat 'economists', who were abandoning the political activity implicit in revolutionary Marxism and concentrating on improving the material lot of the working class. The new 'SRs' referred disdainfully to the economists as 'social-evolutionists' and re-affirmed their own commitment to revolutionary political change.[4]

There were several centres of populist activity in the 1890s.[5] In Petersburg, the most prominent association had been the *Gruppa Narodovoltsev*, active between 1891 and 1897. By the latter date, however, this organisation had all but coalesced with formerly rival SD groupings, in the capital, and arrests only forestalled a formal alliance. In the summer of 1897 a new organisation was busy propagandising the Baltic and Pallizen factories in the city; generally speaking, however, police intervention prevented any lasting progress before the formal establishing of the PSR in Petersburg in November 1902.[6]

Activity in the Ukraine and Volga regions was more durable. Between 1896 and 1898 SRs in Kiev, under I. A. Dyakov, worked among local railway workers, recognising (with many populist groups of the period) that it was necessary temporarily 'to put the peasants to one side'.[7] Significant activity was also recorded (c. 1895) in Penza,[8] Voronezh, Tambov, Vyatka, Nizhnii-Novgorod, Odessa, and so on. The spiritual home of social-revolutionism however was Saratov, the 'Athens of the Volga'. Saratov owed its prominence to its being a common reception point for returning political exiles. Starting in 1896, the local SRs began extending their influence to other organisations: in Petersburg, Moscow, Ufa, Nizhnii-Novgorod and Chernigov. The result was the founding of a 'Northern Union' of SRs with a common manifesto, *Nashi Zadachi* (*Our Tasks*), composed by A. A. Argunov. This document was closely based on the programme of the People's Will and sanctioned terror. Like the Kiev activists, the Northern Union felt it inappropriate to conduct active propaganda among the peasantry and concentrated on the workers and the radical intelligentsia. The journal of the union, *Revolyutsionnaya Rossiya* (the first number of which appeared in January 1901), eventually became the official organ of the PSR. The Northern Union itself was broken up by the police in September 1901; twenty-two of its members were taken, together with the proofs of the third issue of the paper. The leading lights, however, remained at large.[9]

Meanwhile, similar attempts at co-ordination had been taking place in southern Russia. In August 1897 'the first formal SR congress' was held in Voronezh. Delegates from Kiev, Poltava, Petersburg and Khar'kov attended, and there were also links with circles in Moscow, Odessa, Tambov and Ekaterinoslav. Early attempts at hammering out a common platform foundered on the questions of terror and the revolutionary potential of the peasantry. After one or two more fruitless meetings, a 'Manifesto of the SR party' appeared in November 1900, claiming to speak for the entire southern grouping. There was still ambiguity on terrorism but the Manifesto took a more positive view of the peasantry than expressed hitherto, describing work in the countryside as 'necessary and possible'. For all practical purposes, however, the urban proletariat remained at the centre of the group's attention.[10]

A third element in the unification process was the Minsk-based 'Workers' Party for the Political Liberation of Russia'. There had been a circle in Minsk since 1895 but the workers' party dated only from 1899. Its luminaries included two subsequent leading figures of the PSR: E. E. Breshko-Breshovskaya (referred to earlier) and G. A. Gershuni. The Minsk activists opened up western Russia to the SR party, although there were also circles in Petersburg and Ekaterinoslav. A manifesto *O Svobode* (*On Freedom*) appeared in its name, based on the programme of the People's Will. Arrests disrupted the organisation's activities in March 1900, but again leading representatives survived to negotiate a union with the embryonic SR party.[11]

In February 1900 the funeral in Paris of the great *narodnik* Peter Lavrov was the occasion for a meeting of Russian-based and *émigré* populists from organisations based in London and Berne, as well as Paris. The outcome was the founding of the Agrarian Socialist League,[12] dedicated to propaganda work in the Russian countryside and providing an important back-up for the future SR party.

Notwithstanding the absence of a common programme, agreement on important tactical issues, even consensus on the main focus of propaganda and agitational activity, detailed negotiations on unification continued through the second half of 1901, both within and outside Russia. The results can be summarised as follows:

(1) the formation of a united Socialist-Revolutionary Party, drawn from the Saratov, Voronezh, Minsk and *émigré* centres;
(2) the establishment of a central organ, *Revolyutsionnaya Rossiya*, to be published in Geneva under the editorship of V. M. Chernov and M. R. Gots, and carrying the slogan: 'In struggle you will win your rights';
(3) the conversion of the theoretical journal *Vestnik Russkoi Revolyutsii* into a party organ, under the editorship of N. S. Rusanov and I. A. Rubanovich;

(4) the setting up of a Foreign Organisation which incorporated a party training school from the autumn of 1904;
(5) the organisation of an *émigré* Central Committee around the nucleus of the Saratov group and including Chernov, Breshko-Breshkovskaya, Gots, Gershuni, O. S. Minor, N. I. Rakitnikov, and P. P. Kraft.[13]

SETTLING THE TERROR ISSUE

It was pointed out in Chapter 1 that political terror (by which is meant attempts on the lives of prominent representatives of the tsarist bureaucracy and the ruling class) had been a contentious issue among neo-populist groups even before the official birth of the PSR. However, in view of the fact that both the influential Northern Union and the Agrarian Socialist League had come down in favour of the terror tactic it was not wholly surprising that the new party duly established a Fighting Organisation (*boevaya organizatsiya*) headed by G. A. Gershuni and the as yet unmasked arch-provocateur Evno Azef.[14] Consisting of a permanent nucleus of only half a dozen or so individuals, the FO recruited additional members as and when necessary. The core of the worker element mainly comprised artisans from the western provinces, notably Belostok. Both workers and *intelligenty* shared an elitist conception of their mission. Contrary to official party teaching, many were disdainful of other forms of political activity and some had become involved in terrorism as a result of their disillusionment with propaganda and agitational work. The Simferopol' terrorist, Fedor Nazarov, for example, was said to have held the masses in very low regard, believing them to lack courage and to be generally unworthy of the tasks facing them.[15] A second characteristic of FO members was a mystical, almost religious attitude towards terror. The Biblical saying 'Greater love hath no man. . .' was, for example, included in the party obituary of one of their number;[16] while V. M. Zenzinov makes clear in his memoirs that each activist considered his own life to be the proper price for taking the life of another, even if the victim was held in loathing by the people.[17] There were even those, like Mariya Benevskaya, who found involvement in this brand of terrorism compatible with Christian beliefs.

Between April 1902 and February 1905 the Fighting Organisation was responsible for five assassination attempts, four of which were successful.[18] The victims included two ministers of the interior (D. S.

Sipyagin and V. K. Plehve), two provincial governors (I. M. Obolenskii and N. M. Bogdanovich) and the Governor-general of Moscow, the Grand-Duke Sergei Aleksandrovich. Three workers were directly involved in these early attacks: Thomas Kachur, aged twenty-six, from Ekaterinoslav,[19] Egor Dulebov, a twenty-year old locksmith in the Ufa railway workshops and Sikorskii, a twenty-year old tanner from Belostok. Technically the FO continued to operate through most of 1905, but in fact provocateurs 'practically paralysed all terrorist activity from the spring'.[20] The promise of a constitutional regime in October led to the suspension of terror for a time;[21] it was resumed in January 1906, halted again for the duration of the first Duma and resumed once more in July. Several months later the FO was re-formed as the Fighting Detachment of the Central Committee (under the direction of Lev Zil'berberg,[22] and was responsible for the assassination of the Governor of Petersburg in December. At the end of 1907 the FO was revived, but it was never as effective as in the early years of its existence, failing notably in its attempts to kill the Tsar.

To the Social Democrats the SRs' terrorist activity was only more proof, if more were needed, of the party's 'adventurism', but there were a number of theoretical arguments which the Socialist-Revolutionaries deployed in defence of their position.[23] First of all, it was argued, political terror was a temporary substitute or support for an as yet weak and disorganised working class, lacking in effective political allies and therefore incapable of mounting a serious challenge to the ruling regime (or at least, so it seemed before 1905). Even when the workers took to the streets, it was said, they were usually powerless to defend themselves. Hence the FO was temporarily entrusted with avenging acts of violence perpetrated against the working class. A second argument advanced was that the assassination of ministers and government officials served to throw the authorities into confusion, damaging their morale and making them appear vulnerable in the eyes of the masses. Terror was also assumed to have an 'agitational' significance. It drew attention to the revolutionaries and their ideals, conferred prestige on the party and awakened the interest of the more backward and ignorant sections of the toiling classes. There was the additional argument that, if applied over an extended period, terror would either compel the government to make concessions to the revolutionary movement or, conversely, drive it to acts of even greater provocation and thereby make open confrontation between rulers and ruled more likely. Either way, it was felt, the working class would be the beneficiary. The SRs accused their Social Democratic critics of cowardice and hypocrisy with regard to terrorism. They suggested that the Marxists were anxious to share in any benefits accruing from succesful terrorist activity but were unwilling to share the awesome responsibility for carrying out the policy. The point concerning responsibility and control was fundamental to the SRs' evaluation and justification of political terror. They stressed to their own members that acts of terrorism should be carried out only in collaboration with the Fighting Organisation; otherwise the entire business would dissolve into anarchy. Equally important, terror was not to be allowed to steal the limelight from other, less sensational, forms of struggle. Terror was to be integrated into the overall strategy and tactics of the party; it was to constitute a part of the revolutionary movement, not act as a substitute for it.

THE PARTY PROGRAMME

The programme adopted at the first congress which was held at Imatra (Finland) from December 1905 to January 1906 closely resembled, in its essentials, a draft statement which had appeared in *Revolyutsionnaya Rossiya* the previous year.[24] It was divided into two sections; the first took the form of a lengthy theoretical preamble which also set out the party's long-term socialist objectives (the 'maximum programme'). The second outlined the demands for a 'minimum programme'; that is, the less ambitious though still far-reaching goals which the party would promote while the revolutionary working class remained a minority, able to exercise only a 'partial influence' on legislation and on the overall direction of social change.[25]

The programme betrayed notable Marxist influences (to the discomfiture of some delegates), but the terms in which Chernov acknowledged the debt in that direction succinctly express its limitations: 'Marx is our great common teacher in the realm of economics, but we do not feel constrained to make him an idol.'[26] The features in the programme most derivative of Marxism were:

(1) its analysis of the harmful aspects of capitalism: private control of the means of production, direct exploitation of the proletariat through the extraction of surplus value, and the anarchic nature of capitalist competition;
(2) the need for class struggle in advancing the cause of socialism;

(3) recognition of the oppressive and exploitative nature of the State and the role it played in defending the interests of the possessing classes.

Against these similarities, however, must be set a number of fundamental differences, especially crucial in the Russian context. The most significant concerns the SRs' interpretation of the development of history which owes most to the subjectivism of P. L. Lavrov and N. K. Mikhailovsky.[27] The SRs rejected the economic materialism of the orthodox Marxists.[28] They were not prepared to accept, even 'in the last analysis', that economic factors determined the course of history, but held instead that the interaction of a wide range of influences – legal, political, intellectual and economic, were jointly responsible. These influences were woven so inextricably, it was argued, that it was impossible to identify any one as the ultimate cause: they were 'in essence only the different sides of a single process'.[29] Though the SRs were ready to attribute to natural forces a major role in determining the course of history, they were at the same time deeply convinced of the power of 'critically thinking individuals' to exert an influence on its outcome. Derived from this view was the crucial implication that capitalism, though admittedly by now a historical fact, did not have to run its full course in Russia. The timely intervention of the radical intelligentsia could, by shaping and encouraging the class consciousness and organisational ability of the toiling masses, make possible the early realisation of socialism, providing that the revolutionary energy engendered was sufficient to topple autocracy, and was accompanied by the appropriate revolutionary measures.[30]

A second important difference distinguishing social revolutionism from social democracy lay in its understanding of class. According to the SR point of view class divisions in society derived not from the relationship of the subject to the means of production but from his relationship to the means of distribution (source of income, in other words). Here, in fact, was an area in which the SRs felt they had 'a claim to understand Marx better ... than the so-called Marxists'.[31] Their distinctive interpretation of the mechanics of class had important implications for the party's view of class allegiance and class conflict. For not only the industrial and agricultural proletariat but the vast bulk of the small-holding peasantry (as well as elements within the intelligentsia) lived more or less exclusively by their own labour and were equally subject to exploitation at the hands of those in a position to extract surplus value. For the SRs therefore, the notion of the 'working class' was a much broader concept than for the Social Democrats. It encompassed all the exploited[32] on equal terms – there was little mention of the Marxist–Leninist notion of a proletarian vanguard.[33] The socialist-intelligentsia, the small-scale producers in the village and the industrial and agricultural proletariats were to struggle *en bloc* against an equally broad range of class enemies[34] – autocracy and the tsarist bureaucracy, the landed nobility and the bourgeoisie.[35] Having recognised that the mass of the peasantry was not petty-bourgeois in outlook but, potentially at least, fully capable of understanding its real class interests in the light of socialism, the party's immediate task was to raise the peasants' consciousness to the level of the most advanced stratum of the factory proletariat. The SRs emphasised time and again that the industrial proletariat could never achieve any significant victory by relying exclusively on its own resources and that to ignore the revolutionary potential of the peasantry was, in effect, to open the floodgates of capitalism on the Russian countryside, with all the horrors which that entailed.[36]

The third major difference between the rival socialist parties concerned their interpretation of what the Social Democrats termed the 'bourgeois-democratic' phase of the revolution, which would seal the fate of autocracy and remove all feudal remnants from Russia.[37] For the Social Democrats this implied the creation of a constitutional regime which would, on the one hand, concede to the proletariat those freedoms of expression and organisation previously denied them and, on the other, remove all obstacles in the way of the further development of capitalism, an essential prerequisite of the socialist order. The SRs advanced several objections to this scheme. Firstly, it implied that 'all revolutionary tasks must be put off to the very end'.[38] The Socialists were meekly to accept what the bourgeoisie were pleased to concede and to press for nothing more. They were to watch and wait while capitalism did its work and in the meantime content themselves with a reformist-style programme, acceptable even to 'state socialists' and 'economists'. The SRs vehemently rejected this scheme, refusing even to employ the term 'bourgeois-democratic'. They proposed instead that the initial phase of the revolution be used to peg back the encroachments of capitalism, as well as to destroy the vestiges of feudalism. It should propel the country beyond the frontiers of bourgeois democracy and closer to socialism. To help accomplish this bold step the SRs included a demand for 'land socialisation' in their minimum programme. This envisaged 'the withdrawal [of the land] from commodity circulation and [its] conversion from the private property of individuals or groups into the possession (*dostoyanie*) of all the people'.[39] 'Local organs of popular self-government', based on the *obshchina* would then carry out the repartition on an egalitarian basis. The size of each holding would depend on the size of the individual family concerned (the 'consumer norm'). No one would be allowed to increase his share of the land by exploiting hired labour. The non-arable land was to be administered by the higher organs of government rather than the individual communes. Former estate-owners would not be offered compensation but would be entitled to support, pending re-adjustment to the new situation. The forcing through of such a radical proposal would, it was anticipated, undermine bourgeois rule and so hasten its demise. The thinking behind the SR position was neatly expressed by M. R. Gots, in terms reminiscent of Trotsky:

> They [the SRS] should not restrict the scale of the revolution in advance for the benefit of the bourgeoisie, but on the contrary they should turn it into a permanent one, oust the bourgeoisie step by step from the positions it has occupied, give the signal for a European revolution and then draw strength from there.[40]

The SRs' minimum programme was, then, bolder and more far-reaching than that of the Social Democrats. The SDs were hampered by the need to reconcile two contradictory requirements – the facilitation of further capitalist development and the defence of the physical and spiritual well-being of the workers. Theirs, in the opinion of the SRs was a 'reformist' programme, while even the 'minimum' demands of the SRs were revolutionary in character.[41]

The party's minimum programme was not confined to demands in the agrarian sphere. It included the customary political goals – the convocation of a 'constituent assembly', elected directly by all men and women aged twenty and above in a secret ballot; personal inviolability; freedom of conscience, speech, press, assembly and union; replacement of the monarchy by a democratic republic; wide local autonomy and improved federative arrangements with the subject peoples, including the right to self-determination. In the economic sphere, the programme called for progressive taxes on income and inheritance, the abolition of all indirect taxes, save on luxuries, and the removal of all protective duties.[42]

The party also included a section on rights for workers which it believed, for reasons already described, to be in some respects more adventurous than that of the Social Democrats.[43] For instance, not only was there a demand for the immediate introduction of the eight-hour day, but also for a further reduction in hours in those branches of industry considered dangerous or harmful to health. A minimum wage was to be negotiated between 'organs of self-government' and legalised trade union organisations. There were to be comprehensive schemes for social insurance, at the expense of the State and the employers and to be administered by the workers themselves. An elected factory inspectorate would lay down new norms for working conditions and there would be a fresh round of protective legislation outlawing child labour and regulating the employment of women and adolescents. Finally, provision was to be made for trade union organisations to play a gradually expanding role in determining the 'internal organisation of work' in industrial enterprises.

OTHER ISSUES RAISED AT THE FIRST CONGRESS

Factory Socialisation

Ambitious the minimum programme may have been, but it did not satisfy the more radical elements within the party. In fact, there had been opposition to the very notion of separate maximum and minimum demands ever since the publication of the draft programme in 1904. The original source of this opposition was the rebel *émigré* authors (chiefly M. I. Sokolov and E. Ustinov) of the flysheet *Volnyi Diskussionyi Listok* (Free Discussion Leaflet), who advocated an immediate, all-embracing social revolution which would twin land socialisation with the socialisation of the factories.[44] This idea gained considerable popular currency during 1905, especially in western and southern Russia, and was to become the main policy plank of the break-away Union of SR Maximalists the following year.[45] By the time the founding congress was convened there was already strong support for immediate factory socialisation in a number of centres, including Belostok, Minsk, Vitebsk and, in all probability, Ekaterinoslav. The most authoritative and vociferous supporter of the idea at Imatra was 'Poroshin'/Ginzburg, the delegate from Vitebsk. The core of his argument was expressed thus:

The draft programme is based on two different principles; on the one hand, the revolutionary principle – the fundamental restructuring of agrarian relations; on the other, the reformist principle, the partial, not fundamental restructuring of factory relations.[46]

As the reforms contained in the existing minimum programme could all, Poroshin asserted, be achieved within bourgeois society they could in no sense be considered a bridgehead to socialism comparable to the socialisation of the land. Poroshin's solution was uncompromising: the minimum programme must include a demand for 'the revolutionary expropriation of factories and mills and the replacement of private property in them by collective social property'.[47] Another, very influential delegate at the congress ('Bazarov'/N. I. Rakitnikov), was also concerned that factory socialisation was excluded from the minimum programme. In his opinion progress in that direction should not be discounted out of hand; in other words, if circumstances permitted, factory socialisation might be possible at the same time as the socialisation of the land.[48] Other delegates spoke more in terms of the municipalisation of the factory, though still within the frontiers of the minimum programme. 'Abramov', representing Ufa, argued that in an area like the Urals, where the worker's wage contractually took into account the plot of land signed over to him, it would be 'senseless' to socialise the land while allowing capitalist relations to continue in the factories.[49] 'Goretskii'/A. I. Al'tovskii (representing Saratov) held a similar view, arguing that 'the minimum programme must be a programme of social revolution' and that it would be realistic to expect that such a radical reform of property relations as land socialisation would have a far-reaching agitational impact on workers suffering exploitation in other branches of the economy. Goretskii believed that there was already a widely-held conviction among workers that the seizure of factories was a realistic proposition and cited an instance where this had apparently taken place. At some time during 1905, a number of workers threatened with unemployment had taken over the running of two metalworking factories in Saratov, formerly belonging to S. V. Chirikhina and M. A. Makharov. Unfortunately, the only other details supplied about this experiment were that the enterprises concerned were small and that management had been willing to give them up because they were no longer viable. It was not known at the time of the congress whether the experiment had been successful or not.[50]

The arguments in favour of immediate socialisation of the factories were not convincing to the majority of delegates and there were some powerful speeches in defence of the minimum programme as it stood.

'Snegov', for example, representing Kursk, felt that the demands in the minimum section were socialist in nature and certainly radical enough for the time being, while 'Gribovskii' (Vladimir) was one of a number of delegates to point to the formidable technical problems involved in undertaking such an enterprise.[51] The strongest arguments against change came from delegates from the big cities. In fact 'Roshchin'/V. V. Rudnev (Moscow city) pointed out that the speeches advocating immediate socialisation had come from delegates with little or no experience of large-scale industry and with therefore little real idea of the problems involved. Unlike land socialisation, socialisation of the factories required radical change in the organisa-tion of production, apart from cultural acclimatisation to the idea by the workers themselves. Roshchin contradicted the opinion, voiced by the Saratov delegate, that the workers were ready to contemplate such a measure. Throughout the short life of the 'Novorossiisk Commune', he asserted, when the town had been in the hands of the proletariat, no conviction had emerged that the factories were the common property of those who worked in them; a crucial difference from the peasants' attitude to the land.[52] 'Zhelezovskii' (Petersburg) took up Roshchin's point about the need to re-organise production and the difficulty of carrying out such a re-organisation – 'expropriation is not socialisation'. He also drew a distinction between the handing over of isolated factories to the workforce as producer co-operatives and the infinitely more ambitious goal of comprehensive socialisation.[53] As in so many other issues, however, it was left to the party leader himself to deal the decisive blows against the radical case.[54] Chernov drew a distinction between the socialisation of the land, on the one hand, and the socialisation of the factories on the other. It was illogical, he maintained, to press for the parallel implementation of both because one entailed the socialisation of production while the other did not. The real equivalent to land socialisation therefore was the socialisation of urban land. Chernov then moved to aspects of the issue already raised by the delegates from Moscow and Petersburg. Factory socialisation required enormously detailed technical preparations, for: 'The factory is not of course the factory building. The factory is a living productive organism, stretching its tentacles far beyond the confines of the factory walls.'[55] For this reason 'lengthy systematic, organisational work' would be needed. Plans would have to be drafted, accounting based on need rather than competition introduced, and the distribution of productive forces among the various branches of industry organised. But there was also a need for a strong, conscious and united working class, both to execute the necessary measures and to overcome the inevitable resistance. With considerable perspicacity perhaps, Chernov warned against any attempt to carry out such an ambitious programme during a period of crisis and revolutionary upheaval.[56] Like some fellow-delegates before him, the only concession he was willing to make in the direction of the minimal socialisers was to allow for individual cases of municipalisation. The arguments of Chernov and his supporters were certainly shared by the majority of delegates at the congress, though the evidence suggests that there was more enthusiasm for the radical cause among the grass roots.

In the later history of the PSR, calls either for immediate factory socialisation or for far-reaching municipalisation were normally confined to the breakaway Maximalist sections of the party. There are one or two interesting exceptions to this rule, however. In June 1906 the third congress of the Urals *oblast'* adopted a motion calling for: 'the immediate, albeit gradual handing over of declining enterprises in the Urals into the economic management (*v khozyaistvennoe zavedovanie*) of democratically organised local and regional self-governing units. ....' At the same time the view was expressed that a demand for similar municipalisation or 'communisation' of factories elsewhere in Russia should become part of the SRs' minimum programme.[57]

Far more ambitious proposals emanated from the shores of the Caspian in the early months of 1907. In the opinion of the Baku organisation, a whole range of Russian industries were already ripe for immediate socialisation, including the Urals and Donets mining industries, salt and sugar manufacturing and 'without a doubt' the oil and manganese industries of the Caucasus, regarded as particularly suitable because of their monopolistic nature. As far as the oil businesses at least were concerned, social control should be total:

> The oil-bearing lands and the entire oil industry, right to the last sector (*otdel*), that is, the means of transporting the oil, crude oil, kerosene etc. already may and *consequently must be nationalised.*[58]

The Baku comrades enthusiastically informed the party hierarchs that they were already in the process of collating the relevant data and technical information and proposed that the Council of Oil Producers be transformed into a 'Workers' Council for oil enterprises' with the existing bureaucracy becoming subject to popular control. The factory and district committees already in place would act as subordinate agencies to the proposed soviet. The Baku SRs were in no doubt about the attractiveness of the measure as far as the workers themselves were concerned: 'The relevance of this task and its riveting interest will guarantee it the support of the working masses in Baku.' In responding to the idea the editors of *Partiinyya Izvestiya* seem at first glance to have gone considerably further than the line officially extolled at the first congress:

> Our programme envisages the possibility of the socialisation of a few branches of the national economy even within the frontiers of the present order, as far as general conditions provide sufficient guarantees against increasing by such a route the dependence of the working class on the ruling bureaucracy.

Once again, however, the emphasis was placed on the technical and organisational complexities inherent in such an undertaking. Having outlined these difficulties in their answer, the editors concluded by throwing the ball back into the others' court: 'We recommend these questions to the attention of the Baku comrades.'

Factory Terror

Factory terror (the use or threat of violence against the life or property of a factory owner to promote the economic interests of the workforce) is generally associated with the name of N. N. Sokolov, who first disseminated the idea in Ekaterinoslav in 1904, as the urban equivalent of agrarian terrorism.[59] Factory terror was more closely associated with the Anarchists than the SRs during 1905,[60] though the latter may have resorted to it on occasion. The subject was raised only very briefly at the first congress and the rapporteur, Bazarov/Rakitnikov devoted most of his comments to agrarian terror.[61] In the event, neither variant received official approval. The major objection was that it would be almost impossible to regulate; there was also confusion, however, as to what precisely constitued factory terror – the only concrete example cited at the congress was the firing of oil derricks in Baku in August 1905 and this was eventually designated a political act.[62] Factory terror was never officially sanctioned by the PSR, although there was considerable sympathy for it on the ground, especially in the climate of rising unemployment after 1905. Even then, terror against factory owners was most commonly advocated when it was suspected that factories were being closed simply to instil political conformity and labour discipline into the workforce; in these circumstances the application of terror appeared to take on a political rather than an economic complexion.[63]

3 First Acquaintance with the Workers. Propaganda and Agitational Activity on the Ground, 1902–05

INTRODUCTION

The PSR effectively began work early in 1902.[1] By the end of the year there were nineteen urban organisations, scattered across most of European Russia. The majority were in centres with a history of populist activity (Saratov, Kiev, Odessa and Ekaterinoslav, for example);[2] one (Perm') operated jointly with the Social Democrats. Only two well-populated regions west of the Urals were entirely without representation: one was in the far south (Don-Caucasus); the other comprised the northern half of the Jewish Pale of Settlement. During 1903 these regions too were opened up. New organisations were formed in Baku, Tiflis and Astrakhan' in the south and in Minsk, Vitebsk and Belostok in the north-west, while some consolidation was made in the central regions (Orel, Kursk, Bryansk), and in the south-west (Kherson, Azov, Kishinev, and Bessarabia). A group at Zlatoust worked in harness with the Social Democrats.

This rapid expansion owed something to the agrarian disorders of the previous year and to the wave of strikes which swept southern Russia during the summer of 1903.[3] Severe industrial depression, exacerbated by the war with Japan, made 1904 a particularly bleak year for revolutionary movements generally, and, not surprisingly, SR growth was checked. Even so, ten new organisations were founded during that year.

32

With the onset of the revolution party fortunes rose dramatically and expansion was accelerated. By the end of 1905 there were seventy-two groups and committes in Russia, twenty-five of which dated from the revolutionary year itself;[4] four 'unions' (of the North-West, Volga, Caucasus and Siberia), co-ordinated the activities of approximately one-third of them.[5]

ORGANISATIONAL STRUCTURE

As the party's ideology would lead one to expect, no SR organisation concentrated exclusively on the urban proletariat. A report from Odessa in 1902, for example, informs us that the local committee was active among 'workers, peasants,[6] the intelligentsia and the army'.[7] A year later, the Petersburg Committee was casting its net equally wide and as far as the neighbouring provinces of Pskov and Novgorod,[8] while in 1904 the Vitebsk SRs concerned themselves with local 'workers, students and soldiers'.[9] However, generally speaking, workers were accorded the major share of the party's attention and many organisations established an autonomous 'workers' union' (*rabochii soyuz*) to concentrate exclusively on matters of concern to them.[10] Similar unions or groups were formed among other sections of the population wherever and whenever demand seemed to warrant it. Consequently, during 1905 rapid growth in party support resulted in some of the larger organisations rapidly acquiring quite involved structures. In Odessa, for example, the local committee co-ordinated the activity of about eight affiliated bodies, the most important of which was the 'centre' which 'unified (*ob'edinyayushchii*) the activities of the entire Odessa workers' organisation'.[11] Two adjuncts of the centre were the 'Union of Propagandists' (*soyuz propagandistov*) which directed the workers' revolutionary education and a Central Agitators' Assembly. This body co-ordinated activity at the factory and enterprise level in each of the four districts (*raiony*). At least three trade unions (of bakers, joiners, clerical workers and shop assistants) also came under the supervision of the workers' centre, the directing body of which comprised the leaders of each district and trade union (appointed by the committee), a member of the committee itself, and representatives chosen by the workers. In addition to the trades organisations, there were party 'unions' of soldiers, sailors, students and secondary school pupils. The Odessa 'fighting detachment' (*boevaya druzhina*) was also affiliated to the party but probably acted with a considerable degree of independence from the local committee.[12]

The regulations of three workers' centres: Moscow, Kishinev and Penza,[13] appeared in the pages of *Revolyutsionnaya Rossiya* during 1904 and 1905, and they reveal a little more about this type of organisation. In Moscow and Kishinev the workers themselves directed the affairs of the centre, whereas in Penza members of the committee were also entitled to sit on the governing council. The most important requirement for membership was, of course, commitment to the goals of the party with, presumably, some kind of active participation in circle or agitational work. Additionally, each worker was expected to pay a regular fixed subscription into a special fund (*kassa*). Dues were generally levied monthly at an apparently standard rate of 3 per cent of earnings. At Kishinev and Penza at least the candidate also needed the recommendation of two or three card-holding members, and in Kishinev unanimous adoption by the centre itself. The funds were used for a variety of purposes; to maintain the 'conspiratorial' apartment used for circle work and the storing of propaganda; to provide reading matter for a legal and/or illegal library and to assist workers suffering hardship as a result of involvement in the political struggle, or for other reasons (unemployment for example).[14] Apart from administering the fund and issuing proclamations and fly-sheet newspapers, the directors of the workers' centre did, on occasion at least, advise their party committees on the timing and appropriateness of strike action and, presumably, on other matters which directly concerned their members.[15]

FINANCES

Thorough scrutiny of committee accounts is impeded by a number of obstacles. Statements did, it is true, appear regularly in *Revolyutsionnaya Rossiya* and many organisations (though by no means all) provided some sort of return whenever possible. However it would be unreasonable to expect a conspiratorial revolutionary party with an *émigré* leadership to conduct itself with the efficiency and openness of a well-run business. Police activity constantly disrupted political work at local level, bringing it from time to time to an abrupt halt, sometimes for months on end. As a result, committee accounts were issued irregularly and were often incomplete. Nevertheless, there is enough material available to allow for examination of a number of organisations over periods of several consecutive months. The committees of Petersburg and Ekaterinoslav have been selected for the purposes of this study and provide an interesting contrast.

The Petersburg SRs submitted four statements of account for the period 10 December 1904 to 15 July 1905,[16] of which only the first seems to be entirely unabbreviated. A total of 7708 roubles entered the committee treasury between December 1904 and February 1905 (8334r. if the balance brought forward is included). Of this sum, 1465r. was promised in advance to the party's Fighting Organisation (FO). The remainder consisted of 71 contributions from sympathetic individuals and groups. Sufficient information is given about them to permit the construction of a table which divides the sums according to size (Table 3.1).

It will be noted that, of the 71 contributions, 13 constitute approximately two-thirds of the committee's income. At least four of these were group donations: one (of 503 roubles) was collected from among guests at a dinner (*banket*); a second (of 500r.) was presented by lawyers; a third (210r.) came from trainee engineers (*ot studentov-puteitsev*) and the fourth (200r.) from students at the city Polytechnic. Of the contributors in the second category, only three can be postively identified: the Vyborg *raion* organisation (71r.), a laboratory (90r.) and 'doctors and professors' (56r.). Among the contributors of smaller sums were the Pinsk *zemlyachestvo* (16r.), a bank (15r.) and a teacher (2r.).

Expenditure over the same period amounted to 7319r., which left 1015r. in reserve. 2135r. were spent on purchasing weapons (*oruzhie*) and other 'fighting equipment' (*boevye materialy*), and 1033r.[17] on the propaganda effort: to buy a metal press, cyclostyle and relevant accessories; to equip two printing presses, issue mimeographs and other literary items; pay a machine-operator and stock the libraries of workers and propagandists. 383r were used to pay the travelling expenses of party activists (within the city boundaries, in the neighbouring countryside and abroad). Miscellaneous items included the purchase of two overcoats for propagandists and contributions to the district branches of the party (Petersburg, Narva, Vyborg and Vasileostrov).

The accounts for 10 February–1 April 1905 are much less complete. We are told that total income (including balance brought forward) amounted to 6589r. of which 2640r. was spent on arms, 518r. on the workers (*vydano rabochim*) and 439r. on '*tekhnika*'.

The entry for April and May is a little more helpful and invites some general comparison with the accounts of the Moscow Social Democrats cited in David Lane's book.[18] Where appropriate, the SD figures have

Table 3.1 Accounts of the Petersburg committee of the PSR December 1904–Feburary 1905

Number of contributions	Amount of contribution (roubles)						Total roubles
	0–10	11–25	26–50	51–100	101+	Total	
	16	17	11	14 (1261)	13 (4183)	71	6243 (excluding balance brought forward)

Source: 'Denezhnyi otchet Peterburgskogo Komiteta partii Sotsialistov-Revolyutsionerov' (*RR*, no. 61 [15 March 1905], p. 20).

been placed in brackets immediately after those of the Petersburg SR committee. Total income (including balance brought forward) was 11 630r. (8389r.), 5000r. of which had been sent by the Moscow SR committee, and 2000r. donated by a single individual (A. Zet'). As regards expenditure, the committee spent 3595r. (700r.) on the procurement of arms and advanced a further 1000r. for the same purpose. This amount is unusually large, and it is possible that some of the money from the Moscow committee was forwarded to purchase arms for its own use. Of the remainder, '*tekhnika*' and printing expenses consumed 1926r. (1208r.); 381r. (1195r.) went to the districts, and 976r. (830r.) was spent on personnel and organisation.

The final statement covers the period May–July 1905. Total income stood at 6215r., of which 515r. was ear-marked for the Fighting Organisation. There was one major contribution of 2000r. from the Central Committee. Weapons were again the largest single item of expenditure (2385r.), 'conspiratorial' consumed 1048r., workers' assistance 1021r. and printing 506r.

The Petersburg organisation was, then, in a comparatively healthy financial condition, though this does not seem to have helped it make any real impact on the city's working class, before the first half of 1905 at least. By contrast, the Ekaterinoslav committee, which did succeed in exerting at least a sporadic influence on events in the locality, was obliged to exist on a much tighter budget. The accounts presented here are for May 1903 to February 1904; December 1904 to January 1905 and April to July 1905.[19]

Income for May to September 1903 totalled 836r. Of the 37 contributions which comprised this sum only 5 were of more than twenty roubles each, and one of these was a 'special allowance' (*edinovremennoe posobie*) of 240r. from the Central Committee. Twenty-five of the remaining donations were for sums of less than ten roubles. By December the organisation was in debt to the tune of 208r., though a loan of 170r. from an unnamed contributor did temporarily ease the situation. The committee nevertheless had to appeal for help in the pages of *Revolyutsionnaya Rossiya*, explaining that a lack of funds was 'seriously hindering' (*sil'no tormozitsya*) its activities.[29] This appeal does not seem to have elicited much response: income in February 1904 stood at only 200r. and was considerably less than half that sum twelve months later. By April 1905 there was a modest improvement, thanks almost wholly to the 'Union of those desiring freedom', who contributed 101r. out of the total 145r.; and this sum was ear-marked for those in prison. Fortunately for committee, the summer brought a measure of relief: income from May to July inclusive amounted to 979r.

With such limited resources the Ekaterinoslav organisation was obviously not in a position to make an effective contribution to the armed struggle. In fact, the accounts reveal that just 122r. was spent on weapons over the entire period (in July 1905). The production, packaging and distribution of propaganda material, upkeep of a conspiratorial apartment, maintenance of a professional revolutionary staff and distribution of aid to comrades in prison consumed the lion's share of what little resources were available.

Of the two organisations studied there can be no doubt that Ekaterinoslav was the more typical. The Petersburg Committee also functioned as the party's headquarters within Russia, a transit and communications point connecting the *émigré* leadership with their organised supporters within the Empire.[21] An additional advantage enjoyed by the SRs in the capital was access to a greater number of the disaffected or conscience-stirred members of the professional and business worlds who played such an important role in financing Russia's revolutionary parties. As we have seen, the Petersburg Committee could count for support on the students, lawyers, doctors and professors resident there, as well as on occasional but generous anonymous contributions. In a provincial town like Ekaterinoslav on the other hand, more reliance had to be placed on the 'organised' workers (the 'Ekaterinoslav Railway Craftsmen' and the 'workers' centre' for example), or on other sympathisers of limited means. Here a single gift of 100 roubles might breach the dividing line between solvency and debt, and Ekaterinoslav was by no means the only organisation to plead poverty before the readers of *Revolyutsionnaya Rossiya* during this period.

The expenditure of the Petersburg Committee is evidence of the party's commitment to armed insurrection during 1905. The financial statements also illustrate the degree of importance attached to the production and circulation of propaganda, a task which invariably consumed a sizeable proportion of party income. It is to this subject that we now turn our attention.

PROPAGANDA OUTPUT

Petersburg and Moscow were two of the committees which regularly submitted lists of propaganda titles to *Revolyutsionnaya Rossiya* between 1902 and 1905.[22] These lists may not be complete but they are probably representative, both of the range of subject matter covered by the typical urban organisation and of the social strata to which it addressed itself.

The Petersburg Committee submitted the title of eighty-three proclamations between February 1903 and the end of September 1905. Nineteen of these were addressed directly to the workers. Another four were devoted to topical labour issues (trade unions and the eight-hour day for example) and four more tried to elicit sympathy for the class struggle in other urban centres. Thus the total number of items which might be considered 'worker-orientated' amounts to twenty-seven, or 33 per cent of the total. The number of proclamations addressed specifically to other sections of the population: students, soldiers, sailors and peasants was twenty-three (28 per cent of the total), students being the most prominent contributor-recipients.

Turning to subject matter, the material can be subdivided into four categories:

(1) labour-orientated (27 items)
(2) terror (11 items)
(3) the war with Japan (10 items)
(4) attacks directed at the Government and its policies (8 items).

The Moscow Committee listed seventy-nine titles between the summer of 1903 and September 1905. Twenty-five were addressed directly to the workers and two concerned the urban struggle elsewhere,[23] making a total of twenty-seven worker-orientated items (34 per cent). Of the remainder, eighteen (23 per cent) were specifically addressed to other sections of the population: students and the intelligentsia, the army and the peasantry. The subject matter divides readily enough into the same categories as Petersburg: that is, labour-orientated material (27 items), terror (10), the war (9), and Government policy (9).

The 'workers union' in Moscow is one of five[24] known to have produced its own newspaper, *rabochaya gazeta*, six numbers of which appeared between December 1904 and September 1905, the fifth in an edition of 13 000 copies.[25] Quite a wide range of issues was covered, though with a heavy political bias towards those reflecting the various policy planks of the party. The first number, for example, included pieces on 'Autocracy and our Tasks', the nature of popular government and its advantages, 'The Worker and the Peasant Farmer' and 'The Worker and the Shop Assistant'. In no. 3 there were articles on

'Terrorism in Our Times' and verses on the assassination of Count Shuvalov;[26] and in the fourth issue 'What Can We Expect From a State Duma?' But there was also room for workers' correspondence and verses, a 'Moscow Diary' and, on at least one occasion, an employee's account of conditions at his factory. No doubt many Moscow workers welcomed such an enterprise, even if it made few concessions to the 'economistic' aspects of the class struggle.

The main purpose of proclamations, wherever they were produced,[27] was to communicate the Socialist-Revolutionary programme as effectively as possible, thereby eliciting active support for the cause it promoted. But the majority also performed more concrete, practical functions. A considerable number, often addressed to particular factories or enterprises, attempted to persuade the workforce to embark on strike action or, if this was already under way, to turn an economic dispute into a political one. Proclamations were also issued to announce or report on party meetings, particularly if they had been called to celebrate or commemorate the 'red-letter' days of the revolutionary caldendar – the anniversaries of peasant emancipation or May Day, for instance. On other occasions, proclamations might be issued to defend the party from the polemics of their rivals or, again, to reveal particularly scandalous instances of government brutality or injustice. Finally, proclamations often heralded an act of terrorism by the local workers' detachment, or served to warn potential victims of the fate which might await them. The Moscow Committee, for example, issued such a statement in December 1904,[28] warning the Governor, Grand Duke Sergei Aleksandrovich and his Police Chief, Trepov, that, should demonstrators meet with any violence from troops or police, they would be held responsible. Sergei's life was duly claimed the following February.

David Lane has already pointed to the important role played by revolutionary slogans in Social Democratic propaganda and this remains true for the SRs. The slogans in their proclamations too can be broadly divided into those with a positive emphasis and those with a negative one. The main subjects of the negative appeals were the autocracy or Tsar, the Administration/Government, capitalists or the capitalist system and the war, while the positive appeals commonly favoured socialism, political freedom, popular government, struggle, the general strike or terror. SR demands also closely resembled those advanced by the Social Democrats.[29] They included, in the political sphere, the democratic republic, the right to strike, to assemble and to form unions, the right to free education and a free press; and, in the economic sphere, the eight-hour day, wage increases, free and comprehensive insurance, improvements in the standards of hygiene, the abolition of searches and fines, the dismissal of rude foremen, better accomodation, more attention to the needs of working women and the creation of joint worker–employer commissions to examine and determine such matters.

A final question: in what terms did the SRs present the party programme when they were addressing their working-class readership? In an attempt to answer this, a proclamation has been chosen from among those issued by the Kiev Committee. It dates from the autumn of 1903 and is addressed 'To Comrade Workers'.[30]

This particular appeal begins by referring to what was regarded as the most outstanding features of the contemporary political scene: the strikes in southern Russia, the pogroms, the disaffection in the countryside and the severity of the State's response to the revolutionary opposition. Such events, it argues, are indications that the time is now ripe for the 'Russian working people (*rabochii narod*) to embark on their great task: the liberation of the country'. In Western Europe the struggle had been led by the bourgeoisie, but in Russia their interests are too closely bound up with those of the autocracy for them to be reliable allies. The first part of the task is to overthrow autocracy and replace it with a democratic republic; a system of government which implies rule by representatives of the people chosen by general, direct and secret suffrage alongside guarantees of personal inviolability, freedom of conscience, speech, press, assembly and union, and the 'furthest possible development of local self-government.' Under the democratic republic each nation will determine its own future.

This task is too great to be carried out by the urban proletariat alone. As Thomas Kachur[31] put it: 'While the peasant sleeps, we workers can achieve nothing. We are only a few – they are all Russia.' What is needed is an alliance of workers and peasants because, as the members of *Narodnaya Volya* well understood, the two together represent 'an invincible force'.

The proclamation then briefly discusses the oppressive conditions which the peasants had to endure, spelling out the means by which they might win their salvation, and goes on to highlight the role of the third element in what now became a triple alliance – the 'working' (*trudovaya*) intelligentsia, and those members of the governing classes who could be drawn on to the side of the exploited. These three together were to use every means of struggle, both economic and political, to overthrow autocracy, including terror, an essential weapon against a government which ruled by the sword. The usual supportive arguments for terror are then briefly rehearsed.

Once autocracy had been removed from the scene the forces of revolution would have to ensure that there was a fundamental change in the economic structure of the country. Socialisation of the land would secure such a change. For the urban worker, socialisation implied greater security of employment and a more favourable bargaining position *vis-à-vis* the employer, because the influx of cheap labour from the countryside would be halted, or at least considerably reduced. In addition of course, there would be more direct gains such as the eight-hour day, minimum wage, and so on. These would be the fruits of the democratic republic.

The proclamation concluded by pointing to the more distant future, when autocracy had been destroyed and the advance of capitalism checked. The way would then be clear for progress towards the 'promised land' of socialism.

PROPAGANDA CIRCLES

The preparation and distribution of printed propaganda was one permanent feature of revolutionary work. Another was the dissemination of socialist ideas via the *kruzhok* (circle).

How the system operated under normal circumstances can perhaps best be illustrated by quoting from the memoirs of the Moscow party activist, V. M. Zenzinov:

Attached to our committee was a so-called 'group of propagandists', consisting of twelve to fifteen persons, almost exclusively students. Each of them had two or three circles of workers, to whom they delivered a more or less systematic course of lectures on Russian history, politics and political economy. Naturally, everything was related to current affairs and events. The circles were of two kinds; in circles of the first type the lectures were very basic (*elementarnyi*). Often the themes would be broadened or modified, depending on the questions of the participants. The work sometimes turned into acquainting [the workers] with the fundamental principals of astronomy, natural science or even theology, if they asked questions on these areas. But of course, circle leaders tried to steer the conversation on to political topics. In circles of the second kind, study was more systematic – popular books were read on political economy, Russian history and the revolutionary movement. The favourite themes in this type of study were the land question, political terror, and how the PSR differed from the SDs, who also conducted propaganda among the workers.[32]

As the passage indicates, propagandists were expected to tailor their classes to the level of education and particular interests of the participants. Nevertheless, they often appear to have based them on written programmes they had drawn up themselves. In July 1903, for example, the editors of *Revolyutsionnaya Rossiya* published a 'programme for study in workers' circles' which had been sent to them by the Saratov committee.[33] Its aim was to instil 'the conviction that only the working class can help itself, can free itself from centuries of oppression, and that this is possible only by means of revolution, of a general uprising'.[34] Circle propaganda here took two forms – discussion and interpretation of current events in the light of revolutionary socialism, and 'systematic reading on various questions'. It was suggested that the leaders ought to meet prior to each session so that they could consider information and comment taken from the press (revolutionary and conservative). If a particularly complex question was about to rise, one of the propagandists, or alternatively a sympathiser from outside, should present a paper on the subject. The circles were arranged in a system of three tiers, in line with the three stages of the programme. The first was specified for new recruits, the most promising of whom were expected to attend only three to five meetings before moving up. At this stage, it was suggested that the members discuss their own working conditions, before considering the main forms of exploitation (industrial and agricultural) and the means of resisting them.[35] The role of the government and church in the exploitation process would then be explained, as well as the impotence of the working class under the existing legal framework. The solution to these evils – common ownership of the land and of the means of production would then be elucidated, and a picture drawn of the future socialist order. The final meeting might consider unions, strikes, demonstrations and other means of struggle.

The second stage of the programme was much more expansive and ambitious than the first, though built on the same foundations.[36] Discussion and reading was broadened to encompass primitive communism, the growth of social inequality and the origins of class; the rise of modern industry and the development of capitalism; the history of Western socialism; modern phenomena of capitalism (colonies, cartels, and so on) and the threat posed to the Russian rural economy; autocracy, serfdom and emancipation; the new Russian proletariat; working conditions in the towns and on the land; the need for worker–peasant solidarity and the efforts of the Social Democrats to discourage this; the lack of proper working-class representation in factory, village and *zemstvo*; Zubatovism; factory legislation; the revolutionary movement in Russia and, finally, the history of the SR programme and a discussion of its contents. No indication was given of how many meetings might be needed to complete this formidable syllabus!

The third and final stage of the programme was intended to train potential leaders, either as agitators, or as propagandists supervising the elementary stage of the course. A number of ideas which had already been discussed were now to be treated in greater detail, with particular attention given to the party programme and to tactical questions.

The Saratov union of propagandists invited comment on their programme, and suggested that other organisations might present their own versions for publication in *Revolyutsionnaya Rossiya*. Twelve months later (!) a response appeared from a propagandist attached to the influential Kiev committee, who subjected the Saratov article to extensive and searching criticism.[37] Their programme was, the author argued, impractical, out-of-date and insensitive to the realities of the revolutionary underground. In contemporary conditions, he pointed out, an organisation could count on approximately five months of uninterrupted activity and very few workers (if any) would manage to complete such an ambitious course within that time. There was also criticism of a supposed failure to consider the more backward sections of the working class. The attitude of the proletariat during the strikes of July and August 1903 had, this writer believed, indicated that the socialist parties had failed almost totally to politicise the masses, and this factor had now to be taken into account when preparing circle propaganda. It was also argued that the Saratov programme made extravagant claims on the physical resources available to the party. Circle leaders surely needed to teach shorter courses, in order to be released as soon as possible to educate fresh recruits. The main aim should be to convey the essentials of the revolutionary message to the widest possible audience. Finally, the author claimed that the Saratov programme did not reveal a sufficient awareness of the threat posed by the Social Democrats, which had, he believed, intensified since the convening of their second congress. It was essential, he argued, not only that the SR programme be fully and clearly explained, but also that the vilification of its supporters be refuted and social-democratic ideas, counter-attacked.

The interest of this particular article does not only lie in such criticisms, however, but also in the information revealed about how, under ideal conditions, propaganda work was conducted in Kiev itself. Here, workers were recruited either at party meetings or in the course of strikes and other disturbances. They were then invited to join primary or 'flying' (*letuchie*) circles. Each comprised about eight members who would attend six or seven sessions, twice weekly. The agenda for each session was headed as follows:

(1) labour and capital;
(2) the interests of toilers and capitalists;
(3) socialism;
(4) the role of autocracy and the struggle against it;
(5) the SR minimum programme and an explanation of each of its points;
(6) the struggle against autocracy and the bourgeoisie;
(7) the differences between the PSR and the RSDRP;
(8) a short history of the workers' movement abroad.[38]

At the end of this preliminary course, the majority of workers ceased to attend circles, but they were expected to maintain contact with the party. They were invited to attend meetings and demonstrations, to use the library, and to help distribute leaflets. The most promising workers on the other hand, were creamed off and drawn into a more advanced 'propagandist' circle. The aim here was to produce trained agitators who, it was hoped, would serve as a link between the intelligentsia and the newly-enlightened working masses. There would only be three or four circles of this type at any one time. Meetings were spread over a period of approximately three months (twenty to twenty-five sessions). The course consisted of questions, discussion of current affairs and working conditions, reading and analysis of articles in the press and occasional lectures, on subjects such as the peasant programme – considered vital because agitators were often sent from the city into the rural localities. It was intended that, towards the end of the programme, the trainee-agitators would be drawn into practical work, so that they could make use of their newly-acquired knowledge and be of practical assistance to the party as quickly as possible. The dozen or so circle leaders in Kiev met weekly as a union of propagandists (*soyuz propagandistov*), to discuss questions of organisation and significant items in the illegal press and to present papers. Each propagandist was expected to take two or three circles of the first type and to work with a more advanced group.

Generally speaking, SR propaganda circles appear to have been organised along the same lines as those of the Social Democrats, and were no doubt confronted with similar problems. There was a permanent shortage of propagandists, especially good ones. This deficiency was especially acute in the PSR; it arose partly because the security organs gave it their particular attention and partly because its resources were over-extended, being committed to the countryside as well as the town. Circle work operated under circumstances which were trying in other ways. The workers involved often lacked any formal education and had to cope with study of an exacting kind after an exhausting day at the factory or workshop.[39] Furthermore, the atmosphere was continually made tense by the anticipation of arrest – as the Kiev writer reminded us, five months of uninterrupted activity was all that could be expected at the time. Nevertheless, the author conveys the impression that in Kiev at least the union of propagandists was able to live with such difficulties, and to think seriously about its role in the revolutionary movement. Evidently the Kiev activists were ready to adjust their programme to changes in the political climate, and were also sensitive to the danger of alienating the masses from the movement through disinterest or exclusiveness. It is impossible to gauge with any precision how successful they were in this respect before 1905, but there are serious grounds for scepticism. There is evidence to suggest that there may have been as few as thirty workers (excluding railwaymen) who were actually considered members of the party in Kiev, though admittedly such a figure ignores sympathisers on the periphery of the 'flying' circles and may reflect the impact of recent arrests.[40] The organisation may well have experienced difficulty in maintaining links with workers who had been propagandised and had since left the circles. These people may well have ceased to feel important to the party at this point, and lost interest in the movement.

AGITATION

In the first year and a half of the party's existence most SR organisations had to be content with forming circles and distributing propaganda, much of it published by the Central Committee. Such was the case in Moscow, Smolensk, Poltava, the Crimea, Saratov and elsewhere.[41]

In some places however, propaganda work was accompanied by occasional party meetings to rally the faithful. Three were held in Belostok, for example, during June and July 1903. The first was composed exclusively of peasants (70–80 attended); a 'celebration' attracted 100 workers and *intelligenty*, and a third meeting, conducted in Polish and Russian, 100. In addition a special assembly was convened to inform Jewish workers about the SR programme and to counteract prejudiced impressions already being circulated by the Bund. Aprpoximately 400 people were said to have attended this meeting.[42] Similar gatherings were recorded for Kishinev, Vitebsk and Berdichev during the first part of 1903; they became a feature of every party group as it became established.

Judging simply by the number of reports sent in to *Revolyutsionnaya Rossiya*, two of the most consistently active organisations in this early period were those of Kiev and Odessa.

During the first half of 1902 the Odessa SR group distributed proclamations in the 'streets, mills, factories and theatres' of the city, and a demonstration was planned there as early as February, to be held jointly with the Social Democrats. Police activity postponed it once however and prevented its success when the parties did eventually take to the streets. Apparently there were more than 300 arrests in connection with this incident.[43] A second demonstration held in May was only 'partly realised'. Apart from the police the Odessa organisation had to cope with the rivalry of other political parties. The most formidable of them were the Zubatovite 'Independents' but they also had to contend with the Russian Social Democrats, the Polish Socialist Party (PPS), anarchist groups and, from early 1903, a branch of the Bund.[44] The SRs led only one major strike during 1902, at the Brodskii sugar factory (800 workers) in December. *Iskra* carried a report of this incident. Whilst it was conceded that the strike had been 'prepared by the Socialist-Revolutionaries', their organisational work was criticised for being of a 'spontaneous' rather than a 'conscious' character. Allegedly, no attempt had been made to train proper activists to lead the strike. The dispute, which had arisen out of the sacking of one of Brodskii's employees, petered out after three days and was followed by the sending of about 100 workers back to their home villages and by the arrest of up to fifty *intelligenty*. According to *Iskra*, when the latter arrived back at the station following their release, they were greeted by a group of about seventy railwaymen shouting 'Down with autocracy' and 'Long live political freedom'.[45]

During the first half of 1903 the party claimed to be aware of an upswing in support. A bulletin dated March 1903 recorded a growing number of circles and the interest of migrant workers (bricklayers among others) arriving for seasonal work in Odessa. Agitation was also being conducted among the city's bakery workers and an 'assembly' was formed to further their interests. Propaganda was distributed as far as Akkerman and other places in the vicinity, but there was apparently a shortage of activists ready to undertake this work. There were a number of successful meetings. 'Several hundred' were said to have attended a celebration marking the anniversary of the Emancipation Edict (19 February) and a total audience of 500 was recorded for four meetings convened between March and June.[46] Yet despite this promising news, when the organisation was tested during the general strike of July 1903 it was found to be severely wanting. Several leaflets were produced at the time, including one addressed to the tramway workers and another to 'stokers and sailors', but when party members tried to distribute them at a mass rally in the Rubov Gardens they were seized and torn up by the Independents. Several attempts to hold a demonstration were foiled by the police.[47] While the SRs may not have been effectively involved in the main events of the strike this did not exempt them from arrest. Twenty-three people (including nine women) were taken in September, along with the committee's printing press.[48]

Kiev too was a prominent centre of SR activity in these early days. Already in February 1902 a reasonably successful demonstration had been staged by SRs and SDs combined, with an estimated crowd of 10 000 onlookers. Troops were called in, and there was some violence. An attempt was made to repeat the performance the following day, but with less success; there were about 150 arrests.[49]

The SR organisation subsequently concentrated on distributing propaganda, much of it to the local peasantry. At the close of the year there were three meetings, one of 250 people, but a lack of propagandists was complained of. Early in 1903 agitation began among the city's hairdressers; they were advised to form a union and to strike, but there is no evidence as to whether they did so.[50] Many of the party's supporters here were seasonal workers; in the spring they returned to their villages, each carrying leaflets and books to be distributed among *zemlyaki*.[51] An estimated 300 people attended meetings during March, but in the following month there were arrests. At the time there had been talk of an armed demonstration. The question had been discussed in February, but the essential co-operation of the SDs was lacking. In April the 'Jewish National Committee for Self-Defence', fearing it might inspire a pogrom, asked the local organisations to desist from street activity, and the idea was finally dropped.[52] By the time of the Kiev general strike in July, the SRs had been considerably weakened by arrests and they made no impression on events, a point the SDs were anxious to drive home in the pages of *Iskra*. The SRs replied defensively in September. They admitted that their attempt to hold an armed demonstration on 27 July had been a failure. The event had been called too late, after the strike had passed its peak and the site chosen (Sofia Square), was, it was conceded, the worst possible one for self-defence. But the Social Democrats were chided for not making clear to their readership the terrible persecution which the SRs had suffered during that period:

> But the SD committee knows besides that such comrades [those arrested] were not numbered in ones and twos...The SD committee knows how many fighters were snatched from our ranks by the government during the whole of this terrible year, from the very beginning until the last few days.[53]

The SRs pointed out that the Social Democrats too had been unable to lead the mass movement at the time and they bemoaned the economistic aspects of the strike and the opiate nature of concessions wrung from the employers by local workers.

It is true that the mood of the proletariat during the summer of 1903 was hostile to the '*politiki*', epitomised by the SRs. All the more surprising then to find a comparatively robust organisation in Ekaterinoslav playing an active role in the general strike of August 1903. While elsewhere the party appears to have experienced difficulty in gaining a durable foothold in individual factories and enterprises (where it tried at all) this was apparently less of a problem in Ekaterinoslav. There are few references to an organisation here before the summer of 1903 but by that time the SRs had evidently created a number of bases on which they could rely for support.[54] The most notable of these were the railway workshops, the huge Bryansk works, the Ezau and Tube factories and some of the plants across the river at Amur and Nizhne-Dneprovsk – apart from local artisans and seasonal workers: bakers, printers, bricklayers, and so on.

The strike was planned to begin on 4 August[55] and the SRs conducted intensive propaganda and agitation in the days leading up to the event. Proclamations were distributed and the strike discussed in the course of circle work. Close attention was paid by the committee to the advice of the 'workers' centre' during these preparations. There were a number of successful meetings, though at least one was forestalled by the police, who occupied the crossing points of the river.

In the event the strike got off to a false start, with only the bakery workers answering the SRs' initial call. On 7 August, however, things began in earnest. An agitational tour was made of the SR strongholds, beginning with the railways shops, and the response was enthusiastic. From the beginning (at least according to party reports) the SR agitators tried to give the strike a political character:

'Comrades, do you understand that government and tsar act as one with the capitalist exploiters?

'We understand, we see it clearly,' was the reply from the men at the Bryansk factory. Demands, including the eight-hour day, wage increases and provision for general insurance, were presented to the manager. Troops and police were already on hand but on the strike leaders' assurance that the workers intended to behave peacefully SR and SD representatives were allowed to lead the men out of the complex and towards the town centre, stopping at other factories on the way.[56] In the course of the next two hours, speeches were made by agitators from both parties, the SRs calling for a demonstration and speaking out vociferously against the State. This line of argument did not apparently please the majority. The day's events culminated in a meeting at Bryansk Square attended, it was said, by up to 15 000 people. The vice-governor, Kayazev, spoke to the workers without effect and was unable to persuade them to present delegates for negotiations. Eventually the cossacks moved in and violence ensued, leaving a number of dead and injured. The following day another meeting was planned at Bryansk Square but troops and police were already in place. SR organisers toured the artisanal enterprises and bakeries in an effort to stir up support and, together with the SDs, successfully stopped the running of the trams for a time. In the afternoon there were further clashes with the security forces. That evening, the SR committee sent some of its most militant workers to talk to the men in Nizhne-Dneprovsk and both parties agitated in the industrial suburb of Amur, the SRs again instilling a political flavour into their speeches.[57] On the third day there were more meetings, though generally now in smaller numbers to avoid attracting the attention of the police. One SR-led gathering of 500 people was recorded; it probably took place in the workers' district of Chechelev, not in the town itself, and most likely included SD speakers. The strike ended on the following Monday, apparently without any concessions being won.

The two reports on which this summary has been based provide a sufficiently full account of the events in Ekaterinoslav to indicate relative SR influence in the town. Unfortunately for the party such demonstrations of support rarely went unpunished by the authorities: by the end of the year local organisers were talking of the need to rebuild the party there.[58] No doubt the SDs suffered similarly.

Outside the areas just reviewed there were few noteworthy developments in the period of the party's infancy.[59] Most success was enjoyed in areas where the SRs could count on the temporary support of the Social Democrats. In Khar'kov, for example, both committees staged a strike at the locomotive works in May 1902. Some joint proclamations were issued as well as a common list of demands. The strike took place on May Day itself and the majority of employees (there were between 5000 and 6000 in all) left work. There were serious clashes between workers and cossacks and the governor had to be summoned to the scene in person. The event was followed by the predictable searches and arrests.[60]

There was also a measure of common activity in the Urals, where a regional union of SRs and SDs had been operating since the turn of the century.[61] This alliance enabled the SRs to take an active part in one of the most notorious incidents of the period, at the Zlatoust armaments factory (5000 workers). Unrest began over unemployment resulting from a fire in December 1902 when two workshops had been destroyed. The situation was aggravated by the introduction of account books for fines, together with the abolition of legislation which had previously protected the workers' jobs. In March 1903 the SR–SD union issued proclamations calling for a strike, a call which they responded to readily. After three days the state governor (Bogdanovich) arrived but brought no promises of concessions. On the contrary, there were arrests, and when a crowd subsequently went to the gaol to demand freedom for those imprisoned they were fired upon. The two parties intensified their propaganda campaign after this incident, which was given extensive coverage in *Revolyutsionnaya Rossiya*. The SRs also helped to start a fund for the victims.[62]

A second joint SR–SD committee operated in Perm' from early 1902 and focused its attention on the large armaments plant (6000 workers) in neighbouring Motovilikha. Despite the arrest of propagandists and supporters in May after three proclamations had been distributed at the factory, another five proclamations were in circulation by December. In February 1903 five more workers were arrested in connection with these activities, two of them at the Lyubimov boat factory. On 20 February strike began at Motovilikha in protest at the lowering of wage rates and the behaviour of management. By the following day two-thirds of the workforce had joined the stoppage but it petered out four days later because of a lack of funds. The SRs felt that the strike had begun prematurely but were presumably not influential enough to delay the action.[63] Their Perm' organisation is silent from this point on until 1905.

The period from the autumn of 1903 to the end of 1904 was a depressing one for the revolutionary movement as a whole. For the SRs the nadir was reached during the last quarter of 1904, when hardly any activity is reported in *Revolyutsionnaya Rossiya* except for the issue of proclamations, and that often irregularly. The chief reason for the decline was the worsening economic situation, which made workers reluctant to come out on strike even for wage improvements, let alone risk their livelihood by participating in political protest, which most of them failed either to understand or to sympathise with. Only when the depths of despair were reached would they have been tempted to rebel and such moods probably soon passed. Generally speaking the working class was on the defensive. Another, more obvious, reason for the comparative failure of the revolutionary parties was the efficiency of the police. Spies infiltrated SR organisations with ease, and members of the Zubatov unions in particular were used to provide the authorities with information concerning support for the revolutionary parties in the factories.[64] The Minister of the Interior, V. K. Plehve, had pledged to rid the country of these elements on coming to office and his ruthless determination to carry out this mission only added to their problems; until, that is, the SR Fighting Organisation succeeded in asssassinating him in July 1904.

One new form of SR activity to emerge during this period was local urban terror. The first recorded incident occurred in Berdichev (Podolia province) 14 October 1903 when a police officer named Kulishev was wounded.[65] Two weeks later the Belostok police chief was injured in a similar attack. The SRs claimed responsibility for both events. In the Belostok case, the local armed worker detachment perpetrated the attack; it may have been responsible for the Berdichev incident as well. In November 1903 the Berdichev PSR called a demonstration to express 'solidarity' with the killers.[66] Both Jewish and Christian workers were said to have participated and leaflets were distributed to the accompaniment of shouts of 'down with autocracy', 'long live the assassins'. No indication was given as to the numbers present. Three months later there was a strike in Belostok, during which a number of workers were arrested. In response to this the 'Belostok SR workers' fighting group' issued a statement, warning that if the men were not released the new chief of police, Pelenkin, would suffer the same fate as his predecessor. The prisoners, *Revolyutsionnaya Rossiya* proudly reported, were duly released.[67]

In February 1904 there was another extraordinary incident in Belostok, providing further indication of the swelling tide of extremism there.[68] The occasion was the funeral of a former party member. Of the 600 particpants approximately 100 were said to have been Jews. The procession to the cemetery halted at the local prison, and ribbons carrying the designation 'Belostok organisation of the PSR' were placed on the coffin. There were shouts of 'Down with autocracy', 'Long live the fighting organisation', 'long live socialism', and so on. This incident provoked the intervention of the police and a general commotion ensued in the vicinity of the cemetery, during which there were gunshot exchanges between workers and policemen (the SRs had distributed their small stock of weapons beforehand). The clashes were serious enough to merit a visit from the governor the following day. Although there were arrests the SRs considered the event a success, commenting that the town was now buzzing with the news that the police had been fired on by workers. The fighting detachment, presumably responsible for what had happened, received eighty-nine roubles from the local committee between March and May 1904 for spending on arms. According to Spiridovitch, in October two SRs wounded a number of policemen in Belostok with a bomb.[69] No further incident of this type was recorded prior to 1905.

Indications of growing tension and looming confrontation can also be gleaned from information coming out of Vil'no and Odessa. In Vil'no it was reported in September 1904 that a 'terrorist spirit is growing among the Jewish working masses' and that 'the Jewish workers are sympathetic to the idea of terror'.[70] In Odessa early in the same year there had been talk of pogroms, leading the party to discuss the possibility of armed defence.[71] The conclusion was that such action was justified only in extreme circumstances – there must be no waste of the meagre resources available in defence of Jewish bourgeois property for example! However, resolutions were undertaken to accumulate a cache of side and fire-arms, to calculate the strength of forces available to the party and to constitute a force of perhaps 150 men which could be held in reserve. An idea (reported as originating with the SDs) that police stations be attacked, was rejected out of hand – the necessary resources simply did not exist. There is no evidence that the defence force envisaged was ever constituted, unless it was the origins of what later became the Odessa fighting detachment itself.

Evidence of more conventional activity for this period is comparatively hard to come by. Six party meetings of various kinds were reported by the Odessa committee between December 1903 and August 1904. The greatest disappointment was the failure to celebrate May Day, the result of police action beforehand. Some agitation was conducted at a quarry and brickworks in the industrial suburb of Peresyp and at a local salt mine. A group was established at Odessa port in June 1904.[72]

In Belostok only four meetings were held between October 1903 and May 1904. On May Day itself there were several gatherings in neighbouring villages but none in the town, again on account of the police. The largest assembly, one of 200 people, was held in February to capitalise on the recent demonstration and shooting incident there. The SRs were also involved in a major strike in Belostok during November and December 1903.[73] It began among local handweavers, at the time forced to endure a thirteen-hour day and more for low wages. A total of 2000 workers were said to be involved. The Bund and the Lithuanian Social Democrats fought the campaign independently but the PSR and PPS established a joint strike committee. The SRs immediately began agitating for solidarity with the weavers, addressing both other handicraft workers and 'all the steam mills in Belostok'. On 8 December a general strike involving mill-workers, bakers, tailors, compositors, weavers and others was declared. It was short-lived but concessions were won by some of the weavers. At the same time the party organised another strike at a tannery and won the men a reduction in hours and a wage increase.

In the west of Russia Vitebsk, like Belostok, seems to have been a centre of growing SR influence. When the group presented its accounts to *Revolyutsionnaya Rossiya* in December 1904 it claimed to have organised ten meetings between the time of its foundation in August 1903 and its first anniversary. Total attendance at these functions was put at nearly 700. Two hundred people came to the anniversary celebrations and there seems to have been a regular core of between thirty and thirty-five agitators to hand.[74] Another report claimed that 'the number of *intelligenty* is insignificant in comparison with the number of workers'.[75]

In Bryansk, where a strike broke out at the arsenal in September 1903, SR agitational work already extended to other factories and workshops, both in the town and in neighbouring Mal'tsev. The party attempted to give the movement a political flavour via its proclamations, but apparently without success.[76]

The best-documented organisation for this period is undoubtedly the Moscow party, where operations had begun at the end of 1902.[77] Early activity was subsequently described as amateurish (*kustarnyi*) and both SRs and SDs lived very much in the shadow of the Zubatovite movement.[78] In January 1904, however, Zenzinov arrived from abroad to become the guiding spirit of the movement in Moscow.[79] His description of the organisation at that time has already been cited in another context; total worker membership was somewhere in the region of 140.

In February the group was awarded, or awarded itself, committee status, but three months later disaster struck – every one of its members, with the exception of Zenzinov himself, was arrested. Paradoxically this event marked the resurgence of the party, which this time was built on firmer foundations.[80]

On Palm Sunday 1904 the SRs attracted publicity to their cause by scattering 1000 proclamations on the war with Japan from the upper trading galleries (now GUM) in Red Square, when the area was crowded for the traditional religious procession. It was claimed that the economic demands in the leaflets eventually forced concessions from a number of enterprises.[81]

During the summer the propagandists left town to agitate, both in the villages and among the troops – Zenzinov recalls distributing proclamations to entrained soldiers on the Kazan' railway.[82] By the autumn, although there were only about 70 workers in SR circles, morale was probably much higher than it had been during the previous year and important cells had been established at the giant Prokhorov works (6000 workers) in Presnya and the Tsindel' Cotton Mill, as well as other factories, mills and artisanal establishments in the city. A 'workers' union' was created in the autumn, after which efforts seem to have focused on the organisation of a major political demonstration, apparently at the suggestion of the Prokhorov workers.[83] This was scheduled for 5 and 6 December (6 December being the Tsar's name-day). It was in connection with this event that the committee issued its famous warning to Trepov and the Grand Duke Sergei, mentioned earlier. The demonstration centred on Tver' Boulevard (the residence of the Governor-general), but spilled over into neighbouring streets, as far as Strastnoi (now Pushkin) Square. Party leaflets were distributed and there were the usual slogans and banners. Later in the day there was shooting, and other, less serious clashes between the crowd, troops and police. The second demonstration was smaller in scale than the first, and there were fewer incidents.

In one sense the party's efforts to bring the population on to the streets had been a considerable success, but it was noted that 'there were many among the crowd who expressed surprise that there was almost no participation by workers in the demonstration'; an observation with which the local party more or less concurred.[84] The reason, they argued, was not indifference on the part of the workforce, but the stringent police measures which prevented most of them from gaining access to the proposed venue. A number of important approaches had been cordoned off, while those factories which accommodated their employees on the premises were surrounded and the men prevented from leaving. Nevertheless, some workers (it was later alleged) were seen listening to SR agitators in Red Square. Many more would become acquainted with the party and its programme in the turbulent months which lay ahead.

4 The SRs and the Revolution of 1905–7: An Overview

THE REVOLUTION OF 1905

The December demonstrations in Moscow were followed a few weeks later by the dramatic events in the capital, which began with the dismissal of four workers at the Putilov plant and culminated in the shooting of more than 200 unarmed, peaceful demonstrators in front of Palace Square on 9 January. That fateful occurrence, etched in the annals of history as 'Bloody Sunday' ushered in the unprecedented disorders and upheavals of the revolutionary year, 1905. The immediate reply to Bloody Sunday was a nationwide movement of strikes and protests which impacted with particular severity on the peripheral regions of the Empire – Tsarist Poland, the Baltic provinces, Finland and the Caucasus. This was followed by a frenetic period of factory-level negotiations and by a number of investigative commissions of the kind established by senator Shidlovskii in Petersburg. The end of this particular chapter was marked by the publication in February of the 'Bulygin Rescript' which signified the first tentative step on the road to constitutional government. It was not enough to restore lasting stability however. The catastrophic naval defeat at Tsushima in May was a damning indictment of the autocracy and the government, and added fuel to the argument (advanced by both the Left, and by the grand coalition of bourgeois-liberal interests which had been forming since the turn of the year) that more fundamental political changes were needed. Mutiny among the sailors of the Black Sea fleet in June and news of the first rumblings of peasant discontent sustained the pressure on the authorities, who responded in

57

August by promising a 'consultative assembly' and by granting autonomy to the universities. These concessions, coupled more tellingly with the Peace of Portsmouth, which ended the disastrous and humiliating war with Japan, seemed to offer at least the hope of a breathing space for the government. However, it was barely weeks later that the whole of Russia was brought to a complete standstill by the country's first general strike, which had begun innocuously enough with a printers' dispute in Moscow. The working class now demonstrated the lessons of organisation and solidarity which they had learned during their experiences earlier in the year. The convening of the Petersburg Soviet of Workers' Deputies to co-ordinate the strike in the capital was followed four days later by the climactic point of 1905 – the publication of the 'October Manifesto', which granted Russia's first properly democratic constitution. For a few short weeks, known to those who lived through them as the 'Days of Freedom', the peoples of the Empire enjoyed a taste at least of the civil and political liberties long taken for granted in the West. And while it is true that the strike movement ultimately disintegrated, that the leaders of the Petersburg Soviet were eventually herded off to prison and that the workers of Moscow were driven to the barricades in a heroic but hopeless attempt to prolong the revolutionary momentum, the renewal of disorder in the countryside and the threat of a similar repetition of unrest in the cities ensured at least that the country's first parliament did eventually meet, albeit with considerably reduced powers. Never, in fact, would Russia be quite the same again.

One of the SR organisations to benefit most from the developments just described (in the short term at least) was that of Moscow. Indeed, the events of Bloody Sunday augured a dramatic improvement in the party's fortunes here as compared with the situation at the turn of the year. Propaganda circles quickly outgrew the resources of the intelligentsia, and there were soon an estimated 400–500 worker members.[1] The committee felt a need to decentralise and party branches were created at district level. A workers' newspaper was produced, the volume of other propaganda material was increased, and the workers' union drew up a list of twenty-seven demands to government and employers, supported by a call for solidarity with their comrades in Petersburg.[2] In February the committee gained new notoriety by successfully carrying out the execution of Grand Duke Sergei Aleksandrovich – there had already been an attempt on the life of Trepov. Despite the usual bout of arrests, a number of meetings were held to celebrate May Day, sometimes in the company of the

Social Democrats, and another joint gathering took place on 22 May. Altogether during that month some 600 Moscow workers heard the message of the PSR at their various party assemblies.[3] The first armed detachment was formed in May or June and membership grew apace over the following months. Meanwhile, contact was established with the soldiers and officers of the Moscow Garrison. The committee later claimed to have issued 87 000 leaflets between May and July, and by the end of the summer was well placed to take advantage of the second major wave of strikes which was then about to begin.[4]

The growing politicisation of workers throughout Russia after Bloody Sunday led, not surprisingly, to increasing interest in and support for the PSR and its platform, but it also revealed the comparative weakness of party bases in the towns and, especially, in the factories. According to one source,[5] the SRs were partly responsible for leading the January–February strike movement in Riga, Vil'no, Zhitomir, Baku and Belostok, but this writer has been able to find information about only one of these – Belostok. The strike here broke out in February; there was fierce rivalry between the SRs and the Bund, but it was the SDs who initiated developments from their base in the Vechorek factory (500 workers). Meanwhile the SRs distributed leaflets and convened meetings with representatives from the various enterprises. On 17 February they formed a joint 'revolutionary strike committee' with the PPS, but later conceded that this decision had come too late. (The strike had begun on 14 February). None the less the party did succeed in holding a number of meetings, including one which reportedly attracted 800 previously unorganised workers, whom, it was said, responded positively to the SR slogans. On 18 February the party called a mass gathering which was attended by an estimated 12 000–15 000 people. Agitators from all parties addressed the crowd. Afterwards there was a march into the town, accompanied by shouts of 'down with the police', 'down with the capitalists', and slogans in praise of the Fighting Organisation.[6]

A small amount of material is also available on the activities of the SRs in several other centres during the January–February period. In Saratov, the local committee and workers' union made a joint decision to agitate for a strike on 11 January, and a major stoppage began the following day among the factories and smaller enterprises. Significantly, however, although a 'central strike committee' was formed, there were no SR members, suggesting very weak support among the settled local workforce. The party was therefore powerless to prevent the SDs from declaring the political strike at an end after one or two days and were consigned to the side-lines, complaining bitterly that the Social Democrats listened only to the least conscious workers.[7]

The SRs in Bryansk were able to report more favourably.[8] Agitation began here on 13 January and six leaflets were produced in support of the strike call. Both Social-Democrat and Social-Revolutionary orators addressed a number of meetings, one of which attracted a crowd of 300. On the advice of the Bezhetsa workers' union (Bezhetsa being a large industrial suburb outside Bryansk) the committee sanctioned the launching of a strike on 25 January, centring on the giant rail-producing plant (10 000 workers). This first attempt was a failure but agitation was stepped up and the party's perseverance was rewarded with a one-and-a-half month stoppage which began at the end of February. Other factories joined the strike and, according to *Revolyutsionnaya Rossiya*, used the demands produced by the Bezhetsa SR union. Regular mass meetings were held, attracting crowds of between 6000 and 12 000 people. The SRs claimed to have directed the proceedings at this stage, alleging that their slogan 'down with autocracy' was now widely approved of by the workers, and that the population outside the town was anxious to join in future protests.

In Smolensk the party had to vie both with the Russian Social Democrats and with the Bund for control of the strike, which in any case burnt out after only two days.[9] The report in *Revolyutsionnaya Rossiya* provides some information on the likely sources of party support in the town. It was said that on 17 January a few organised workers of the PSR persuaded forty men at the Kovalev metal workshop to strike, before moving on in turn to four printing works (total employees 253), a bakery and 'many other small craft shops'. The party also seems to have had sympathisers at a local bobbin factory and at the railway workshops in Strogan, a short distance away.

At Krasnoyarsk too, SR support seems to have been concentrated in the railway workshops.[10] A two-day strike occured here in January but collapsed because (according to the SRs) the Social Democrats failed to deliver the local artisans and shop assitants.

The details of three strikes involving SRs were reported during May 1905. In Minsk the party claimed to have led the movement, most probably from the workshops of the Moscow–Brest railway (800 workers).[11] Meetings were held there daily, addressed by party agitators who steered the drift of their speeches gradually from economic to political positions.

SR activity in the Baku strike movement seems to have been limited to distributing leaflets (about 2250 copies in all), but it was said that support for the party was increasing there 'daily'.[12] There were 'hundreds of conscious members' many of them recent converts from social democracy. They had been attracted to the PSR, it was said, by the party's agrarian programme and by the more aggressive means of struggle which it advocated.

In Saratov the SRs were trying hard to compensate for their failure in January. They began holding preparatory meetings for a projected strike just before Easter, and on 27 and 28 April intensified their campaign by distributing two proclamations (3500 copies in all). A workers' assembly, held on the eve of May Day, attracted 200 people, but the celebrations on the day itself were a fiasco. The proposed strike, which ran from 2 to 7 May, was for the SRs more or less a repeat performance of the events earlier in the year. The party benefited somewhat from the publicity – agitators were able to address crowds of up to 1000 people – but was unable to influence the course of the strike itself, which soon lost its political flavour and dissolved into a number of separate economic disputes.[13]

One centre where SR support had increased noticeably by the early summer was Odessa. Here it was reported that 'the number of workers being agitated in an organised fashion, attending meetings, reading literature, and in general ready to answer the call may be reckoned in thousands'.[14] All four city districts had their own branches by June and one or two of these were estimated to enjoy more support individually than the entire city organisation only two years previously. The technical resources of the party had also improved and the committee had a supply of arms, part of which had been transferred to the workers for the purposes of target practice! There had not been a general strike here at the beginning of the year, but there was an upsurge of industrial action during June and July. Previous to this, strikes which had developed had tended to be purely for economic gain; the workers would only listen to party agitators as long as they talked about immediate improvements in conditions (*o dele*). The SRs blamed this narrow attitude partly on the *zubatovshchina* and partly on the Social Democrats. They accused the latter of having only recently been arguing in favour of peaceful strikes, to the detriment of more militant means of struggle. Some economic strikes had been led by the SRs, it was admitted, but in general that party's strategy had been to work for a large-scale political strike which would set the stage for full-scale rebellion.

The Odessa reports claim that the mood of workers began to change in favour of the PSR towards the end of May. Meetings were held regularly, sometimes several times a day in the Peresyp district, and there was the beginnings of a 'mass transfer' of former SD supporters into the ranks of the SRs. One of the reasons for this, it was supposed, was the desire on the part of younger workers to become involved in the activity of the armed detachments. 'Dozens of energetic and revolutionary-minded SD workers asked to be accepted by our armed guards, in spite of the fact that they were not in agreement with our programme.' They had to be turned down, however, allegedly because of the level of demand from SR members.

The political conflagration which the SRs had been anticipating, finally materialised on 14 June and endured for four days. It took the form of a general strike which in turn fed the mutiny on board the *Potemkin*. Unfortunately the available sources do not permit us to trace the role of the SRs in these events with any precision. The party organisation was weakened by arrests on 12–13 June, and by the discovery of a bomb factory several days later.[15]

On the evidence available, the summer of 1905 was a period of only modest success for the PSR, and in terms of numerical support they were almost always well to the rear of their Social-Democrat rivals, and sometimes had to admit to poor organisation. This was the case in Ekaterinoslav, where a strike was launched on 20 July.[16] The party appears to have preserved the bases it had established there during the pre-revolutionary period. As many as seventy representatives from enterprises in the factory district attended a meeting of the 'workers' centre' on 19 July and the railway workshops, the engineering plants in Amur and the Bryansk factory all featured prominently in the strike. There was a certain amount of violence, though the report in *Revolyutsionnaya Rossiya* plays down this aspect, arguing that 'only' five bombs were thrown, none of them causing any damage! The local party committee blamed a delay in the issuing of demands for the failure of the strike, but they may well have alienated many workers by attempting to instil into the event too political a flavour.

Elsewhere, strike activity during the summer months was reported from Ufa, Riga (where the SRs claimed to have made a considerable impact), Bryansk, Novozybkov and Kiev, but doubtless many other organisations were simply too pre-occupied to send in regular bulletins to *Revolyutsionnaya Rossiya*.[17]

FROM REVOLUTION TO REACTION

In the months following the promulgation of the October Manifesto the PSR was transformed from a 'Party of conspirators' into a 'party of the great working masses'.[18] By 1907 it was able to boast 50 000 active members and the peripheral support of up to 300 000 sympathisers. It disposed of a regular income which at one time approached 100 000 roubles and the equivalent of four times this sum had been spent on arms alone during 1904–5. Party publishing houses and the local organisations themselves successfully produced and distributed impressive quantities of books, pamphlets, leaflets and newspapers – a Petersburg workers' paper *Trud* appeared in editions of 20 000–25 000 copies between September 1906 and March 1908.[19] According to calculations based on archival sources,[20] the urban membership of the PSR represented about half the total of 50 000. Six centres claimed more than a thousand worker-members each: Petersburg, Moscow, Baku, Sevastopol', the Mal'tsev industrial district (Bryansk) and Rostov. Another seventeen organisations counted at least 300 'organised workers' at the height of their influence.[21]

Unfortunately, by the time representatives of the Central Committee conveyed these promising statistics to the Socialist International in Stuttgart (August 1907) the party had been overtaken by a wholly adverse trend in events. Even at the height of the revolution progress had been sporadic, uneven, and fraught with every kind of organisational difficulty. While local centres everywhere were flooded with supporters their leaders generally failed to capitalise on this success by consolidating the party's position in the soviets, factory commissions, trade unions, councils for the unemployed, and so on. In Moscow, well in advance of the collapse of the armed uprising in December 1905 the local PSR had been split wide open by the activities of an 'opposition' which would eventually lead to the complete disintegration of the party there. Organisations in the south and west of Russia especially were torn by internecine strife, this time as the result of the spreading 'Maximalist' heresy, while centres where the party remained intact were constantly subject to disruption through arrest, harrassment and intimidation of every form. The PSR was also short of effective, purposeful direction from the top during these crucial moments in its history: the 'founding' congress, it will be recalled, did not meet until the very last days of December 1905 when the revolutionary momentum was already on the ebb, and even then it failed to issue policy directives in areas vital to the development of the labour movement. However, it was not until 1907 that the government delivered its knock-out blow, in the form of the *coup d'état* of 3 June. Constitutional niceties were dispensed with as the second Duma was disbanded, a radically revised electoral law introduced and a counter-revolutionary offensive of unprecedented ferocity launched against town and countryside alike.

All the left-wing opposition parties reeled under these blows but none more so than those advocating terror against the State. The police began to intensify their campaign against the PSR in June, raiding party organisations in Krasnoyarsk, Mogilev and Petersburg, where the entire committee fell into the hands of the Okhrana. In July it was the turn of Samara, Odessa and Sevastopol': fifty-four SRs were arrested at a conference there. In August, the police moved against organisations in Viatka, Revel and Krivoi-Rog; in September, against those in Saratov, Yaroslavl', Nizhnii-Novgorod, Khar'kov, Ekaterinoslav and Ufa; in October, Voronezh and Tiflis; in November, Rostov-on-Don; in December, Nikolaev, Kazan' and Kiev. In fact the majority of these places (and a host of others) were raided several times during this period and again many times subsequently, with the result that by the time of the first SR party conference in August 1908 their entire organisation lay in ruins.[22] There would be no genuine revival before the onset of war in 1914.

THE MAXIMALIST SPLIT

Between 1904 and 1906 the PSR became tainted with two, unrelated heterodoxies. The first, introduced by the *Russkoe Bogatstvo* group,[23] led ultimately to the formation of the Popular Socialist Party. The second, known as Maximalism, exercised a much more pervasive and disruptive influence, especially among workers of the southern and western provinces, and led in turn to the forming of a breakaway 'Union of SR Maximalists' in October 1906.[24]

Doubtless some of the radical traits which coloured the Maximalist deviation were long present in the psychology of various strata of urban worker. The origins of the doctrine itself, however, can be traced to the Geneva group of *émigré* intellectuals led by M. I. Sokolov (Medved') and E. Ustinov (Lozinskii). In 1904 the Geneva colony contributed to the debate surrounding the SR's draft programme by arguing in favour of 'agrarian terrorism' – spontaneous or organised attacks by the peasantry on the estates of landowners. By the summer of the following year they had become estranged from the mother party and, through the medium of the journal *Volnyi diskussionyi listok* (free discussion leaflet) were advocating broader programmatic and tactical changes, incompatible with the orthodox SR approach.[25] The essence of what became known as 'Maximalism' consisted, first, in a demand to include factory socialisation in the party's minimum programme, as a means of achieving outright socialist revolution; and secondly, in the adoption of 'economic' (that is, factory and agrarian) terror as a complement to political terror. Maximalism came to acquire two other distinctive characteristics: a principled hostility to participation in any kind of 'bourgeois' democratic assembly and a tendency to substitute the 'minority initiative' for the masses in the making of social revolution.[26] Sokolov's group formally left the PSR in December 1905 and made a home for themselves in terrorist Belostok, where the local SRs were quickly won over to the Maximalist ideology.[27]

By this time, however, Maximalism was threatening to emerge in a different guise elsewhere in Russia. In Moscow, an 'opposition' to the official SR committee had formed in the autumn of 1905 and included some 'outstanding' members of what was then the party's largest urban organisation: Vladimir Mazurin, Margarita Uspenskaya and D. V. Vinogradov.[28] The split in the Moscow organisation was originally nothing to do with Maximalism; it was caused by demands for the 'democratisation' of the local party and for the greater involvement of workers in its affairs.[29] Following the first party congress, however, this once internalised dispute began to have broader repercussions. On the grounds that it had not been properly represented at that assembly, the opposition refused to recognise party resolutions and, from bases in the railway and Sokol'niki districts began, soon after, to engage in 'private expropriations', a practice outlawed by the party.[30] The spectacular robbery of 800 000 roubles from the Moscow merchant bank, an enterprise masterminded by Mazurin and Vinogradov, drove the opposition on to a collision course with the party hierarchy. By May 1906 the Moscow PSR had split into two separate organisations and the Opposition issued its own 'Platform'.[31] At the same time, the latter's extremist tactics made it increasingly susceptible to Maximalist tendencies and to infiltration by Maximalist groups. This 'riff-raff', as Uspenskaya caustically described them, were soon predominant in at least some districts.[32] Meanwhile, the Opposition had tried with some success to entice other party organisations to leave the PSR by offering financial inducements. The Petersburg armed detachments received money from this source and the Opposition had further success in Ryazan', Stavropol' and Ekaterinoslav.[33] Already by the autumn of 1906, however, the entire Moscow organisation had begun to disintegrate, and although an orthodox committee continued to function for several months more, the PSR in Moscow was essentially a spent force.[34]

Maximalism ultimately left few organisations untouched,[35] but the damage it inflicted varied from one centre to another. At the very least, the proximity of Maximalist or Anarchist influences tended to radicalise local party opinion, especially on the sensitive question of factory terror, thereby bringing it into conflict with official party thinking.[36] In some places (Smolesnk, for example) a minority of SRs began to call themselves Maximalists, while agreeing to adhere to party discipline and not to engage in Maximalist tactics. Elsewhere, the hopelessly lax conditions of entry into the SRs' combat detachments allowed Anarchists and Maximalists to infiltrate more or less at will and their ideological peculiarities may often have gone unnoticed or been waved aside. While this kind of influence was often confined to the combat wing of the party, acts of factory terror, private expropriations or extortion, carried out in the name of 'SRs', obviously had a damaging effect on the morale of the orthodox, and caused confusion about what was permissible in the party. At worst, Maximalism captured the imagination and sympathy of an entire organisation, leaving little more than a rump remaining faithful to the official party line.[37] While the latter often outlived the former, the damage to the party as a whole was irreparable and no organisation ever fully recovered from such a trauma.

In the course of his attempt to 'characterise' Maximalism, Victor Chernov advanced a number of reasons for its apparent irresistibility for so many workers.[38] First, he argued, both Maximalism and Anarchism were primitive responses to an as yet nascent or undeveloped capitalism. Both tendencies found a special resonance among the ruined peasantry – those 'unsocialised, bitter and restless' elements not yet integrated into the urban proletariat. Secondly, at the turn of the century the SRs had offered the only revolutionary alternative to Social Democracy and had therefore tended to attract a variety of fringe extremists who later came to identify themselves more accurately as Anarchists or Maximalists. SR approval of certain forms of terrorism had earlier served to blur some of the distinctions between themselves and these groups. Finally, Chernov cited the appeal of

Maximalism to workers who delighted in 'spontaneity' and direct action, and who were willing to put their faith in the power of minority initiative.

Chernov's theory about 'primitive rebels' may have been more appropriate to the case of handicraft workers than to peasants not yet 'boiled in the factory cauldron'.[39] The ruined artisans of western Russia suffered from a capitalist system which was not only underdeveloped but whose representatives also specifically excluded them from its midst while, at the same time, undermining their existing livelihoods. Is it purely coincidence that Maximalism made such sweeping inroads in the White Russian provinces?[40] As far as Chernov's second hypothesis is concerned, it is certainly true that the failure of the PSR to define its programme and tactics unambiguously at an early stage had left it open to elements which had little kinship with the mainstream of the party. Even had it done so, however, its sanctioning of terror was enough to attract a wide spectrum of marginal fellow-travellers, little interested in ideology of any kind, but thirsting for the excitement and romance of action.[41]

LOCAL SR TERROR: 1905–07

Local, mainly urban-orientated, SR terror arose not from any specific party initiative or directive but as a spontaneous response to the Bundist Hirsch Lekkert's attempt on the life of the Governor of Vil'no in 1902. Within a year, SRs in Belostok had formed their own terror unit and soon after carried out an attempt on the life of the local police chief.[42] Belostok quickly became synonymous with bomb attacks and shooting incidents, though anarchists and non-aligned groups, rather than SRs, were responsible for many of them. Outside the Jewish Pale of Settlement, however, there is little evidence of organised SR terror before 1905.

This situation changed dramatically in the turbulent atmosphere of that year and there was a spectacular increase in terror and militia activity of every kind. According to Spiridovitch,[43] there were at least twenty-one local SR armed detachments (*boevye druzhiny, letuchie boevye otryady*) by the end of the year. To this number one can add the half-dozen or so 'flying detachments' formed at regional level. A semi-official party compilation (and not a complete record) itemises more than 200 terrorist operations executed between 1905 and 1907.[44] Well over 150 of these were the work of units operating within

European Russia. While workers did not usually play the initiating role in their formation they were certainly active participants, being directly responsible for at least a third of the incidents in the survey. Students and *intelligenty* were the other main component, though soldiers, sailors and peasants also figure prominently in some specific organisations. Almost all the available evidence highlights the extreme youth of the worker element: most seem to have been in their late teens or early twenties when active; almost all were male. The largest number of documented cases occurred in Petersburg (17 incidents), Sevastopol' (16), Odessa (13, mainly in 1905) and the towns of the northern Pale of Settlement (26). The victims were mostly government officials of varying rank and seniority and, predictably, members of the various branches of the security forces. Other prime targets were military and naval personnel and the omnipresent *provocateurs*.

Armed detachments were formed not solely with the intention of dispensing revolutionary justice. This is particularly true for the situation in 1905, when combat activity embraced a much larger proportion of urban party activists than later and when units more closely resembled a workers' militia than a 'hit squad'. In the larger cities, separate detachments were formed at district and even at factory level and, such was their popularity, there were even occasions when prospective recruits had to be turned away.

The principal responsibility of the armed units (according to a Petersburg organisational blue-print)[45] was to serve as the elite vanguard of the anticipated armed uprising. Only the most dedicated and conscientious members were to become involved in actual terrorist operations. The remainder were to occupy themselves with drill, firearms and explosives training and logistics. In the event, only in Moscow and a handful of other centres were the SRs presented with any opportunity of fulfilling the role of armed insurgents, and in these instances the lesson was painfully driven home that without the active support of at least sections of the regular armed forces (notwithstanding the sympathy of broad sections of the working class and even the general public) their efforts were doomed to failure.

Of the many subsidiary activities of the combat units perhaps the most routine (during 1905 at least) was the protection of speakers at public meetings. In August 1905, for example, a contingent of fifty Moscow *druzhiniki* fired on cossack troops moving in to seize a local party official.[46] Revolutionary firebrands (and many ordinary workers for that matter) also needed protection from intimidation by Black

Hundred gangs and other right-wing organisations. In the autumn and early winter of 1905 the Nevskii district of Petersburg was the scene of frequent confrontation between right and left-wing forces, while in Saratov during the October general strike a Black-Hundred inspired pogrom provoked the intervention of a detachment of forty SRs who, together with a smaller contingent of SDs, armed with bombs and revolvers, successfully repelled the marauders.[47]

The armed detachments were also occasionally involved in various kinds of sabotage. In Petersburg in December 1905, for example, a number of *druzhiniki* attempted (unsuccessfully) to prevent the dispatch of the Semyannikovskii regiment to suppress the Moscow uprising, by destroying bridges on the Nikolaevskii railway. SRs in Baku were more effective in employing this tactic. During the autumn of 1905 fierce clashes between the Azerbaijani and Armenian populations of the city led to the temporary shut-down of the oil industry. When the employers attempted to recommence work on the drilling sites the fighting detachment of the Baku committee distributed a printed warning, threatening the destruction of oil-well installations if this occured. When this warning was ignored, members of the combat unit set fire to derricks in the Balakhany district. According to one report, fifteen were destroyed in a single day.[48]

One last function of the detachments (and the most controversial one, in revolutionary circles at least) was the 'expropriation' of government money and military equipment for revolutionary purposes ('state' expropriations). In practice the term embraced raids on banks, post offices, military pay convoys, state liquor stores, and so on. State expropriations were approved by the party only with considerable reservation, however (despite the desperate need for money and the considerable popularity of the tactic among activists), and 'private' expropriations were outlawed entirely.[49]

Local terror brought only mixed blessings to the PSR and there are sound reasons for drawing up an overall negative balance. The degree of autonomy accorded the detachments (even by the local committees to which they were theoretically answerable) often resulted in the complete breakdown of party discipline and control. Consequently, on occasions when the Central Committee decided to suspend terror for tactical reasons, it found itself quite unable to enforce the policy at local level, where incidents continued unabated. This was not the only problem: many detachments, irrespective of origin, were easily deflected from their original purpose and quickly degenerated into criminal cells pure and simple, indulging in everything from armed robbery and the misappropriation of funds to extortion and outright lawlessness. The autonomy of the terorist wing also deprived party officials of the opportunity to screen prospective recruits as to their seriousness and ideological suitability. The result (as we have seen) was that SR detachments became an easy target for infiltration by Maximalists, anarchists and others who hijacked them for their own purposes. Thereafter the SRs were frequently suspected or accused of terrorist acts which they had neither knowingly sanctioned nor condoned and the party was brought into disrepute as a result. The same lack of overall supervision led to the detachments becoming 'seedbeds of provocation', a soft touch for the police who were thereby able to infiltrate party organisations at will and break up painstakingly constructed conspiratorial networks.

For all these reasons the third party council, convened in July 1907, officially dissolved the armed detachments and abandoned local terror.[50] This decision was by no means universally popular. A number of delegates were in favour of structural reform and tighter controls rather than the disbanding of the detachments altogether, and their view reflected a considerable sympathy for the terror tactic in working-class society as a whole, particularly in the face of administrative repression, unemployment and political 'filtering'. However, though combat activity continued unabated in the Urals for a time,[51] it was never officially resurrected by the party as a whole.

5 The Socialist-Revolutionaries in Petersburg – A Case Study

INTRODUCTION – CITY AND WORKFORCE

In the period under discussion Petersburg was at once Russia's administrative capital, largest city and most important commercial and industrial centre. Its population rose from 1 439 600 in 1900 to over 2 million on the eve of the First World War – an increase due almost wholly to peasant in-migration.[1] As late as 1910, less than 25 per cent of those belonging to the peasant *soslovie* (estate) had been born in Petersburg; another quarter had lived there more than ten years.[2] It was primarily industry which drew people to the city in such large numbers. Following Witte's policy of 'forced industrialisation' the urban workforce increased from about 70 000 in 1890 to more than double that figure ten years later. By 1913 approximately 242 000 workers would be employed in over 950 factories.[3]

Petersburg's labour force may be divided into the following categories:

(1) factory workers departing each summer for the countryside;
(2) factory workers residing in the city for an extended period but intending eventually to return to their villages;
(3) 'cadre' proletarians – children of Petersburg-born workers who had severed all economic ties with the countryside; At the turn of the century, approximately 85–90 per cent of Petersburg workers were engaged in year-round factory labour, but no more than 10 per cent had been born in the capital;[4]

71

(4) non-factory, permanently settled labour: domestic servants, artisans, public transport employees, construction workers, and so on (about 400 000 by 1913);

(5) seasonal migrants employed on a casual basis as carpenters, bricklayers, stevedores, and so on (100 000 arriving annually).[5]

Of the factory labour force, about 40 per cent was employed in the metallurgical and engineering industries. Here there was a strong tendency towards large-scale enterprises – 55 per cent of Petersburg metalworkers were employed in units of more than 1000 by 1913.[6] The financial control of these plants came increasingly to rest in the hands of powerful joint-stock companies and international banking concerns like the Russo-Asiatic and Meyer and Co. Twelve of the largest factories were under direct military or naval management: the Baltic Shipbuilding Plant (5200 workers in 1914), the Obukhov Steel Works (4500), the Izhorsk factory at Kolpino (3000) and the State Pipe Works (5500) being prominent examples. Many, though by no means all, enterprises in the metal/engineering group had adapted to utilise advanced technology, producing everything from machine tools and steam engines to sophisticated weaponry and telephone equipment. Prosperity ebbed and flowed with the fluctuations in demand. 1901–2 and 1906–8 were years of acute depression during which thousands of workers lost their jobs and entire factory departments were forced to close. By way of contrast the period immediately preceding the war was one of confidence and expansion, bolstered by a substantial increase in defence orders, contracted with private firms as well as State-controlled suppliers.

Metalworkers were among the highest-paid workers in Petersburg, though of course there were considerable differentials within the industry. *Masterovye* (skilled craftsmen of the artisanal type, such as pattern-makers), *slesari* (fitters) and *tokari* (turners) received the highest wages: the hierarchy then descended through caulkers, foundry workers and draughtsmen, down to the *chernorabochie* (unskilled) and *ucheniki* (apprentices). Within the factory environment, all workers were conscious of a hierarchy of status running parallel to that of skill and in their turn, even lower-ranking metalworkers rated themselves above workers in other branches of the industry.[7]

The Petersburg metalworking industry underwent a number of significant changes after 1905, when the innovative methods and profit-maximalising ethos of the American F. W. Taylor were introduced on a far more ambitious scale than before in the city's leading engineering plants.[8] The intention, the 'rationalisation of industrial organisation', threatened to replace the traditional 'universal' metalworker, expected to be familiar with all the skills involved in the crafting of metal, by more specialised, unskilled or semi-skilled machine-operators. The new changes account for the huge influx of cheap adolescent and female labour in the period immediately prior to the war. 'Taylorism' (or the 'Amerikanka' as it was referred to by the workers) envisaged, and to some extent accomplished, a whole range of 'improvements' in the running of the major Petersburg plants: the replacement of outmoded or defective machine tools, the introduction of labour-saving and sophisticated technology (automatic hammers, electric-powered hoisting cranes, acetylene welding and metal-cutting equipment, and so on); the reorganisation of the shop lay-out, special 'rates bureaux' to fix new, competitively-orientated wage structures, time-and-motion studies, punch-clocks, automatic closing gates to repel latecomers and closer surveillance and supervision of the workers' performance on the shop floor. The comparatively relaxed (and often chaotic) atmosphere of the traditional Petersburg factory, which conceded something at least to the status of the metalworker as craftsmen, yielded to a conveyor-belt mentality where men became increasingly subservient to the dictates of the machine. No doubt the encroachments of Taylorism contributed something to the increasing unrest in the industry in the decade preceding the First World War.

The second largest employer in Petersburg, accounting for about 23 per cent of the work force, was textile manufacturing. Over half the workers here were women and the majority were unskilled and poorly educated.[9] Not surprisingly, therefore, wages were much lower than for metalworkers and hours were longer. Cotton-spinning enterprises were larger on average than those in the metallurgical industry but there were fewer giant plants; the biggest tended to be groups of factories under common ownership – for example, the Nevskii Spinning Manufacture (7500 workers in 6 factories) and the 'Voronin, Lyutsh and Chesher' group (4400 workers in 6 factories).

Food-processing, chemicals, printing and paper manufacture were the other major industries of the capital. Again, women (and juveniles) played a much larger role than in metallurgy (only 1.3 per cent of metallists in 1900 were women, but they comprised 45 per cent of workers in the clothing industry).[10] Factories ranged greatly in size, but again there were a number of very large enterprises – for example, the Nevskii Mechanical Shoe factory (2700 workers), the State Paper

Manufactory (3200), the Laferm (2500) and Bogdanov (2000) tobacco plants and the George Borman chocolate factory (1000).

EARLY HISTORY, 1902–05

There was already a considerable history of populist and neo-populist activity in Petersburg before the turn of the century, but the first SR organisation was not formed there until November 1902.[11] During the first six months the committee distributed a number of proclamations among the students and workers of the city, as well as initiating a handful of circles at the Putilov plant. These first, tentative steps were brought to an abrupt halt in May 1903 when the police made two crucial interventions against the organisation; the first to forestall a May Day demonstration, the second to ensure that celebrations to mark the city's two hundredth anniversary would not be marred by an unseemly or embarassing incidents.[12]

How quickly the party recovered from these early set-backs is difficult to assess, but there is no record of any more proclamations until November 1903. in the same month a letter from a Petersburg worker to the editors of *Revolyutsionnaya Rossiya* claimed to know of SR activity 'on Vasilevskii Island and beyond the Nevskii Gates', at the same time denying an allegation printed in the Social-Democrat newspaper *Iskra* that the SR committee was 'mythical'.[13] But more precise information on SR support in the factories is extremely hard to come by, above all in the party's own press. Certainly a group survived at the Putilov plant and the official factory history records that the party's stock rose somewhat after the assassination of Interior Minister Von Plehve in July 1904.[14] There is also evidence of support in 1904 at the opposite end of the city, specifically in the electro-technical shops of the large state Pipe (Trubochnye) works in Vasileostrov.[15] The best-known SRs at the Pipe works were Aleksandr Mityukin, dismissed in February 1905 for distributing illegal literature, and two foundry workers, the brothers F. E. and S. G. Kononov. S. G. Kononov was subsequently to enjoy a colourful revolutionary career which included membership of the Petersburg soviet.[16]

While the SRs were clearly anxious to recruit as many workers as possible into their organisation, the 'commanding heights' were exclusively an intelligentsia preserve before 1905.[17] The following biographies of committee members discovered by this writer may therefore be considered as typical.

A. A. Bitsenko-Kameristaya

Born 1875 in Ekaterinoslav *guberniya*. Completed gymnasium and pedagogical courses before working for the SR organisation in Smolensk (1902–3). Member of the Petersburg committee, 1903–4, when she was arrested. Subsequent revolutionary career included membership of the Moscow committee during 1905.

M. I. Bulgakov

Born c. 1884. Student and member of the Institute of Highway Engineers. Was twice a member of the Petersburg committee during 1902–4, and served as a propagandist among the workers. Arrested for involvement in an abortive conspiracy to kill Plehve in January 1904.

L. P. Loiko-Kvashnina

Born 1854 in Perm'. Her revolutionary career began in 1877 with membership of 'Zemlya i Volya'. She was involved subsequently with *narodnik* groups in Ekaterinburg, Kazan and Khar'kov for which she served several prison terms. She joined the Petersburg PSR as a committee member in 1903, working as a propagandist until her eventual arrest in February 1907. Her later revolutionary career took her as far as Baku (c. 1910).[18]

The intelligentsia-student monopoly of committee posts led predictably to frustration and possibly resentment on the part of the working-class membership,[19] and does not seem to have been fully justifiable in terms of the organisation's social composition. The material in PKS has in fact revealed that as much as one-third of members joining the party before 1905 may have been manual workers. Relations improved to some extent at the end of 1904, when a 'Council of Representatives' began to argue the workers' views before the committee. As an article in *Trud* later recalled: 'Here for the first time the workers themselves began to participate directly in party work.' It was not until October 1905, however, that the council began to play a deliberative role in the affairs of the organisation.[20]

THE REVOLUTION OF 1905

In December 1904 a strike over the dismissal of four workers at the Putilov plant triggered off a sequence of events which were to lead ultimately to the tragedy of 'Bloody Sunday'. Inevitably there would be diverging and sometimes contradictory accounts of the origins and development of Father Gapon's 'Assembly of Russian Factory and Mill Workers' and of the circumstances surrounding his followers' ill-fated attempt to present a petition to the Tsar on 9 January.[21] As far as the SR role in the episode is concerned, the following at least can be advanced with a reasonable degree of confidence.

Firstly, the influence on the movement of Petr Rutenberg, who led the SR group at the Putilov factory and stood at the head of the procession on Bloody Sunday, had until then been negligible.[22] Secondly, before 9 January the SR committee distributed at least one proclamation containing the strikers' demands (which both SRs and SDs subsequently claimed to have influenced) together with the petition itself.[23] Thirdly, local representatives of the PSR attended a meeting of the second branch of the Assembly of Mill workers on 28 December 1904[24] and party agitators also took part in a number of subsequent mass meetings, though their contributions were doubtless received with the same mixture of suspicion and hostility as were those of the Social Democrats.[25] Finally, neither the Socialist-Revolutionaries nor any other political party played anything approaching a leading role at the time. In fact, membership of Gapon's organisation was far in excess of the PSR and RSDLP.

Be that as it may, the shooting down of hundreds of unarmed demonstrators in front of Palace Square on 9 January transformed the situation overnight, to the decided advantage of the revolutionaries. Marching in the vanguard of the nationwide strike movement which ensued, the workers of the capital hastened to improvise factory committees which duly presented their employers with far-reaching demands for improvements in wages, hours, conditions of service and the ordering of industrial relations. This stage of the movement culminated in the election by over 150 000 workers of delegates to the Shidlovskii Commission, originally intended to review labour grievances but subsequently abandoned by the government when it threatened to evade the constraints imposed upon it.

The ignominious and unexpected retreat by the authorities provided the revolutionary parties with an unparalleled opportunity to build their own organisations as well as to contribute to the creation of a genuine mass movement for the first time.[26]

The most detailed description of the impact these momentous events had on the SRs in the capital is contained in the memoirs of Aleksei Buzinov, a member of the Nevskii district organisation.[27]

Buzinov was a second-generation Petersburg worker. His father's origins were in Smolensk province but he had since severed all connections with his birthplace. In the early 1890s Buzinov senior was employed in the forge at the Semyannikov (Nevskii) shipbuilding plant. His wife too worked in a factory and the family lived almost literally in the shadow of the Pal' textile Mill. When Buzinov died prematurely his son was taken on at the forge in his place, after a police official had been bribed to add two years to the age on the boy's passport (he was actually only twelve at the time).

Buzinov had worked at the factory for about ten years before he personally became aware of arguments about factory conditions on the shop floor (among metalworkers, not forge-workers, incidentally). But whereas before Bloody Sunday the majority had rallied to the defence of the Tsar in the face of opposition from isolated individuals, afterwards 'Social Democrats and Socialist-Revolutionaries ... recruited into circles intensively'.[28] Buzinov first joined an SD circle but was disappointed with the propagandist's preference for discussing political economy to explaining the differences between the various political parties. When the Grand Duke Sergei Aleksandrovich was assassinated by an SR in February, the event was greeted with 'boundless rejoicing' at the factory as a suitable revenge for Bloody Sunday.[29] So when Buzinov completed his circle training it was to the SRs that he turned. At first he was required only to pay membership dues to the party's representative in the engineering section (one Novitskii). But, as the organisation continued to expand, and additional groups were formed, there came the point when Buzinov was elected to the factory committee as representative of the forge. He was now expected to present a weekly report on the state of morale in the shop as well as the demands his co-workers were making. At this first committee meeting (probably during the early summer of 1905), Buzinov learned that the SR's Nevskii district organisation had just been 'rebuilt', presumably after recent arrests. Now, not only a *raion* committee functioned again, but three *podraion* organisations; one based at the Nevskii Works itself, the others probably centring on the Obukhov Steel plant and the Aleksandrovskii Machine Building Factory (all were SR *podraiony* after 1905). According to a soviet source, the SRs at the Obukhov Works were fanatical extremists who persistently urged 'small adventurist advances'. The same author asserts that the majority of the workforce, having previously fluctuated between economistic and SR positions, were by the summer veering decisively towards the Bolsheviks.[30] This at least seems unlikely, because when the soviet emerged in October the Mensheviks were much the stronger faction there and the SRs too appear to have retained their influence.

Elsewhere in the city support for the Socialist-Revolutionaries is, unfortunately, very difficult if not impossible to measure. There is no evidence at all for the northern districts. In the south-west of the city (Narva-Petergof) the party would seem to have been weaker than in the Nevskii *raion*. At the Putilov plant, the largest of the city's factories, there were cells in the instrument, pattern and wagon shops (and probably elsewhere) but the organisation as a whole has been assessed as feeble during the summer of 1905, partly at least because of repression.[31] In other areas there were probably a number of major factories still without an SR committee, as appears to have been the case at the Franco-Russian plant in Kolomenskii *raion*, for instance.[32] Of course this does not necessarily imply a lack of sympathy for the party in such enterprises; the SRs always emphasised the extent to which they were hindered by a shortage of propagandists (and money).

Inevitably the party had to contend with intense competition in its efforts to recruit members, mainly from the Social-Democratic factions, both of which were numerically stronger. The SRs received less financial support from the bourgeoisie than their rivals, and there is some evidence to suggest that they may have spent proportionately more of their income on arms.[33] These factors must adversely have affected the efficiency and scale of their operations among the workers. Relations between Social Democrats and Socialist-Revolutionaries were generally acrimonious, but this by no means excluded occasional marriages of convenience, especially at *raion* and factory levels where there was probably more blurring of party lines. For example, although on May Day 1905 the SRs were supposed to have issued a proclamation calling on workers *not* to join in celebrations organised by the RSDRP this was probably as much the result of confusion as intransigence, for the following month a major strike at the Putilov factory was preceded by consultations between the parties – and the same thing happened again in July.[34] Moreover, there is evidence of more fundamental and enduring co-operation in the Nevskii *raion*. During 'Potemkin Week' (June 1905) representatives of the rival parties agreed to form an intra-party workers' committee to co-ordinate their activities, and to provide more consistent leadership. This committee continued to exist until October, when it was apparently transformed into the *raion* soviet.[35]

Throughout 1905 the PSR was committed to a strategy which aimed to promote the overthrow of autocracy by means of an armed uprising.[36] This commitment was reflected alike in the allocation of funds for the provision of weapons and explosives, in the stepping up of the terror campaign and in the phraseology used in the party's press and propaganda output. Early in the year a number of socialist organisations, including the PSR, were involved in a complex arms deal arranged by the Finnish patriot Konni Zilliacus, with the assistance of the Japanese military attaché in Petersburg.[37] A substantial quantity of guns, explosives and ammunition were to be landed by ship in the Bay of Finland the thence transported to the capital to be collected and distributed by the SRs. Weapons bought from firms in the USA, Germany and Switzerland were assembled in due course, together with a decrepit steamer called the 'John Grafton'. But in August 1905, after a series of blunders and misadventures, the ship ran aground off the coast of Finland and was subsequently scuttled in an effort to avoid detection. Some of the cargo was eventually recovered by the Russian authorities, but little if any by the revolutionaries.

The financial accounts of the Petersburg committee reveal considerable expenditure on arms during the first half of 1905 – 11 700r., in fact, between December and July.[38] Presumably much of it was used to pay for the armed detachments of workers formed by the party from the summer of 1905 onwards. By the end of the year there were units in most if not all large factories with SR organisations. The main purpose of the detachments was to form the vanguard of the anticipated insurrection, but secondary activities included the protection of party speakers at meetings, the organisation of resistance in the face of attacks from Black Hundred gangs and, later, the assassination of officials held responsible for particularly brutal acts of repression. The history of the unit attached to the Nevskii factory is probably fairly typical.[39] Formed late in the summer of 1905, it was supplied with a 'large number of (rather primitive) revolvers' known significantly as 'John Grafs'. An 'instructor' organised weekly target practice in the surrounding countryside, a favourite spot being the woods at the rear of the Thornton factory across the river. In addition, members were expected to attend two or three 'theory' classes in which they were taught to clean and operate their weapons, as well as the rudiments of manufacturing explosives. Here the Nevskii detachment was assisted by three local student chemists, who filched the necessary materials and set-up a 'laboratory' in a private house made available to them by a sympathiser. The workers were meanwhile responsible for making bomb casements. So, by the autumn of 1905 SRs in the Nevskii *raion* at least were actively preparing for the eventuality of rebellion, though how effective such preparations were is highly debatable.

A Summary of SR Activity before October

Although the SRs were active in a number of districts at the beginning of 1905, they were quite unable to influence, let alone direct the great events of January and February. Like the Social Democrats however, the party benefited from an increase in worker radicalism after Bloody Sunday. The rate of expansion and consolidation varied considerably from one district to the next, and was ultimately determined by the degree of police effectiveness. From admittedly fragmentary evidence the Nevskii district would appear to have been something of a stronghold, in some contrast to the Narva district, where the SRs had begun their activities three years previously. And, no doubt, there were many factories where the party could only count on a handful of members, even if latent support was considerable. It would be especially interesting to know how matters stood in the heavily working-class district of Vyborg, as evidence from the 1906–7 period has revealed impressive levels of SR support in many of the metalworking plants there. Propagandists were certainly operating both here and in the neighbouring Petersburg district during the summer of 1905, but how effectively is not known.[40] Of the two remaining districts (Moskovskii and Vasileostrov) the former was to be important to the PSR from October onwards.

Although it is quite impossible to estimate numbers for the Petersburg organisation as a whole during this period, growing instances of co-operation with the more powerful Social Democrats may indicate a substantial increase in the influence of Social-Revolutionism as the year progressed.

For some time before 1905 the PSR had argued for armed rebellion as the only means of overthrowing the autocracy and taking the revolution beyond the 'bourgeois' limits recognised by the Marxists. In Petersburg, commitment to this strategy is evident in the allocation of very substantial sums for the purchase of arms, and in the formation of factory-based worker detachments. Generally speaking, however, most SR activity before October consisted of propaganda and agitation.[41] The majority of party activists and organisers in 1905 were students at the city's university and Technological Institute. There were hardly any full-time revolutionaries and relatively few professional people, with the notable exception of teachers.[42] The party also benefited to a degree from the break-up of the non-party Northern (school) Students Group, though the SDs took the lion's share of the former membership.[43]

The Renewal of Working-Class Unrest

In September 1905, the printing workers and railwaymen of Moscow and Petersburg initiated what was to develop into an empire-wide general strike. As the movement gained momentum the strikers' economic demands, hitherto predominant, became increasingly enveloped within bolder political ones. Everywhere there were calls for freedom of speech and assembly, for an end to capital punishment, for a democratic republic. By mid-October, with the entire country at a standstill, with the economy – already seriously weakened by the disastrous war with Japan – suffering daily reverses, and with support for the regime at a dangerously low ebb, only two options remained open to the government if revolution was to be avoided; the imposition of military dictatorship or the granting of a constitution. Having earnestly but fruitlessly explored the possibility of dictatorship, the Tsar agreed with great reluctance to authorise the 'October' Manifesto. Four days previously the Petersburg Soviet of Workers' Deputies had held its first meeting.

The SRs and the Petersburg Soviet of Workers' Deputies

Collectively the SRs played no part in the birth and early development of the Soviet. There are several explanations for this. As has already been pointed out, the party was of more recent origin than the RSDRP, and its ties with the urban working class were weaker. Secondly, the SRs' over-zealous anxiety to avoid economism led them to neglect the very organisations on which the Soviet was built, namely the embryonic trade unions and mutual aid societies. Thirdly, the age structure of the Soviet may be of relevance. From the (admittedly modest) quantity of biographical data we have been able to examine, most of the SRs' working-class activists would appear to have been much younger than the average Soviet factory deputy (twenty-six years). For instance, of a sample of twenty-seven worker activists who joined the Petersburg organisation before 1906, twenty- four were aged between seventeen and twenty-two in 1905.[44] So although the

PSR did not lack skilled and literate worker-members, they may have been too young and politically inexperienced to have attracted mass support in the factories at a time when individuals generally counted for more than parties. Finally, the SRs' poor representation in the Soviet may partly have been the outcome of their underestimating its revolutionary significance, though there is no firm evidence that this was the case.

Numerical Strength in the Soviet

Here one can offer only approximations. A police report dated 4 November 1905 estimated twenty-five SR deputies at that time as opposed to fifty SDs, while the Social Democrats' own newspaper *Novaya Zhizn'* gave the SRs only 13 per cent of the total membership (about 70 out of 562 deputies) at the height of the Soviet's influence.[45]

Ten SR deputies are identifiable by name. They are:

B. I. Bryukkel
Age 25; first generation worker and deputy at the Rechkin Wagon Works (Moskovskii *raion*).

A. I. Feit
Age 41; professional revolutionary; member of PSR Central Committee and of the Soviet Executive.

N. D. Avksent'ev
Age 27; professional revolutionary; prominent agitator in Petersburg during 1905; member of Soviet Executive Committee and later of PSR Central Committee.

S. M. Khachko
Age unknown; pharmaceutical assistant and member of the Soviet executive.

A. K. Piskarev
Age unknown; metal worker; former elector to the Shidlovskii Commission and member of the Soviet Executive; later prominent in the Metalworkers' Union; deputy for the Ozoling factory (Moskovskii *raion*).

P. F. Sokolev
Age unknown; chairman of the Sanitation Workers' Union.

S. R. Korneeva-Brodskaya

Age 18; student; SD agitator in Poltava before working for the PSR in Petersburg.

S. G. Kononov

Age 22; smelter; member of '*soyuz bor'by*' in 1899; member of PSR from about 1902; deputy for the Pipe Metal Plant (Vasileostrovskii *raion*).

A. N. Kotlov

Age 25; second-generation worker (turner); member of workers' circle from 1900; member of Soviet Executive.

I. Romanov-Romantsev

Age 22; first generation worker (turner); member of Gapon organisation; later headed SR Narva combat organisation; deputy at the Putilov Metal Factory (Narvskii raion).[46]

SR Policy and the Soviet

The leading SR deputy, N. D. Avksent'ev gave the following summary of the party's attitude to the Soviet during his trial:

> The representatives of the party did not have the right to vote; moreover they didn't want it. Their role was that of advisors, of theorists to the Soviet. They tried to marry their own power to reason with the collective reasoning of the Soviet. The proletariat executed its will by itself, it couldn't have been otherwise. The party renounced the right to influence this will 'positively', that is through voting. It relied on its intellectual authority. Outside, the party put its press and agitators at the Soviet's disposal. The task of the agitators was to see that Soviet decisions were adopted in the factories, to make them accessible to people of all points of view, to analyse them and to explain their *raison d'être*. The party tied its actions closely to those of the Soviet. It couldn't act in any other way as a party of the masses, because the Soviet personified the will of the proletariat, being itself a proletarian organisation; only this will could sanction the actions of the party. During the October days, the party wedded its own cause to the Soviet's, and took pride and satisfaction therein.[47]

The SRs were insistent, then, on Soviet autonomy. When the Bolsheviks attempted to impose their own party programme in

October the SRs drew up a letter of protest in which they demanded that the Soviet continue to represent the interests of all workers, irrespective of party affiliation. Implicit in this was a rejection of the Social-Democratic claim to be the sole legitimate representative of the proletariat.[48]

On the major tactical questions, the advice of the SR leadership ran consistently contrary to the actual policy line adopted by the Soviet. Firstly, the Party opposed the campaign to introduce the eight-hour day in Petersburg factories, even though the SRs were firmly committed to the idea in principle (the local committee had issued a proclamation supporting it back in August).[49] The party leadership now argued that by confronting the government head-on, without waiting for rebellion in the countryside, the Soviet was inviting failure – the proletariat would (to use Chernov's word) 'overtax' itself.[50]

The same logic was subsequently used to oppose calls for a second and third general stike in November and December 1905.[52] Outvoted in the Soviet, the SRs may have loyally supported industrial action where it was popular, but they also attempted to push through their own factory resolutions in favour of land socialisation, stressing the interdependence of interest between the urban proletariat and the toiling peasantry. The Soviet's own newspaper, *Izvestiya* contains a number of SR resolutions for the first half of November 1905; in the engine-construction, cannon, gun-carriage and shell shops of the Putilov plant; at the Semyannikov (Nevskii), Erikson (Vyborgskii), Ozoling (Moskovskii), Artur Koppel' (Moskovskii), Shreder (Vasileostrovskii), Langenzipen (Peterburgskii) and Vestingauz (Town) factories; on the railways; in the unions of clerks and accountants and pharmaceutical workers.[53] If SR policy frequently seems to have been at odds with the decisions of the Soviet, there were occasions when their approches coincided. The party supported calls for the non-payment of taxes and withdrawal of savings deposits, for instance, as well as the unilateral introduction of the democratic freedoms of speech, press, assembly, and so on. It was also involved in Soviet projects to help the unemployed, though there is little information available about the nature and extent of SR participation.

The SRs and the Collapse of the Soviet

Throughout the comparatively short life of the Soviet, the SRs continued to form armed detachments of workers. By the end of the year there is evidence of *raion* fighting organisations in the Nevskii,

Narvskii and Moskovskii districts – there were almost certainly others. In November the Nevskii detachment was receiving instruction on the 'history and theory of barricade fighting', drawing up a plan of the neighbourhood and stockpiling saws and axes.[54] When the Soviet leadership was arrested on 3 December there was confusion as to where the authority to call an insurrection would now lie. Shortly afterwards, members of the detachment were informed of the party hierarchy's decision to abandon plans for an armed uprising in Petersburg on the grounds that the workers were for the moment too exhausted to undertake an enterprise of such magnitude. A small group then left, with the approval of the Petersburg Committee, to join the rebels in Moscow, while the local detachments of Narvskii and Moskovskii tried unsuccessfully to prevent the despatch of the Semyannikov regiment to Moscow by destroying bridges on the Nikolaevskii railway line.[55]

Had there been a rebellion in Petersburg in December 1905, the preparations of the SRs would certainly have been inadequate. Though a large quantity of weapons had been ammassed, many had apparently not been distributed. More important, attempts to propagandise the military units stationed in the capital had met with only marginal success and the morale of some of the fighting detachments was said to be low. When the general strike collapsed early in December, government retribution was swift. On 9 December the police uncovered two bomb factories and less than a week later over fifty members of the *druzhiny* (combat units) were arrested and their arms confiscated. Before the end of the month there had been two more devastating raids by the police.[56] As the Petersburg organisation reeled under these and other blows and the uprising in Moscow disintegrated, the party leadership turned once again to the countryside.

THE WORKING CLASS ON THE DEFENSIVE – JANUARY TO SEPTEMBER 1906

The decision of the Petersburg Soviet to press for the immediate introduction of the eight-hour day at the beginning of November 1905 had provoked a prompt response from the city's industrialists. Sixty-three[57] firms threatened to lock out their employees in the eventuality of a strike; in fact over seventy[58] factories shut their gates, creating immediate large-scale unemployment. The new resolve displayed by both government[59] and employers proved effective in bringing about the collapse of the campaign and, as we have seen, the demise of the Soviet itself.

Having tasted victory in December, the owners set about recovering ground lost to them during the revolution. Their business association, the 'St Petersburg Society to Promote the Improvement and Development of Factory Industry' exerted pressure on the government to dilute pending proposals on factory and welfare reform.[60] The terms of the Trades Union Law of March 1906, which imposed severe restrictions on working-class organisation,[61] were reassuring in this respect.

Meanwhile, management and government continued to mount a more direct assault on the now faltering labour movement. In the course of January 1906 up to 40 000 Petersburg workers found themselves at least temporarily out of work;[62] while more than 1700 were under arrest.[63] A survey of the Vyborg district several months later revealed that less than a third of the unemployed were victims of production cut-backs, while over half were on the streets as a result of political activity of one kind or another.[64] In the case of workers locked out of their factories, written guarantees of good behaviour were required before re-employment was considered. Even this opportunity was denied the hardened politicals who were 'filtered' from the labour workforce permanently. Some long-term unemployed returned to the countryside,[65] but not in numbers large enough to ease the pressure on those left behind; migrant workers continued to arrive in the capital even at the height of the depression.[66] Those remaining in Petersburg had to rely for the most part on hand-outs from factory committees and party and trade union organisations; *zemlyachestvo* may also have had a role to play. Further relief arrived in April when the city Duma agreed to allocate half a million roubles for the provision of soup kitchens and the financing of a number of public works projects, to be partly administered by representatives from the 'Council for the Unemployed'[67] (*sovet bezrabotnykh*). In this way several thousand jobs were found. But of course this was at best no more than a palliative which faded into insignificance as the recession deepened in the metalworking industry during the second half of 1906.[68] From then on even those fortunate enough to remain in work were faced with wage reductions, intensified production schedules and, in many cases, a three or four-day working week.

The SRs and the Onset of the Reaction

For the SRs in Petersburg the first half of 1906 was one long tale of harassment and arrest. The rout of party forces at the beginning of the year (referred to earlier) had not been confined to sections involved in terrorist activity. Repression was so severe in the Obukhov *podraion*, for example, that even in the summer of 1906 the SRs attributed the 'insignificance' of party work there to the arrest of conscious workers in the previous December and January.[69] Shortly before the convocation of the First Duma (April 1906) the Petersburg organisation was again severely mauled.[70] In Kolomenskii *raion* leadership now passed into the hands of a twenty-year-old unskilled worker who had only entered the party's ranks the previous autumn; no doubt similar tales could be told elsewhere.[71] Then, after the dispersal of the Duma and the failure of the insurrection in Kronstadt and Sveaborg in July, the SRs suffered once more at the hands of the security forces.[72]

Their response was to set about training new student and worker activists, so that by the autumn several dozen organisers, agitators and propagandists may have been available for service.[73]

In spite of all the disruption, the SRs succeeded in maintaining a measure of continuity in at least some districts during the pre-October period.[74] The extent of the party's support among the working class is impossible to assess on the available evidence, but the scale of operations to come suggests that considerable foundations had already been laid.

SR Terrorism during the first half of 1906

Bolsheviks and SRs in particular had begun to respond seriously to the growing threat posed by right-wing forces in Petersburg towards the end of 1905. In January 1906 the SRs were responsible for the murder of one of the Black Hundred leaders at the Nevskii shipbuilding factory and for a bomb attack on a cafe frequented by members of the 'Union of the Russian People'.[75] In February several SR conspirators shot and killed an engineer at the Putilov plant for his role in ordering dismissals,[76] while in March a twenty-year-old metalworker, V. N. Fedorov, was put on trial for the murder of another member of the URP, again at the Putilov factory.[77] The memoirs of Aleksei Buzinov provide some additional information on terrorist activity during the period. Buzinov had rejoined the Nevskii SR detachment after returning from Moscow, and was now living on false papers. He took part in a number of operations – the commandeering of a printing works on the Mytinskii Embankment, the murder of a policeman in the Vyborg district and the assault on the black-hundred leader at the Nevskii factory referred to earlier.[78] Buzinov claims that as many as a dozen attacks on members of the Okhrana and police by the Petersburg organisation were nipped in the bud, resulting in many arrests.[79] Two other terrorist incidents in September and October are mentioned in PKS (see Appendix); one was an attack on the paymaster of the frontier guard corps, the other, an expropriation at a government liquor store.[80] These are the only specific instances of expropriations this writer has discovered for the period, but there is compelling evidence to suggest that, in the Nevskii *raion* at least, the practice was rife before the autumn, when efforts were made to reduce party involvement.[81]

REGENERATION: SEPTEMBER 1906–FEBRUARY 1907

The customary return to Petersburg of the student population in the autumn of 1906 enabled the SRs to replenish their ranks with a new in-take of propagandists and organisers. At the same time the party announced its intention to launch a workers' newspaper, which appeared under the title *Trud* (Labour) in September and was destined to become the SRs most impressive labour publication before the First World War. Between September 1906 and March 1908 nineteen issues of the paper were circulated in editions of 20 000–25 000 copies.[82] According to contemporary accounts *Trud* was eagerly devoured by SRs and SDs alike and proved immeasurably valuable to the former, both as an instrument of propaganda and as a unifying centre for the myriad off-shoots of the organisation which would otherwise have fragmented under the difficult political conditions. The pages of *Trud* are a uniquely detailed record of the life of one local SR organisation during this important period and will be drawn on extensively throughout the remainder of this chapter.

The PSR underwent rapid growth during the autumn and winter months of 1906. The City Committee was soon confronted with the task of co-ordinating the activity of several thousand members and a great many more sympathisers, distributed among nine district organisations and well over eighty factories and workshops. In addition there were separate sections of students, railwaymen, shop-assistants and print-workers to contend with, as well as an independent combat organisation and units devoted to peasant and trade union affairs. Police activity seems to have abated somewhat during this period with the result that party meetings and assemblies were convened with unaccustomed regularity. A city conference met on some half-dozen occasions before repression intensified again in the spring, while the Council of the Workers' Union (referred to earlier) also held regular sessions until March or April 1907.

An Overview of Party Activity in the Autumn

Vyborg, Petersburg and Vasileostrov districts

Vyborg appears to have been the best organised of the northern districts in the autumn of 1906. One reason for this was an increase in the number of party workers after the summer holidays; according to a report presented to the Council of the Workers' Union in October there were now 'many propagandists' in Vyborg.[83] Consequently the SRs were able to reach most of the major factories and mills in this very large district. The exception was the borough of Okhta which, because of its remoteness, tended to be neglected. Vyborg had recently been subdivided again into four *podraiony*, mirroring the rival SD organisation.[84] The local leaders reported that party relations with the masses in this foremost bastion of Menshevism were 'indisputably better' than in the past, and that the party newspaper found a wide readership. Unfortunately no membership estimates are available, but a *raion* assembly held in mid-October 1906 was attended by representatives from ten of the largest factories: Nobel, Parviainen, Orudiinyi, New Lessner, Baranovskii, Erikson, Petersburg Metal, Arsenal, Rozenkrants, Shell; together with a delegate from the Okhta *podraion*. Other enterprises with SR organisations *not* represented at this particular meeting were the Mal'tsev textile mill, where the committee had dispersed following a recent strike; the Tove, Feniks and Kornilov factories and the Voronin and Chesher mills. At least ten factories had their own party library but committees, circles and funds were not evenly spread. Apart from the progress described above, the *raion* committee had been able to establish 'firm ties' with the Council for the Unemployed.[85]

Reports from the two other northern districts (Petersburg and Vasileostrov) paint a similarly optimistic if not so detailed picture. The Petersburg district had been sub-divided into two *podraiony* to facilitate party work. The organisation there was described as 'solid' and increasing in size.[86] In Vasileostrov there was a recovery under

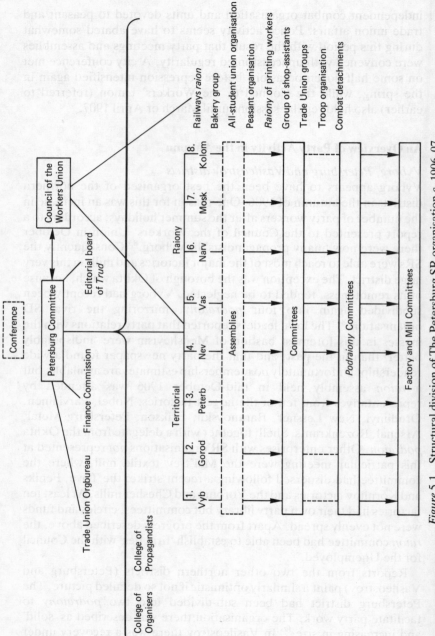

Figure 5.1   Structural division of The Petersburg SR organisation c. 1906–07

91

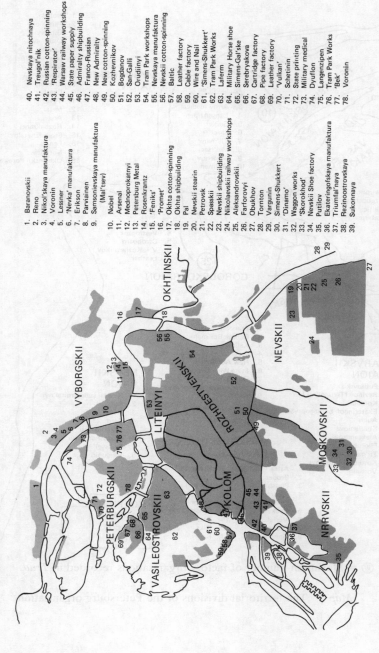

1. Baranovskii
2. Reno
3. Nikol'skaya manufaktura
4. Voronin
5. Lessner
6. 'Nevka' manufaktura
7. Erikson
8. Parviainen
9. Samsonievskaya manufaktura (Mal'tsev)
10. Nobel
11. Arsenal
12. Mednoprokatnyi
13. Petersburg Metal
14. Rosenkrantz
15. 'Feniks'
16. 'Promet'
17. Okhta cotton-spinning
18. Okhta shipbuilding
19. Pal
20. Nevskii stearin
21. Petrovsk
22. Spasskii
23. Nevskii shipbuilding
24. Nikolaevskii railway workshops
25. Aleksandrovskii
26. Farforovyi
27. Obukhov
28. Tornton
29. Vargunin
30. Simens-Shukkert
31. 'Dinamo'
32. Waggon works
33. 'Skorokhod'
34. Nevskii Shoe factory
35. Putilov
36. Ekateringofskaya manufaktura
37. Triumfal'naya
38. Rezinoostrovskaya
39. Sukonnaya
40. Nevskaya nitochnaya
41. Treugol'nik
42. Russian cotton-spinning
43. 'Respirator'
44. Warsaw railway workshops
45. State paper supply
46. Admiralty shipbuilding
47. Franco-Russian
48. New Admiralty
49. New cotton-spinning
50. Kozhevnikov
51. Bogdanov
52. San-Galli
53. Orudinyi
54. Tram Park workshops
55. Nevskaya manufaktura
56. Nevskii cotton-spinning
57. Baltic
58. Leather factory
59. Cable factory
60. Wire and Nail
61. 'Simens-Shukkert'
62. Tram Park Works
63. Laferm
64. Military Horse shoe
65. Simens-Gal'ske
66. Serebryakova
67. Cartridge factory
68. Pipe factory
69. Leather factory
70. 'Vulkan'
71. Schetinin
72. State printing
73. Military medical
74. Dyuflon
75. Langenzipen
76. Tram Park Works
77. 'Bek'
78. Voronin

Map 1 St Petersburg factory locations

92

Key ⑩ = Maximum number of factory organisations recorded in *Trud*.

Map 2   The territorial divisions of the Petersburg organisation

way. The organisation now had a new *raion* leader and was said to be 'firm' (*prochnaya*). Overall, party influence was, according to one report, 'increasing noticeably',[87] while in the Baltic *podraion* matters went even better. Here the local representative claimed that SR influence prevailed 'in all factories' and was growing 'frighteningly'. In addition to five factory committees, all with their own funds, there were eighteen propaganda circles, six libraries and a mutual assistance fund. The SRs were, it was claimed, making inroads into Social-Democrat territory; some SDs had already joined the party and their cells were being undermined by effective SR work.[88]

Neva, Moscow and Narva districts

The Nevskii *raion* was the SRs' principal stronghold in the south of the city. Work there focused on three major plants: the Semyannikov (Nevskii), the Obukhov and the Aleksandrovskii. Overall, the organisation comprised up to 1000 'fully-organised workers' in the autumn of 1906 and the income of a single *podraion* (the Semyannikovskii) stood at 500 roubles.[89] The *raion* committee had its own printing facilities and in October issued a proclamation in support of the Soviet deputies on trial; an appended resolution contained 3000 signatures.[90] Here, as in other districts, gravitation towards the PSR was remarked upon. There was also a party representative on the Council for the Unemployed.[91]

In the neighbouring Moskovskii *raion* a mood sympathetic to the SRs was noted everywhere.[92] In November 1906 there were committees in nine factories: Rechkin, 'Skorokhod', Mal'kiel, Pintsh, Ozoling, Astra, Koppel, Riks and Glebov and ties at four more – Broder, Pastor, Keller and the Gas Works. The SRs at the Rechkin factory were encouraged by the state of morale there, claiming that this erstwhile Menshevik stronghold was now 'leaning decisively' towards their own party. Elsewhere however there were cases of organisations not being able to take full advantage of the generally favourable atmosphere. The committee at the Mal'kiel factory, for example, though long-established, felt unable to record any real advance, while a representative at the small Julius Pintsh metal factory complained of a shortage of party workers. The overall impression, confirmed by the *raion* accounts which show a fall in income from 111 roubles in August to just 18(!) roubles in September, is of an organisation convalescing in an atmosphere favourable to recovery. In the Moscow district too the party was represented on the Council for the Unemployed.[93]

In contrast with most other districts Narva, which encompassed the giant Putilov and Treugol'nik plants, was never to experience a major breakthrough by the SRs, which partly explains why information on party activity there is comparatively scarce. A new (fourth) *podraion* serving the small factories was established in the autumn and was said to be prospering.[94] There was a marginal improvement in the party's affairs here towards the end of the year but this proved to be only temporary.[95]

Town district

There is no information on party work in the town (central) district until December 1906. By then there were cells at twenty-five enterprises but activity was restricted by lack of funds.

Okrug (hinterland) organisation

Unlike the Social Democrats, the SRs had no formal *okrug* organisation and evidence of their presence has been found in only one of the outlying industrial settlements, Kolpino (25 km south-east of Petersburg).[96] Kolpino was the site of the Izhorsk shipbuilding and armaments complex. The SRs maintained an organisation of sorts there for a considerable period but its location, together with the difficulty of the surrounding terrain, made sustained revolutionary activity difficult. During the autumn of 1906 local activists were attempting to establish propaganda circles in the factories, but were constantly being harassed by the police.[97]

Railway and Print Workers' Sections

The SRs had considerable support among the railway workers of the Petersburg junction but repression on the railways was so severe during the autumn that the party found it almost impossible to preserve any of its organisations for any length of time.[98] SR influence on the Petersburg–Warsaw line, where the workshops had long been a party bastion, was said to be 'somewhat stronger' than that of the SDs, while the organisations on the Nikolaevskii and the Moscow–Vindava–Rybinsk lines were in disarray following police activity. The position on the Baltic railway was a little better, with some advances being claimed at the expense of the Social Democrats who traditionally dominated the line.[99]

An organisation of SR print workers existed only from August 1906, but by October its representative on the CWU already claimed to speak for 20 enterprises (unspecified), 8 of which had committees. The printers also had their own library and fund.[100] Shortly afterwards the 'council' of SR printworkers reported that the number of affiliated shops had increased to nearly thirty. Work was said to be going well and a special organiser had been appointed to co-ordinate party work.[101]

This brief survey has aimed at measuring the relative strength of the various SR district organisations in the autumn of 1906. The major weaknesses may be summarised as:

(1) a shortage of experienced organisers and propagandists;
(2) a decline in the number of worker-activists as a result of filtering and administrative exile;
(3) inadequate finances;
(4) frequent breakdowns and shortages in the supply and distribution of illegal literature;
(5) vulnerability to infiltration by the police.

To which one should add:

(6) the failure to contain 'economic' terror (expropriations) referred to specifically only by the Nevskii *raion* organisation, but possibly affecting party work elsewhere.

Summary

Evidently then, in spite of a number of organisational deficiencies, some of which were unavoidable given the political and economic conditions, the popularity of the PSR measured either in terms of activists or sympathisers increased appreciably during the autumn of 1906. This trend may be explained to some degree by the following factors.

Factors Specifically Favourable to the SRs
(1) Increasing levels of unemployment and short-time working gave weight to the SR's argument that only the immediate socialisation of the land would effectively stem the influx of cheap peasant labour and so increase the job security and bargaining power of the proletarian worker.
(2) SR terrorism, directed against members of the URP and senior factory personnel held responsible for lockouts and dismissals, continued to be popular with large sections of the capital's

workforce who were happy to see vengeance meted out on their behalf.[102]

(3) Internecine warfare within the RSDRP could only have assisted its political rivals.

Factors Favourable to the Revolutionary Movement as a Whole

(1) The behaviour of the Government during the summer of 1906 (the summary dissolution of the Duma, the introduction of field courts martial and of fresh punitive expeditions into the countryside, the unspoken but transparent *entente* with the employers to suppress the urban labour movement) were all fully consonant with the Marxist and neo-Marxist predictions and evaluations of the revolutionary parties and arguably increased their credibility.

(2) The refusal by the authorities to assume responsibility for alleviating the effects of unemployment, lock-outs and short-time working, together with their obvious reluctance to introduce significant factory and welfare legislation, gave the revolutionary parties the opportunity to fill the breach (as far as they were able) and in so doing gain the trust – or at least the sympathy – of thousands of workers who could expect help from no other quarter but the black hundreds. The means by which the breach was filled included the forming of party-sponsored institutions such as trades union, co-operatives, and the Council for the Unemployed; the symbolic revival of proletarian democracy through elections to a new 'Soviet'; the provision of educational opportunities for workers (propaganda circles and factory libraries – often made available to non-party members;) the setting-up of soup kitchens and mutual-assistance funds; the organisation of collections for those in need, and the publicising of strikes.

THE SRs AND THE WORKERS' CURIA ELECTIONS TO THE SECOND DUMA (JANUARY 1907)

The Election Campaign

The imperial decree announcing the dissolution of the first Duma in July 1906 provided for a new assembly to convene on 20 February 1907.[105] It was to be preceded by fresh elections, which for workers in Petersburg entailed the following: first, the direct election of factory 'representatives' (*upolnomochennye*) to a workers' *curia* or college; second, the election by these representatives alone of *vyborshchiki* (electors) to a city college also containing representatives from the other social estates; third, the election of the deputies themselves by the city college.[106] The franchise, already a narrow one, was to be further pared-down on the eve of the elections. Women were entirely excluded, as were men under the age of 25 and workers at enterprises with fewer than 50 employees. Factory workers with less than six months' continuous employment, the unemployed, artisans and other non-factory workers (bakers, for example) were all disqualified. Finally, no worker was allowed to vote in another *curia* even if he was able to meet the prescribed property qualification.[107]

Each factory with between 50 and 1000 workers were allowed a representative in the *curia*. Enterprises with more than 1000 workers were allowed one extra representative for each additional 1000 employees, so that, for example, the Pipe factory with approximately 5200 workers would elect five *upolnomochennye*.[108]

The SRs boycotted the first Duma but their decision turned out to be ill-advised, at least in the countryside, where there had been considerable enthusiasm for participation.[109] Consequently, after the Duma was dissolved the party chose to review its position. It was originally intended that a projected second party congress would make the final pronouncement, but because the government was demanding electoral lists from many areas earlier than expected, the matter was placed on the agenda of the second party council, which met in October 1906. The council opted for participation in the election campaign but postponed a decision on whether to take up seats in the Duma. It was emphasised that the decision to take part in the campaign was based solely on tactical considerations and was not meant to imply a positive response to the government's overtures. The aim was to expose the Duma as an unrepresentative and ineffective body, while at the same time using it as a public platform from which to agitate and organise the masses in preparation for a future armed uprising. Political terror, which had been suspended during the first Duma, was this time to be sustained, on the grounds that the government itself was conducting its own campaign of violence against the people.[110]

The arrangements for the Petersburg campaign were finalised at a conference in November 1906, which was attended by members of the central committee and representatives of the city and *raion* organisations.[111] An elected *orgbyuro* was to form an 'Electoral Central

Committee' consisting of representatives from the party central committee, the city committee and special precinct (*uchastok*) committees. Each committee was to create its own executive commissions to handle the literary, financial, legal and agitational aspects of the campaign. The precinct committees seem to have worked closely with the existing *raion* committees; indeed, membership may have been interchangeable in some cases.

Well in advance of the November conference, local party organisations had begun to canvass the view of workers on the Duma. As early as 6 September representatives of the Vyborg district proposed issuing a leaflet which would, among other things, invite workers to express their opinions on the subject.[112] Then, in mid-October, a *raion* assembly discussed the Duma question.[113] From this meeting it emerged that local workers were broadly in favour of participation, albeit with certain reservations. The New Lessner spokesman, for example, reported that although party members at his factory were in favour of entering the Duma, ordinary workers were more sceptical. On the other hand, representatives from the Baronovskii and Rozenkrants plants were more anxious to extract assurances that no SR would be involved in 'organic' (that is, legislative) work in the assembly. Only one delegate (from the Ordnance factory) was firmly against participation. He argued that the government would never allow socialists into the Duma and that, even if it did, they would find it impossible to behave as revolutionaries in such a chamber. The party should therefore press ahead with the task of overthrowing autocracy; once this was achieved the road would be clear for the convocation of a genuine democratic assembly. The Vyborg organisation eventually decided (by eleven votes to one with one abstention) to support participation in the Duma. This view turned out to be typical: by the time the Council of the Workers' Union discussed the question in November, opinion had been canvassed in eight districts and was found to be overwhelmingly in favour of entry.[114]

Following these meetings the campaign gathered momentum. An 'Assembly of Organisers', also meeting in November, was able to report considerable progress, in some districts at least.[115] On Vasileostrov, for example, a 'significant increase in SR work' was reported. Special *raion* and factory bureaux were already arranging meetings to explain the significance of the Duma, and an electoral leaflet had been issued. In the neigbouring Petersburg district 'Duma circles' had been organised, a flysheet was in preparation and electoral candidates were in process of selection. In Kolomenskii *raion* too the party was in good shape. A recent 'increase in intelligentsia resources' had enabled work to begin at new enterprises, while advances made elsewhere were being consolidated. An election leaflet had been issued here too, but agitational bureaux were still being formed. Elsewhere things may have taken longer to get off the ground, but by December at the latest electoral propaganda and agitation were under way in every part of the city.[116]

Once the campaign had been properly launched, the SRs were anxious to draw their most dangerous opponents into debate at open-air factory meetings. As early as 27 October the Menshevik-controlled newspaper *Sotsial-demokrat* reported clashes at two plants in Kolomenskii *raion* (Galernyi Island and New Admiralty) while claiming at the same time that SR agitators were not in evidence elsewhere.[117] In the Moscow district, of five large *massovki* held during the second half of December (at the Rechkin, Pastor, Pintsh and A. Koppel factories), two at least involved speakers from both the major left-wing parties, while in January the liberal newspaper *Rus'* singled out the Glebov electrotechnical plant as the scene of particularly sharp clashes.[118] On the Petersburg side the story was much the same, with eve-of-election rallies sometimes lasting five or six hours. Here Bolsheviks and Mensheviks fought one another as well as the SRs.[119] The largest gatherings of all (and perhaps the fiercest confrontations) took place in the Neva district, where the SRs were already well-entrenched. Two meetings, held there in December 1906, attracted audiences of about a thousand each. In the course of one of a banner exhorting the electorate to 'vote for PSR candidates' was hoisted above the crowd. It showed a peasant and a proletarian jointly pulling apart the chains which constrained an exhausted woman and her starving child, while in the background the countryside had been set alight by cossacks involved in a punitive expedition – surely as powerful a statement as any of the need for the unity of all toilers in the face of the common enemy. According to the memoirs of the SR, Aleksei Buzinov, a popular venue for pre-election meetings in this southern part of the city was the Kornilov school (home of the district soviet in 1905). Here the Socialist-Revolutionaries were represented by 'Norskii', an expert on the land question, while their Popular Socialist allies put up V. A. Myakotin (a participant at their own founding congress). Buzinov claims that the Social Democrats failed to put in an appearance at the Kornilov debates. Even if this is true, there can be no doubt that the arch-rivals came face to face on the premises of many of the larger plants during the election period.[120]

Over and above the flysheets produced by the district organisations the Petersburg committee issued its own election propaganda (some seven leaflets in all) varying in content from acerbic and wide-ranging onslaughts directed at every representative of the non-socialist camp to straightforward explanations of the party's philosophy and programme.[121] Several numbers of *Trud* also appeared in the course of the campaign and naturally considerable space was devoted to electoral issues.[122] The paper's overall message can be summarised thus: since the promulgation of the October manifesto the government had been cynically trying to out-manoeuvre its opponents and had succeeded in restoring the essentials of autocratic power. As a part of its policy that same government now aimed to secure a 'black-hundred' Duma by stage-managing the elections and unleashing a campaign of violence and intimidation against the Left. The response of the SRs must be to win seats in the Duma so that the assembly's powerlessness and irrelevance might be exposed. Sooner rather than later autocracy would have to be forcibly overthrown and replaced by a democratic republic. Only then would genuine freedom be possible.

It will be recalled that the party hierarchy had chosen not to halt terrorist operations during the election period, on the grounds that the government had refused to suspend its own war against the revolutionaries. On 21 December the central Fighting Organisation struck, assassinating the Governor of Petersburg, General V. F. von der Launitz. Six days later it was the turn of the chief Military Prosecutor, Pavlov, killed by members of the party's Northern Combat unit.[123] The Petersburg detachments were also active, being responsible between November and January for the deaths of two police agents (a provocateur and a spy), a police officer and the governor of the Deryabinskii prison.[124] The impact of these events ensured that political terror would be one major issue in the campaign. According to a prominent Menshevik observer,[125] others included agrarian reform, the relevance and effectiveness of political strikes, the place of armed rebellion in the strategy of revolution and the conduct of the SDs in the factory commissions. The clear impression derived from material preserved in the SR Central Committee archive, as well as from published sources, is that the main thrust of the party's challenge stemmed from its agrarian programme of land socialisation.[126] Urban workers were supposed to benefit from this policy in a number of ways. First, the anticipated satisfaction of the peasants' land needs was expected to reduce the influx of surplus labour into the towns, a factor which had been effectively depressing wages and removing security of employment. Second, the creation of more prosperous conditions in the countryside would, it was hoped, stimulate internal demand for manufactured goods (farm machinery as well as consumer items). Third, socialisation would provide the industrial worker with a valuable bargaining counter: if he were not offered a fair deal at the factory he could threaten to return to the countryside and claim his share of the redistributed land.[127]

As the campaign progressed SR organisers became increasingly confident of the outcome. A reporter from the Moscow district asserted in December that victory was assured in at least nine factories. In Petersburg *raion* there was said to be 'tremendous sympathy' for the SRs, while on the railways success was considered 'certain'. Similar confidence emanated from Vyborg.[128] There were problems too, of course. In the Narva district, for example, where a lack of finances had delayed the start of the campaign, the party organisation was riddled with spies and continually harassed both by the police and the black hundreds. On the railways, despite the evident sympathy of the workers of the SRs, there was also little money, as well as too few *intelligenty* activists to fight the elections adquately; while in the remote industrial settlement of Kolpino (home of the Izhorskii Armaments Complex) the Social Democrats remained firmly in control, despite the efforts of the local SR organisation. Nevertheless, in the overall context these were relatively minor setbacks, in any case compensated to some extent by a heartening increase in support from the student population.[129]

The Elections

Voting in the workers' *curia* took place in two stages. On 7 January (1907) workers in the city's small and medium-sized enterprises went to the polls. The following week it was the turn of the larger plants together with the factories located in the district (*uezd*). According to a report in *Rus'* on 9 January,[130] turnout on the first occasion was as low as 40 per cent. The main reason, it was alleged, was that insufficient forewarning of the precise date and time of the elections had been given by the authorities. There were also complaints (relevant to both stages) that some workers had been deliberately laid off on the eve of polling day to prevent them from taking part.[131] After the elections a number of successful candidates were expelled from the capital before they could participate in the second stage.[132]

As David Lane has already pointed out, nothing approaching a complete set of election returns exists for the workers' *curia*.[133] Where information from individual plants is cited by liberal newspapers, no distinction is usually made between the various parties, while the evidence of the left-wing press is often contradictory, incomplete or inaccurate. The best collection of data to survive was assembled and analysed by a Menshevik, Andrei Mikhailov, and first appeared in a party journal (*Otzvuki*) in August 1907.[134] Information from this source is reproduced in Tables 5.1–5.3. Clearly the statistical detail should be treated with a certain amount of caution.[135]

The calculations are based on the following evidence:

(1) three preliminary meetings of SD *upolnomochennye*;
(2) specially prepared questionnaires completed by the secretaries of all *raiony* and *podraiony*;
(3) newspaper accounts, the reports of other parties and miscellaneous information.

Altogether, detailed evidence was amassed from 147 enterprises (representing 115 000 workers) and more general information from 192 enterprises (126 000 workers). Completely excluded from the survey were printing workers, who generally put up independent candidates; the employees of the San-Galli and Kozhevnikov factories and the Nevskii and New cotton mills; workers from five factories in the Moscow district where the SRs are known to have won. Votes cast for 'SDs' and 'SRs' who fought the elections on a 'non-party' or 'anti-party' ticket, together with 'sympathisers', appear under 'non-party' in the tables.

Evidently the SRs performed remarkably well in the workers' *curia*, bearing in mind that they were contesting Russia's most industrially advanced and proletarianised centre. Though they were beaten overall by the Social Democrats, they still managed to pick up well over a third of the total vote, more than either Bolsheviks or Mensheviks taken separately. What was more upsetting for the SDs, however, was not so much the size of the SR vote, though that was disconcerting enough, but the fact that this 'petty-bourgeois', 'rootless' and peasant-orientated party had been most successful in the largest metallurgical and engineering plants, traditionally the Social Democrats' most reliable stomping ground and the nursery of the most conscious cadre proletariat.[136] If we combine the state-owned with the privately-owned categories of metal-working plants, for example (see Table 5.2), we find that the SRs took fully 45 per cent (11 238) of the votes cast, compared with 24 per cent for the Mensheviks and only 13

Table 5.1 Petersburg workers' *curia* elections: votes cast in numbers and percentages divided by type of enterprise

Type and number of enterprises	Mensheviks SD No.	(%)	Bolsheviks SD No.	(%)	Non-fraction SD No.	(%)	Total SD No.	(%)	Total PSR No.	(%)	Non-party No.	(%)	Total
11 factories under military and naval management[1]	2759	21.2	632	4.8	—	—	3391	26	6653	51	2996	23	13040
24 other large metal factoires[2]	3222	26.5	2767	22.7	210	1.7	6199	50.9	4585	37.7	1385	11.4	12169
19 textile factories	815	29.7	629	22.9	289	10.5	1733	63.1	769	28	243	8.9	2745
93 other enterprises	2785	32.6	1301	15.2	1711	20.1	5797	67.9	1216	14.3	1519	17.8	8532
Total	9581	26.2	5329	14.6	2210	6	17120	46.8	13223	36.1	6143	16.8	36586 (including 100 KDs and Rs)

Source: A. Mikhailov, 'Vybory vo vtoruyu Dumu v Peterburgskoi rabochei kurii', *Otzvuki* (August, 1907)
[1] Nevskii Shipbuilding, Obukhov, Orudinyi, Snaryazhatel'nyi, New Arsenal, Gil'zovyi, Pipe, Baltic, New Admiralty, Galernyi Island, Military-Medical.
[2] Putilov, Zhelezoprokatnyi, Langenzippen, Geisler, Franco-Russian, Khaimovich, Possel, Gvozdilnyi, Rozenkrants, Simens and Haliske (two factories), Petersburg Metal, Phoenix, Old Lessner, Erikson, Nobel, Kreiton, Rechkin, Chugunoliteinyi; Warsaw, Nikolaevskii and Baltic railway workshops, Aleksandrovskii wagon construction.

Table 5.2 Petersburg workers' *curia* elections: votes cast in numbers and percentages divided by size of enterprise

Size of enterprise enterprises	No. of enterprise enterprises	Total number of workers in enterprises	SD Mensheviks		SD Bolsheviks		SD Non-fraction		Total SD		Total PSR		Non-party		Kadets or Rightists		Total
			No.	(%)	No.	(%)	No.	(%)	No.	(%)	No.	(%)	No.	(%)	No.	(%)	
from 50 to 100	21	1571	446	43.9	139	13.7	41	4	626	61	—	—	363	35.8	KD 26	KD 2.5	1015
from 100 to 300	50	9079	941	25.1	844	22.5	641	17.1	2426	64.7	693	18.5	593	15.8	KD 38	KD 1	3750
from 300 to 500	22	8219	1338	45.4	458	15.6	157	5.3	1953	66.3	674	22.9	318	10.8	— KD	— KD	2945
from 500 to 1000	23	15852	1113	32.2	927	26.4	35	1	2095	59.6	932	26.5	483	13.7	6 R	0.2 R	3516
1000 and over	33	80000	5723	22.6	2961	11.7	1336	5.3	10020	39.5	10924	43.1	4386	17.3	30	0.1	25360
Total	147	115000 (approx.)	9581	26.2	5329	14.6	2210	6	17120	46.8	13223	36.1	6143	16.8	70 KD R 30	0.2 KD R 0.1	36586

Source: A. Mikhailov, 'Vybory vo vtoruyu Dumu v Peterburgskoi rabochei kurii', *Otzvuki* (August, 1907)

per cent for the Bolsheviks. The only obvious consolation for the SDs was that their opponents had been comparatively less successful in the private engineering plants than in the multi-purpose government-owned factories which employed the largest numbers of unskilled migrant workers. While the SRs seem also to have been unable to leave their mark on the smallest enterprises (evidently the preserve of the Mensheviks) this should not necessarily be put down to a straightforward rejection of the party by these workers. It may well have been the case that because the SR organisation in Petersburg was of more recent origin than that of the Social Democrats, and because the party had fewer propagandists at its disposal, a decision was made to concentrate available resources on the larger, more strategically important factories, where contact could most easily be made with the maximum number of workers. What this implies is that, given more time, the SRs would have been able to penetrate smaller factories successfully too.[137]

The electoral evidence also reveals that the party's performance among textile workers, though respectable, was less impressive than in the metal industry, and that the party received even fewer votes from enterprises in the 'miscellaneous' category. Other extraneous evidence seems to confirm that the SRs failed to make much headway in the chemical, glass, rubber and leather industries of the capital (see below). Again the explanation may lie in the fact that many of these factories were small and therefore for practical reasons beyond the pale of SR influence. As far as textile workers are concerned, a recent writer, analysing the results of two municipal elections in Moscow in 1917, found a negative correlation between the number of SR votes in a particular precinct and the number of textile workers, together with a corresponding positive correlation in the case of the Mensheviks.[138] In this instance, the large proportion of women in the textile industry may have been an important factor. It is arguable that working-class women may have been less attracted to the extreme radicalism of the SRs than their male counterparts, and that land socialisation may have been of less interest to women, because a smaller proportion retained a direct economic interest in the land. However, such a hypothesis must be excluded in the case of the Petersburg elections because women were ineligible to vote. An alternative explanation has therefore to be found. Evidence presented by David Lane for the Trekhgornyi textile mill in Moscow indicates that about 28 per cent of workers there had been employed at the factory for five years or more, and that this category comprised nearer two-thirds of workers in some of the more specialist shops. Skilled workers were certainly a minority in the textile industry but their significance was probably disproportionate to their numbers – they were probably more likely to vote in elections than unskilled workers, for example. The Trekhgornyi data also reveal that fewer workers (about 20 per cent of the total) had direct and regular contact with their villages than one might have expected.[139] A more recent study of Petrograd workers during the 1917 revolution has introduced evidence to show that there were by then more hereditary proletarians in the textile industry than in metalworking.[140] Our impression (to be substantiated below) is that the 'typical' SR recruit was probably young, moderately skilled, of fairly recent urban origin and with continuing ties in the countryside. While there can be no doubt that the textile mills contained large numbers of 'peasant' workers who might therefore be expected to sympathise with the SRs, the evidence discussed here indicates that the complexion of the textile labour force was highly variegated. It included a significant element of settled workers who would have tended to associate more closely with the Menshevik Social Democrats than with the PSR.

Table 5.3 reproduces the election results by geographical locality, though unfortunately without distinguishing between the Bolshevik and Menshevik vote. Generally speaking, impressions derived from the *Trud* concerning the extent and durability of SR strength in the various *raiony* are confirmed here. The results may also reflect the

Table 5.3 Petersburg workers' *curia* elections: party support by geographical locality

Raion	SR (%)	SD (%)
Narvskii	15.8	64.9
Town	22.2	59.8
Petersburgskii	23.6	54.4
Vyborgskii	41.4	54.3
Moskovskii	59.4*	36.1
Nevskii	33.1	28.3
Vasileostrovskii	53.1	41.2

*+ 5 SR factories
Source: A. Mikhailov, 'Vybory vo vtoruyu Dumu v Peterburgskoi rabochei kurii', *Otzvuki* (1907)

impact of the SRs' vigorous electoral campaigning. In the Narva district, for example, where the electoral machinery was set up late and where there had been a number of other organisational problems, the party's performance was relatively poor, contrasting sharply with the outcome in the Moscow and Vyborg districts where the SRs were comparatively well-entrenched. Perhaps one might have expected a victory of more decisive proportions in the Nevskii *raion*. The likely explanation here is that the local party organisation had always been confined to a handful of large factories, where the SRs duly received a large share of the vote. Outside these concentrations the party was unable to make its presence felt, leaving the field relatively clear for the Bolsheviks and Mensheviks.

Election Post-Mortem

After the elections were over, the Social Democrats in particular were anxious to discover and analyse the reasons for the rebuff they had received at the hands of so many voters. The explanations they discovered not only reveal much about the weaknesses of their own party but also something about the nature of the SRs' appeal.

First of all there were accusations of dishonest electioneering. An open letter to the editors of the Menshevik paper *Nash Mir*, for example, alleged that at the Obukhov factory the SRs had 'avoided open struggle' with their rivals and promoted their candiates not as members of the PSR but as 'non-party'. At the Okhta powder works, on the other hand, they were supposed to have slandered their Social-Democrat opponents by describing them as 'disguised bourgeois' who wanted to take the land away from the peasantry 'to sell it at a good price'.[141] Other SDs, notably Lenin, preferred to derive comfort from arguing that the SRs' success, though a chastening experience, had been no more than a flash in the pan:

> A 'revolutionary' petty-bourgeois party is incapable of solid and persistent work among the proletariat; at the slightest change in the workers' mood it disappears completely from the horizon of the working-class suburbs.[142]

There were those who took the SR threat more seriously. A representative from the (Bolshevik) Semyannikovskii *podraion*, for example, admitted that the SRs there were better organised for the campaign than his own party,[143] while a number of Menshevik writers reluctantly conceded that there was widespread, if misguided, support for SR policies on the land and on terror.[144] Martov even conjectured that with greater organisational resources enabling them to 'engage in battle on all fronts' the SRs would have been even more successful.[145]

While Bolsheviks and Mensheviks were ready to agree that the SRs posed no long-term threat to the future of Social Democracy, they insisted on blaming each other for their temporary set-back. For Lenin the sole culprits were the Mensheviks, for concluding an electoral agreement with the Kadets, ostensibly to prevent the possibility of right-wing gains (the 'black-hundred danger').[146] Lenin argued that this pact seriously damaged the credibility of the Social Democrats during the campaign. In Vyborg, for example, the SRs had won the sympathy of many workers by taunting the Mensheviks with accusations of 'kadetism', while on the other side of the city at the Nevskii shipbuilding and Rechkin factories their candidates were similarly embarrassed. To drive his point home Lenin produced evidence which purported to show that where Bolsheviks had fought the elections alone they had succeeded in holding off the SR challenge.[147] Needless to say, the Mensheviks rejected Lenin's analysis, though there can be little doubt that they were acutely embarrassed by the 'kadet issue', especially as in the event the right wing picked up so few votes.[148] They argued that it was the Bolsheviks who had discredited the party during the campaign. The workers had been unable to see any real differences between SRs and SDs because the Bolsheviks had taken over SR slogans and policies for themselves. This had had such a deleterious effect that at the traditionally Menshevik Obukhov factory the (Menshevik) candidate had been heckled with cries of 'It's not a workers' party we need but land'.[149]

Martov's analysis throws yet another light on events.[150] He wrote to Axelrod that pre-electoral agitation had gone 'wretchedly' (*velas'-izruk von plokho*) claiming (with considerable exaggeration) that not a single leaflet calling on workers to vote for Social-Democrat candidates had been issued by the party. He complained that party workers had been complacent, taking an SD victory for granted. They had overlooked the fact that the secret ballot presented workers with an opportunity to 'escape' from the party's tutelage, and that they had used this to register their resentment and disillusionment. Moreover, party work, together with morale, had deteriorated since the dissolution of the first Duma and local organisers had begun to behave 'despotically', particularly in the supposedly neutral factory commissions; this the SRs had successfully exploited. Martov also complained about the 'very low' (*ves'ma nevysokii*) level of political consciousness shown by the SD vanguard in his altogether negative and gloomy prognosis.

So much for the Social Democrats' version of events. For their part the SRs acknowledged that they had received 'a much larger share of the vote' than anticipated and only regretted that their organisational resources had not permitted them to reach an even greater number of workers, and that the electoral system had been so heavily weighted against them. Their success they attributed to their policies rather than to the personal appeal of their candidates. The popularity of 'land and freedom' they argued, exposed the fallacy in Lenin's assertion that a proletariat remote from rural ties already existed in St Petersburg.[151]

Social and Political Implications

The election evidence provides important clues as to the nature and social composition of SR support among Petersburg factory workers. By its very nature, however, it can do no more than reflect the political preference of a part of the working class, registered on a single occasion after an unusually intensive barrage of party propaganda and agitation. The findings might therefore do no more than measure the dimensions of a transient tidal wave of sympathy for the PSR, in which case they cannot serve as a reliable indicator of party support over an extended period. Fortunately there is a method, though admittedly a far from perfect one, by which the Mikhailov evidence can be tested. There is sufficient information in the *raion* and factory reports submitted to *Trud* to permit the compilation of a factory index, consisting of enterprises known to have had organisational ties with the party at some time during the period September 1906 to March 1908. The completed index, containing eighty factories in all, is reproduced here as Table 5.4.[152]

Seventy-five factories have been located in a Petersburg factory directory for 1914 which provides information on location, size and production speciality.[153] This information is reproduced in the index. In order to compare the data there with the industrial make-up of Petersburg as a whole we turned to the statistical evidence compiled by James Bater from the directory used here.

The results provide confirmation of at least two impressions derived from the Mikhailov material. First, that the SRs were most closely associated with large factories. Second, that the party was particularly

Table 5.4 Petersburg factories with known SR ties, 1906–08

Name	Type	No. of workers (1914)
Gorodskii raion		
Cardboard factory		?
V. I. Kozhevnikov	cotton fabric and cloth	700
Leather factory		?
San-Galli	machine-building for tobacco factories	1000
'Svet'	stove and cooking pieces etc.	40
Vestingauz	printing	355
A. M. Zhukov	machine construction, foundry, oil	240
Kolomenskii raion		
Bor'man	chocolate and biscuit	1000
Durdin	beer and malt	480
Franco-Russian	shipbuilding	2100
Kalinkina	beer and mineral water	1200
New Admiralty	shipbuilding	1850
Russian Cotton-Spinning	cotton-spinning	3600
State Paper Supply	printing and paper	3200
State Liquor Store	—	?
Kolpinskii raion		
Izhorskii	metalworking (steel parts, armour, shells, torpedo-boats)	3025

111

Moskovskii raion

'Astra'	oil (coconut, castor, lamp, oil cake)	500
Broder	?	37
Gas works	—	?
Glebov	electro-technical	150
Keller	vodka distillery	100
A. Koppel	truck, waggon building	500
Mal'kiel	?	c.300 (1906–7)
Ozoling	mechanical (iron and copper parts, machine equipment, transmission parts)	140
Pastor	foundry and mechanical	250
Pintsh	metalworking	150
Rechkin	wagon construction and metal parts	2000
Riks	wall paper, paper dyeing	200
'Skorokhod'	shoes	2700
Syromyatnikov	chocolate and confectionery	350
K. F. Verfel	stone and bronze decorative items	65
A. F. Zass	propellor caps	66

Narvskii raion

Aleksandrova	metal	82
Arkhipov	bone-burning	400 (1907)
T. L. Aukh	cloth	200
Ekateringof	cotton-spinning	950
Kharlambov	metal	c. 65 (1907)
M. Konradi	chocolate and confectionery	500
Pilorubnyi	?	?

Table 5.4 Petersburg factories with known SR ties, 1906–08

Name	Type	No. of workers (1914)
Putilov	rail, general metalworking, shipbuilding	13 382
Til'mans	?	?
'Treugol'nik'	rubber	11 000
Voronin (Rezvoostrovskaya)	weaving mill	922
Nevskii raion		
Aleksandrovskii	waggon building and machine	3 300
Card factory	—	?
Maksvel	cotton-spinning	3 000
Nevskii Shipbuilding	—	3 500
Obukhovskii	steel and ship parts	4 500
Pal'	cotton-spinning	2 057
Vargunin	stationery	750
Peterburgskii raion		
Bek	cotton-spinning	990
Geisler	electrical and telephone	800
Gofman	rod and strip (frame)	170
Langenzipen	machine building and foundry	1 200
Leont'ev	cloth-printing	500
Mel'tser	furniture	250–300
Military Medical	medicaments, surgical instruments	1 000+
I. Sautam	cloth	65
Til'mans	metalworking	?

Vasileostrovskii raion

Baltic	shipbuilding (fitting and bodies)	5 200
Laferm	tobacco	2 500
Cartridge factory	machine and cartridge	1 200
Pipe factory	pipe	5 500
Vyborgskii raion		
Arsenal	machine, military equipment	1000+
P. V. Baranovskii	machine, cartridge and pipe	800
Chesher	cotton-spinning	900
L. M. Erikson	telephone, telegraph and signal equipment	1500
'Feniks'	machine, tools, hydraulic presses engines, steam hammers	500
Cartridge Case factory	pipe and mechanical	?
Kornilov	china and ceramics	400
New Lessner	machine building, iron foundry	1260
Mal'tsev (Sampsonievskaya manufaktura)	cotton-spinning	2865
Okhta	gun-powder	1000+
Petersburg Metal	general (steam engines, turbines)	3 000+
Nobel'	machine building and diesel motors	1000
Armaments factory	gun, machine construction (cannon and parts)	1000
Parviainen	machine and foundry (piano frames, screw propellors)	1600
Rozenkrants	metal-rolling	2000
Ordnance factory	equipment, supply	?
Tove	?	?

attractive to workers in the metal industry. These conclusions will now be substantiated.

The factories contained in the index represent about 8 per cent (1913) of the total number of industrial enterprises in Petersburg but over 54 per cent of the labour force. The contrast between number and size is even more striking in the metallurgical and engineering group, where 'SR' factories account for only 13 per cent of the total plants but fully 80 per cent of the workforce. The same trend can be observed in other major industries but is much less pronounced. The corresponding figures for textile manufacturing are 15 per cent and 40 per cent and for the food and drink industry 7 per cent and 30 per cent. The average factory in Petersburg in 1913 employed 203 workers, the average in the file, 1300 workers.

Next, the industrial distribution of workers in the index was compared with that of Petersburg as a whole. The results are shown in Table 5.5.

The paramountcy of metal workers in the index is self-evident and considerably exceeds their share of the labour force as a whole. So who were these workers and what were their political interests likely to be?

On the face of it there was something in the SR programme to attract all workers, even the *cadre* proletariat. The party's minimum demands in the field of worker legislation included a working day of eight hours or less, a negotiated minimum wage, unrestricted trade union activity, comprehensive social insurance, an elected factory inspectorate and the participation of workers in the internal running of their factories.[154] Apart from these officially sanctioned demands, some of which were more adventurous than those advanced by the RSDLP, local SR workers' organisations called for such reforms as the abolition of factory searches, the fixing of rents, the provision of schools and reading rooms on factory premises and the construction of lodgings for the unemployed.[155] Moreover, land socialisation, though ostensibly a 'peasant' measure, was expected to benefit even settled workers to some degree. But the PSR was not exclusively or indeed primarily concerned with the aspirations of the *cadre* proletariat. It consistently emphasised the shared origins and culture of worker and peasant, their interdependence of interest and their common subjection to exploitation. While acknowledging that the urban worker was part of the 'most militant element' of the oppressed class,[156] the SRs refused to recognise the vanguard role assigned to the proletariat by the Social Democrats, and instead stressed the indispensability to the revolution of an active worker–peasant alliance conceived as a partnership of

Table 5.5 Distribution of workforce in factory index compared with Petersburg as a whole

Type of industry	% of Petersburg labour force	% of labour force in SR index
Metallurgy and engineering	40	60
Textiles	23	17
Food and drink	10.5	6
Paper and printing	12	3.8
Chemicals	8.5	3
Total	94	89

equals. The collapse of the soviet movement in 1905 and of the Bolshevik-inspired general strike of July 1906 (both attributed to the lack of active support from the peasantry) were grist to the SRs' mill in developing this argument.[157]

Obviously the sense of common identity and mutual interest supposed to hold worker and peasant together was least experienced by the *cadre* proletariat. In a leaflet dated April 1905 the SRs posed a series of rhetorical questions which clearly reveal where instead they considered their major urban constituency to lie:

> Where do we workers ourselves originate? Aren't the majority of us *muzhiks*? Don't we have families in the countryside? Don't we send money there? Don't we make trips back home?[158]

Evidently then, the SRs were appealing primarily to workers who retained economic as well as cultural ties with the village, most of all perhaps to those owning a *nadel*, even if they did not actually cultivate it themselves. Even in Petersburg in the period under discussion, this 'nadel-owning' group constituted as much as 40 per cent of the workforce in some factories, something which not all Social Democrats seem to have appreciated.[159] Furthermore, workers with rural ties were by no means exclusively confined to the unskilled and poorly educated strata of the industrial population.

The biographical entries in the directory of the Society of Political Prisoners[160] provide some clue as to the type of worker likely to belong to the party *aktiv*. They include twenty-one members of the PSR engaged in the metalworking industry of the capital at some time during the period c. 1902–14.

We find that over 60 per cent of this (admittedly small) sample were under twenty years of age when they joined the party and that almost all were less than twenty-five. While only a small proportion (about 6 per cent) were genuinely *cadre* proletarians (that is, second-generation Petersburg-born) the father in about half the cases was either specifically described as a worker, or possessed a skill appropriate to industrial work. A little over half the sample were fitters (*slesari*) but turners, joiners, draughtsmen and machine-builders are all represented.

These were for the most part skilled workers. The remainder were mostly from the 'hot' shops (forge workers and smelters). There are no *chernorabochie* (designated unskilled workers). Virtually the entire sample had enjoyed at least a primary education; not much less than a third had attended factory or technical schools. By the time they joined the PSR most were probably nearing the end of a factory apprenticeship and would therefore already be fully acquainted with the peculiar rigours and rhythms of industrial life.

To pinpoint the location of SR support within individual factories, reference was made to the party's financial accounts which occasionally record membership dues by shop. Unfortunately only a single example relevant to Petersburg is extant. It lists contributions from the Nevskii shipbuilding factory during May 1907. The details are reproduced in Table 5.6.

Table 5.6   Accounts of the Semyannikov *podraion* of the PSR, May 1907

Shop	Contribution (roubles)
electrical	12.70
steamer-assembly	7.65
wheel shop	6.40
steamer-mechanical	4.61
boiler house	4.21
iron-shipbuilding	3.54
new mechanical	3.30
stamp forge	3.25
forge	3.09
engine assembly	3.05
bolt shop	2.85
copper brazier	2.79
engine repair	1.68
iron foundry	1.41
sail shop	0.90
paint shop	0.90
Total	62.33

It has proved impossible to obtain a detailed breakdown of the labour force at the Nevskii plant, but information is available for the Baltic shipbuilding factory, which may be comparable.[162] A large majority (about 80 per cent) of the workforce there belonged to the peasant estate (*soslovie*), that is they were still under the legal jurisdiction of their native villages even though they actually resided in the city. However, there were considerable fluctuations in the proportion of 'peasants' from one part of the plant to another. The highest percentages were recorded in the carpentry (98 per cent), shipbuilding (95 per cent), rigging (89 per cent) steel foundry (89 per cent) and boiler shops (86 per cent); the lowest in the pattern (50 per cent), electro-technical and repair (67 per cent) and joining (68 per cent) sections. This second group, together with the mechanical and brazier shops, was considered by the manager, Major-General Ratnik, to represent the more sophisticated aspects of factory production and so to contain the largest proportions of skilled workers.[163] If the evidence from the Baltic plant holds good for the Nevskii shipbuilding works, we may conclude that support for the PSR was drawn from a large number of shops, representing a considerable range of skill levels and experience. This broad trend can be found elsewhere.[164] A comparison with accounts from metalworking plants in Sevastopol' (Admiralty shipyard), Votkinsk and Bezhetsa (Bryansk), for example, would seem to indicate that the most consistent source of support for the SRs was to be found in the 'mainstream' metalworking departments; that is, the mechanical, construction and assembly shops.

This ties in fairly closely with the evidence from the Society for Political Prisoners. The fitters and turners who formed the largest single groups of metalworkers in that source would presumably have been distributed through most of the mainstream workshops; fitters in fact represented 16.5 per cent of the total labour force at the Baltic factory (1906) and formed the largest single group there.[165] Also interesting is that none of the skills most closely associated with a long work *stazh* at the Baltic – pattern-working, engineering, finishing and machine-operating – occur in the PKS sample. In fact, the skills which are represented there were often acquired beyond the confines of the city. The management of the Baltic factory, for example, took on recruits from rurally-situated railway workshops as well as seasonal shipbuilding workers on the Volga. These men were not so highly-valued as city-trained workers and often served as assistants (*podruchnye*) to the already established fitters, turners and braziers.[166] They were, nevertheless, skilled and educated workers, of a type likely to be susceptible to the political ideas and slogans of the Socialist-Revolutionaries.

When the Duma election results were analysed it was noted that the SRs received their greatest share of the vote from workers in the state-owned plants. Because they were generally larger and less specialised than the engineering factories, state enterprises took on much larger numbers of unskilled and semi-skilled workers. In 1901, for example, 75 per cent of the labour force at the Putilov works

Table 5.7 Distribution of workers at the Baltic factory according to length of service (1906)

Trade	Total workforce		Length of service (%) of whole group)					
	no.	(%)	Up to 1 yr	Up to 5 yrs	Up to 10 yrs	Up to 15 yrs	Up to 20 yrs	More than 20 yrs
All workers	4551	100	13.9	51.4	25.9	5.2	2.1	1.5
Fitters	751	16.5	8.9	48.7	32.6	5.1	2.7	2.0
Carpenters and moulders	500	11	11.8	45.4	33.0	7.4	1.6	0.8
Assistants	487	10.7	10.7	68.8	18.3	1.4	0.6	0.2
Drillers and loppers	460	10	0.4	70.2	26.3	2.0	0.9	0.2
Oborshchiki	394	8.7	0.3	39.6	50.0	6.3	3.0	0.8
Machine operators	310	6.8	19.7	33.9	27.1	8.7	3.5	7.1
Riveters	203	4.5	18.2	70.5	7.3	2	1.5	1
Apprentices	207	4.5	52.7	47.3	—	—	—	—
Blacksmiths and strikers	184	4	25	42.4	17.9	9.8	2.2	2.7
Caulkers	141	3.1	14.2	67.4	12.1	3.5	1.4	1.4
Painters	139	3.1	5.8	72.6	18.0	2.2	0.7	0.7
Unskilled	127	2.8	18.9	63.7	12.6	1.6	2.4	0.8
Engineers and stokers	114	2.5	18.4	22.8	32.5	18.4	6.1	1.8
Iron-smelters	105	2.4	32.4	28.6	26.7	9.5	2.8	—
Joiners	107	2.4	6.6	57	28	4.7	2.8	0.9

Source: Rashin, Formirovanie rabochego klassa Rossii, p. 503.

earned a basic wage of less than one rouble a day, compared with 20 per cent at the Lessner factory and 24 per cent at Wire and Nail. The state plants took a correspondingly smaller share of the most highly qualified workers: at Putilov, for example, only 1.1 per cent of the workforce earned more than two roubles a day. The corresponding figures for the Lessner and Wire and Nail factories were 13.5 per cent and 11.4 per cent.[167]

What final conclusions may be drawn about the social and occupational background of SR supporters in the Petersburg metal-working industry? It would seem that party members were to be found in most sections of the average factory, but that they were less well represented among workers with the highest technical skills and with the longest work *stazh*. The core SR supporters were the fitters, turners, smelters and forge-workers in the major metalworking departments. There were probably fewer party members among the unskilled (including those who had most recently migrated to Petersburg) precisely because these workers tended to be the least politically conscious. However, the known association of the SRs with peasant interests, conceived even in the vaguest terms, may, on occasions such as the second Duma elections, have enabled them to mobilise the unskilled migrant with greater ease than the more urban-facing Social Democrats. Finally, the evidence of the Society of Political Prisoners, though by no means conclusive in itself, would seem to bear out Social Democrat assertions that such support as there was for the PSR from among the *cadre* proletariat was largely a temporary phenomenon. Pooling all the information available, the background of a 'typical' SR metalworkers might be sketched in the following terms.

He had migrated from Tver province or from another part of the Central Industrial District where there was a high level of literacy and a tradition of seasonal wage labour, and was in his late teens or early twenties when he joined the party. After receiving an elementary education in the village, he had acquired a metalworking skill (or at least some work experience), possibly in the local railway repair shops, alternatively at a rural factory or handicraft enterprise, or at a technical school in Petersburg. In this last instance he was probably enrolled either by his father, who may himself have had some experience in industry, or by another close relative or kinsman to whom he would then have been entrusted. At some time between the ages of 13 and 16 he would have begun several years' apprenticeship in one of the major metalworking factories. Though now living in the city, he may have been in line to inherit a *nadel* in the countryside. This would have been cultivated for him by relatives or friends, who would in return expect to receive a portion of his wages, or possibly some 'luxury' items obtainable only in Petersburg. Generally speaking, his financial obligations to the village were a considerable drain on his income, but fulfilling them did at least provide some measure of security in case of unemployment. For such a worker, the main attraction of the PSR lay in its strong identification with 'land and freedom', a slogan as resonant in the factories of Petersburg as in the villages of Tver and Ryazan.[168]

Postscript

The workers' *curia* duly assembled on 1 February 1907. After what was evidently a stormy session, all fourteen places in the city college were awarded to the Social Democrats.[169] Petersburg's working class was eventually represented in the Duma by a Bolshevik from the Okhta powder works, I. A. Petrov.

THE PETERSBURG SRs AND THE TRADE UNIONS

The place of the trade unions in Socialist-Revolutionary strategy will be discussed elsewhere;[170] here we are concerned only with the party's involvement in the Petersburg labour organisations. At the outset it can be said that the PSR was slow to become active in trade union work and was never able to overcome the predominance of the Social Democrats in that sphere. The SRs had initially been reluctant to lend their full support to the nascent 'legal' labour movement because they believed that trade unions would be unable to operate effectively under autocratic conditions.[171] When these conditions were relaxed and the party reversed its policy, it failed to communicate a coherent trade union policy and strategy to the masses with sufficient urgency and clarity.[172] In part the outcome was that the SRs were often unable to generate enthusiasm for union work, even among their own activists. On the basis of other evidence presented in this study, for example, one would at least have expected them to play a major role in the union of metalworkers. Yet even here, though the party did participate in discussions in a number of factories preliminary to the founding of the union and was at times strongly represented in that body afterwards, there is no evidence to contradict the recent assertion that 'from the start it was a predominantly Social Democrat operation'.[173] The same probably goes for the majority of trade unions in Petersburg.

A partial exception was the union of bakery workers, where the SRs constituted a significant force, intermittently at least, before the First World War. Their 'power base' here rested on the large bakeries of the Moscow firm of Filippov. The Filippov bakeries were of the 'mass producing' type, employing a labour force 'tied predominantly to the countryside and not so (politically) conscious as the Germans' (owners of the smaller, more specialising artisanal establishments). Following a successful and well-supported strike in June 1906 which obviously enhanced the union's reputation among the workers, 'two courses' (SR and SD) vied for control of its ideological direction. According to the standard Bolshevik history,[174] the SRs (led by a 'fanatic' called Solovev) soon began agitating for a second strike, arguing that the employers had already recovered most of the ground lost to them after the initial dispute. The repsonse within the union's ruling body was cool, but at a secret delegate conference held in Finland in the spring of 1907 the pro-strike line was overwhelmingly endorsed. The industrial action which duly followed was this time disastrous for unions and workers alike. The strike was crushed by a judicious blend of lockouts and repression, to which the SRs allegedly responded with acts of sabotage and 'terrorist struggle'.[175] Comprehensive defeat resulted in a mass exodus from the union (once 6000 strong) with the 'peasant' bakers allegedly leading the way. This did not, however, signal the permanent demise of SR influence in the union: in 1913 approximately half the executive belonged to that party.[176]

No doubt the SRs exerted periodic influence in a number of other unions during the 1906–7 period, but they achieved effective control of only two major organisations: the Union of Post and Telegraph Employees (for which, unfortunately, precious little information is available) and, more importantly, the All-Russian Railway Union (ARRU).

From its inception, the ARRU was largely in SR hands – by the end of 1905 the party already held more places on the central bureau than any other organisation.[177] The Petersburg branch of the union was no exception to this trend; here too the SRs exercised a 'remarkably large' influence.[178] At the end of 1906, despite exceptionally difficult political conditions, there were still 2391 members, with sympathisers 'exceeding the number of members many times'. The majority (1254 – 54 per cent) were workshop and repair employees, 752 (31 per cent) were 'line personnel' (drivers, guards, points operators, and so on) and only 385 (16 per cent) were clerical and administrative staff (including engineers). The author of the press report from which these figures are taken claimed that they belied an impression given currency by the SDs that the ARRU was a predominantly 'middle bourgeois' or 'petty bourgeois' organisation. More accurately perhaps, they show that the ARRU was by no means a distinctively 'white collar' union.

By the time the activities of the union had been severely curtailed by a virtual state of martial law on the railways,[179] as well as by the customary shortage of finances (in part attributable to the bourgeoisie cutting off their support). Monthly income was reduced to 700–800 roubles per month, though in fact there would shortly be a remarkable, if temporary, revitalisation.[180] The SRs 'controlled' all lines operating within the Petersburg junction with the exception of the Baltic, which was firmly in the hands of the Social Democrats. Menshevik-led attempts to reverse the balance of forces were directed towards encouraging the membership of the ARRU to desert the official organisation and to join a rival, Social-Democrat sponsored 'non-political' union, a policy which apparently enjoyed only limited success in Petersburg.[181] Meanwhile the SRs were able to tailor the platform of the ARRU to suit their own requirements by including a 'political' statement which called for 'full civil freedoms' and popular representation, guaranteeing 'the involvement of the entire people in the running of the country'. Almost nothing is known of the local history of the union after March 1907, save that (predictably) inter-party rivalry continued to play a debilitating role.[182]

SR union activities in Petersburg had at first (in 1906–7 that is) been overseen by a party *orgburo*; by September 1908 this had become a 'professional commission' consisting of one representative for each union, meeting once a fortnight.[183] The commission maintained ties with 18 trade unions at that time – in numerical terms not much of a shortfall on the previous year.[184] Support within them was sufficient for the SRs to claim five seats on the Central Bureau of Trade Unions, including the position of secretary. The party was strongest (according to its own estimates) in the Unions of metalworkers, marble workers ('entirely in the hands of the PSR'), coach-makers, hatters, confectionary workers, gold and silver-smiths and shop-assistants. Ties with the textile workers were said to be 'very weak'. This was also the case with the print-workers' union: of 86 nominees to its 'delegates assembly' only five were SRs. Judging by the contributions of other groups to party funds the SRs also had a following among tanners, tramway workers and tailors.[185]

The SRs faced two major problems in their union work. One consisted in persuading party members to join in the first place (and convincing them that it was worthwhile remaining after the revolutionary movement had subsided); the second lay in persuading suitable candidates to stand for executive posts. Only a comparatively small number of party members are known to have held senior positions in any major union, though it should be borne in mind that most of the available sources are not favourable to the SRs. In 1908 the secretary of the metalworkers' union was an SR and, two years later one Zatorskii, previously vice-president, was promoted to the top post.[186] The union also records in its roll of honour the name of an SR activist in the Moscow district and former member of the soviet, A. Piskarev. No other members of the party appear to have won and held on to any position of distinction, however. In the other unions the story is much the same. In 1910 an SR was among those attending the All-Russian Congress of Handicraftsmen as a representative of the Petersburg Woodworkers' Union,[187] and it will be recalled that, shortly before the war, half the governing body of the bakery workers' union was composed of SRs. The party was also represented on the board of the builders' union in 1914.[188] Sad to say, not all party members gave the unions such commendable service. During 1908–9, for example, SRs were held responsible for several cases of embezzlement and theft from the metalworkers' union, the union of draughtsmen and the ARRU.[189]

To sum up, information on SR trade union activity in Petersburg is too fragmentary to permit any but the most tentative conclusions. The available evidence suggests that at best the party was substantially represented in about half the trade unions of the capital and 'predominant' in a quarter of them. Here at least they conducted agitation, probably intermittently, with limited resources and with varying degrees of success. With the exception of the Union of Post and Telegraph workers and the ARRU, the SRs were unable to dominate any major trade union. Many party members were apathetic about joining the unions.[190] This was partly due to confusion (initially at least) about where precisely the SRs stood on the issue, also because more overtly political forms of action were more to the taste of many party members and because the most immediately appreciable benefits of trade union membership were of a kind more likely to appeal to workers without alternative means of support in the countryside. The SRs suffered from an additional, related handicap: relatively few of their activists could boast much union experience. Consequently, even in cases where support for the party was sufficient to entitle it to fill executive positions from within its own ranks, it was often unable to provide candidates with the necessary qualities of reliability, competence and dedication.[191]

HETERODOX CURRENTS IN THE PETERSBURG ORGANISATION

In Petersburg the earliest recorded defections to the Maximalists date from 1906, though there may have been Maximalist circles two years earlier.[192] By January 1907 the SRs felt that Maximalism had become enough of a threat to merit a lengthy refutation in the pages of *Trud*.[193] While the present writer discovered only a single instance of desertion *en masse* from the PSR (the case of a factory organisation in the Kolomenskii *raion*),[194] the reason may be that the party was anxious to draw a veil over similar scandals to protect both morale and its own credibility. Whatever the extent of the defections (and they do not seem to have been too serious) the attraction of Maximalism in Petersburg appears to have lain more or less exclusively in its uninhibitedly adventurist tactics rather than in any particular element of its programme.[195] This no doubt helps to explain why the fighting detachments of the PSR were more susceptible to Maximalist influence than other parts of the organisation. A certain amount of confusion was probably caused by the local party's own somewhat equivocal attitude towards Maximalism. For example, while it was expressly forbidden for a member of the PSR simultaneously to be a member of a Maximalist organisation, individuals leaning towards Maximalist positions but willing to submit to party discipline were tolerated. Furthermore, 'close technical agreements' with the Maximalists (presumably in the field of terrorist operations) were considered 'desirable'.[196] Evidence of the influence of Maximalism on SR fighting units can be found in the Buzinov memoir already referred to in this study. According to his account, there were one or two Maximalist circles in the Nevskii district early in 1907, and supporters of the tendency had already infiltrated the party's terrorist cells and begun using their weapons for Maximalist-style operations (usually private expropriations). When the local SR detachment was broken up as the result of a major provocation, all party members were ordered publicly to surrender their firearms, on risk of expulsion. One or two *druzhiniki*, however, chose instead, to lend their services to a Maximalist group led by 'Ira' and took part in an expropriation at the house of the chief of police in March 1907.[197] Examples such as this were probably to be found in other parts of the city. They highlight the weaknesses of local combat organisations – the ideological confusion of many of their members, their susceptibility to provocation and infiltration and the difficulty of exercising effective overall party control. Coincidentally, in March 1907 an official resolution of the Petersburg organisation called for the disbanding of *raion* units and the formation of a single detachment, to be directly subordinated to the city committee.[198] This plan was virtually still-born: in July all local combat activity was officially halted, ostensibly because of a shortage of arms.[199]

By now, for reasons which will be outlined below, many supporters of the party were inclining towards open advocacy of outlawed tactical positions. The Petersburg delegate to the third party council (July 1907) reported a strong current of opinion in favour of economic (factory) terror and private expropriations.[200] The accuracy of his observation is confirmed by a contemporary resolution passed at an assembly of the Town district.[201] The party hierarchy in the capital was soon registering its concern by devoting space in *Trud* to these very issues.[202] However, the emotional tide continued to run directly in the face of official policy. In February 1908 the Narva *raion* committee voted in favour of factory terror and for large-scale private as well as state expropriations,[203] while at the party conference in August one of the delegates noted that 'half the workers of Petersburg' now approved of economic terror.[204]

THE DISINTEGRATION OF THE SR ORGANISATION, 1907–08

The early months of 1907 witnessed the high-water mark of SR activity in Petersburg. An organisation of 6000 members,[205] the Socialist-Revolutionaries could now claim with justice to be arch-rivals of the Social Democrats in the most highly proletarianised and industrially-advanced of Russian cities. As we have seen, this unpalatable fact was driven home to the SDs in the course of the workers' *curia* elections to the second Duma; the same phenomenon was to be remarked on again and again by the SRs themselves well into the spring. Yet within a mere twelve months barely the foundations of their organisation remained intact and the prospects for reconstruction appeared remote. Two factors, acting as corroding agents within the party, were primarily responsible for this dramatic change in fortune; one was the devastatingly effective intervention of the security forces, the other the advancing industrial recession.

When the second Duma, with its unexpectedly large left-wing representation, began work in February 1907, revolutionaries both inside and outside the Tauride Palace became a particular source of embarassment and concern to the government. In response to this situation the police carried out a series of raids over the ensuing months, concentrating their efforts on organisations like the PSR, which sanctioned terrorism in its war against the state. As a result, that party alone estimated its losses at 300 activists (students and workers) for the first half of the year.[206] Obviously arrests on this scale caused untold internal damage, besides dealing a devastating blow to morale. The network of ties established between the various parts of the organisation was constantly being disrupted, fear of infiltration by provocateurs caused suspicion and ill-feeling, virtually all forms of protest and assembly were made impossible, printing presses were silenced and propaganda circles, where they survived at all, were unable to meet regularly. Within a few months the workers were left almost entirely to their own devices and generally proved unable or unwilling to carry out many of the tasks previously undertaken or overseen by the intelligentsia or the party professionals.

The second corroding agent at work within the PSR during 1907–8 was the deepening recession in the metalworking industry, which brought in its wake the familiar corollaries of unemployment, short-time working and wage-reductions.[207] One immediate casualty was party income as supporters found themselves unable to pay membership dues or to contribute to the cost of newspapers and literature. Bereft of money as well as leaders, district and factory organisations were scarcely able to keep afloat, especially as they could not, as in the past, turn to the city committee for financial help.[208] In the longer term the evident failure of the revolutionary leadership to find a way to combat the police onslaught, together with the seemingly inexorable industrial decline, convinced many workers of the futility of revolutionary politics and led eventually to desertion on a large scale. Already by July 1907 party membership had declined to about 4000; at the time of the first party conference just a year later it was in the region of 1400.[209] Though the party continued to maintain a foothold in the city up to the First World War it was unable to recover its former strength before 1917.[210]

128

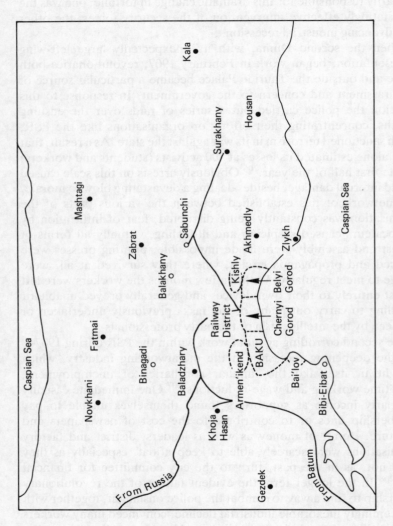

Map 3 Baku and its environs

6 Five Organisational Profiles

THE SRs IN BAKU

City and Workforce

Formerly an Iranian possession, the Caspian port of Baku was finally ceded to the Russian Tsars in 1806.[1] Its population grew from a mere 15 000 in 1875 to more than 334 000 in 1913,[2] an increase mainly attributable to the development of the oil industry with which Baku quickly became synonymous. Systematic drilling began during the 1870s: by the turn of the century the surrounding oil fields were producing more than those of the entire United States.[3] This period of remarkable growth was, however, followed by a serious and pro-longed contraction. Output dropped by 11 per cent between 1901 and 1903 and took a further dive in 1905. There was to be no substantial improvement before the First World War – production levels in 1913 had still not surpassed those attained during 1901, allowing Russia's American competitors to forge ahead.[4]

The population of Baku was markedly heterogeneous. In 1903 the native Azerbaijanis comprised about 54 per cent of the total inhabitants, Armenians 20.5 per cent and Russians 20.3 per cent.[5] There were smaller minorities of Georgians, Daghestanis, Volga Tatars and western Europeans (French, German, English). Despite the kaleidoscope of nationalities, Baku was no ethnic melting-pot: the major groupings strove to retain their separate identities in a fiercely confrontational atmosphere which, not infrequently, spilled over into unrestrained violence of the kind seen between Armenians and Azerbaijanis during 1905.

129

Table 6.1   Distribution of Baku labour force, c. 1906–07

Category	No. of workers
oil	42 000–50 000
metalworking	7 000
Caspian Merchant Fleet	6 900
food	3 500
port	2 000
cotton-spinning	2 000
railways	2 000
artisan sector	500
printing	450

Altogether, there were about 80 000 workers in Baku and its environs, distributed as shown in Table 6.1

The majority of Baku workers (64 per cent in 1913) were male migrants: from rural Azerbaijan, Persia, the Volga provinces and the Caucasus. The proportion of migrants was even higher in the oil industry.[7] Many workers continued to own land in the countryside and to maintain a family there; some were employed in Baku only on a seasonal basis. Generally speaking, Russians were the most settled or proletarianised nationality and Azerbaijanis the least. The appalling environmental conditions in Baku might encourage one to suppose that the 'push' factors of over-population and rural poverty were the main generators of migration here. Nevertheless, it must be borne in mind that, though prices in Baku were above the Russian average, so too were wages; so much so in fact that there must have been a considerable incentive for skilled workers to make the long trip down to the grime-sodden shores of the Caspian.[8]

The Baku oil industry, together with a third of the population, was dispersed over a scattering of settlements encircling the outer reaches of the city. The most important of these were Balakhany, Bibi-Eibat, Surakhany, Sabunchiny and Binagadi. The oil district was the domain of the industrialists, who were responsible for 'everything from roads and water supply to medicine and schools'.[9] Russian and Armenian firms predominated by the turn of the century but effective financial control was increasingly located in foreign hands – British interests alone were responsible for 60 per cent of total capital investment by the time of the revolution. In 1900 just six firms: Nobel bros,

Mantashev, the Caspian-Black Sea Corporation (Rothschild), the Baku Oil Society, the Caspian Company and the Society for Drilling Russian Oil and Liquid Fuel, accounted for 50 per cent of production. By the time of the First World War further mergers and consolidations created a situation fast approaching monopoly, with the bulk of production being concentrated in the hands of three giant concerns: the Russian General Oil Corporation, the Royal Dutch-Shell group and Nobel bros.[10]

By Russian standards, the individual oil enterprises (there were over 300 in all) were on the small side: in 1913, 55 per cent employed 50 workers or less and only 9 per cent more than 300 workers.[11] Among the largest were Shibaev (710 workers), Oleum oil extraction (500), the Bibi-Eibat Co. (487), Nobel (428), Bering engineering and contract drilling (368), Mantashev (320) and the Caspian-Black Sea Corporation (300).[12] In 1907 Russians comprised 25 per cent of the oil-workers in Baku, Armenians 24 per cent and Azerbaijanis 48 per cent.[13] Russians and Georgians predominated in the most skilled occupations, Russians accounting for 67 per cent of workers in oil processing and 48 per cent of metalworkers but only 20 per cent and 13 per cent respectively of those employed in oil extraction and contract drilling. (These latter occupations were dominated by the Azerbaijanis.) About 25 per cent of Armenian workers were highly skilled and were mainly employed by Armenian-owned firms such as Mantashev and Mirzoev.[14] Occupational divisions reflected the educational level of the various nationalities – nearly 84 per cent of Georgians and 51.3 per cent of Russians were literate but only 34.9 per cent of Armenians and a mere 5.5 per cent of Azerbaijanis.[15] Wage-levels conformed to this same hierarchy, with Azerbaijanis receiving only 73 per cent of the average wage earned by Georgians and 81 per cent of that earned by Russians.[16] As the more skilled workers were able to substantially increase their basic wages by earning bonuses however, the real difference between the nationalities was probably even more accentuated.

An Outline History

While the Social Democrats had begun work in Baku as early as 1898, an SR group was not formed there until the spring of 1903. The founder members evaded arrest for only a few months and the party played no more than a peripheral role in the general strike which took place at the end of 1904.[17] Support at that time was concentrated among artisanal workers though there were also some factory cells, at the Mirzebekiants tobacco plant (800 workers), for example. Evidently the SRs enjoyed little influence in the city before the revolution. However, by May 1905 local activists were already claiming the support of 'hundreds of conscious workers', including (it was said) former SDs who were defecting to the PSR 'sometimes individually and not uncommonly in entire groups'. These workers allegedly preferred the SRs agrarian programme and their more robust stance on tactical questions.[18] The welcome growth in support brought with it additional resources. In June 1904 the income of the Baku committee had stood at only 243 roubles; less than twelve months later receipts totalled 928r and in July 1905 exceeded 1500r.[19] Yet despite these hopeful signs a later report could only describe progress before the middle of 1905 as 'uneven' and it was not until the arrival of central committee member O. S. Minor in the autumn that the party began to reassert itself.[20] The SRs were fortunate in being able to count on the financial and to some extent political support of two nationalist parties based in the Caucasus, namely the Armenian Dashnaktsutyun and the Georgian SR federalists.[21]

Early in 1906 work was interrupted once again but this time the tide turned decisively, thanks largely to a one-off donation of 8000 roubles from the Caucasus *oblast'* committee.[22] The availability of funds sufficient to maintain up to fifteen professional propagandists heralded a broadening and intensification of activity far in excess of what would otherwise have been possible. The number of circles increased, regular agitational meetings were held, ties were established with the factories; trade union, combat and student sections were reconstituted. The organisation was divided into six district branches: city, Belyigorod, Chernogorod, The Port and the outlying oil settlements of Balakhany and Bibi-Eibat. The timely improvement in finances coincided with continuing revolutionary disorder in Baku – in direct contrast with the situation in many other parts of the country where resistance had either already been crushed or was beginning to weaken.[23] From now on, it was claimed, SR influence grew 'not daily but hourly' as 'one factory after another' lended its support. By March 1907 there were already 700 'conscious, organised workers', led by eleven professional activists and sixty agitators; a labour newspaper, *Molot* (later *Oblastnya Izvestiya*) was distributed in editions of 5000 copies and up to 400 000 leaflets were to appear in the course of just two years.[24] The increasing popularity of the PSR was underlined by its key role in a strike by sailors of the Caspian Merchant Fleet, a movement which took the toughest military measures to break.[25] By early summer sixty enterprises were considered to be within the party's ambit and its influence was said to extend to 10 000 workers. A report in the September issue of *Znamya Truda* referred to 1200–1500 'organised workers' in addition to the 670 members of a newly-affiliated Armenian section composed of defectors from the Dashnaktsutyun party.[26] A Soviet source has conceded that the party was 'quite strong' among the Caspian sailors and the artisans in the small workshops.[27] There can be no doubt, however, that SR strength, like that of the Bolsheviks, was drawn primarily from workers in the oil fields and (perhaps to a lesser extent) from the skilled employees of the refineries and processing plants.

Oil firms known to have had organisational ties with the PSR include Nobel bros., Shikhovo, the Bibi-Eibat Company, Mantashev, Oleum, Mukhtarov, Shibaev, Votan, Lianosov, The French Society, The Caspian Black Sea Corporation and the Russian Caucasus Company.[28] Outside the oil industry the party also worked among the shop assistants and railwaymen of the city. Like its Social-Democrat counterpart the Baku PSR was essentially a Great Russian organisation, but from May 1907 onwards there was also a sizeable contingent of Armenian members. In contrast the SRs enjoyed only weak support among the indigenous Azerbaijani population; an independent SR Muslim section (known as *Ittifag*) does not appear to have survived beyond 1907.[29] Party reports stress the occupational mobility of the Baku workforce, its strong ties with the countryside and its aversion to the undeniably inhospitable urban environment.

The Social Democrats' response to the remarkable increase in SR influence was contradictory. On the one hand, extra activists were despatched to the city in an effort to combat the 'SR danger' and to retake the 'citadels' which had been 'demolished', while, on the other, the threat was played down with claims that support for the PSR had passed its peak and was in case rooted exclusively among the petty-bourgeoisie. To this jibe the SRs could retort that in Baku, as in Petersburg, it was precisely in the large industrial enterprises that they predominated, while Social-Democrat support was confined to the smaller firms.[30]

Clearly the Socialist-Revolutionaries were a force to be reckoned with by the second half of 1907; boasting the organised support of perhaps 2000 members widely dispersed over the city and including important bases in the strategically vital oil industry, disposing of a monthly income well in excess of 1000r and operating an impressive propaganda machine.[31]

When political reaction and industrial depression did eventually set in, however, the consequences for the revolutionary movement in Baku were no different from anywhere else in Russia. Demand in the metallurgical industry began to fall off during 1908 and the employers immediately resorted to the familiar expedients – lay-offs, short-time working and lock-outs. The oil industry was, in its turn, severely affected by a sales crisis. Fierce competition from abroad depressed prices more or less continuously for three years, and annual output had still not passed the 1901 level by the outbreak of war. Over 13 000 workers were laid off during 1908–9, while those remaining found it increasingly difficult to defend concessions wrested from employers during the revolution. The infant trade union movement was an early casualty. The Baku Union of Oil Workers, for example, which had once boasted 9000 members, was left with just 20 by 1910.[32] The exodus from the unions was inevitably accompanied by the abandonment of revolutionary politics. By common consent the 'crisis in party work' in Baku can be dated to May 1908 when the government finally abandoned plans for a long-projected oil industry conference.[33] Several weeks previously Prime Minister Stolypin had written to the viceroy of the Caucasus, I. I. Vorontsov-Dashkov, complaining of the disintegration of law and order in the region and singling out Baku, where 'daily tens of murders and expropriations occur openly and the guilty remain free'.[34] By June 1908 virtually all leading SR activists were under arrest and the organisation was left almost penniless. Not only the intelligentsia deserted the cause but also many skilled, conscious workers. In such a climate even fewer of the 'grey masses' were likely to remain – with the result that by the spring of 1909 total membership was reduced to about 470.[35]

Aspects of Organisational Activity before the Reaction

Agitation

Generally speaking, the SRs were too weak to play a leading role in the Baku labour movement before 1906. As late as August of that year the Social Democrats could attempt to stage a political strike without, apparently, consulting their 'comrades in struggle' the SRs. However, this initiative failed to win mass support and when the SDs called a second strike in September to protest against the introduction of field courts material they sought the co-operation of all revolutionary parties in Baku: SRs, Dashnaks, *Hummet* (Bolshevik Muslims) and *Ittifag* (SR Muslims). The outcome this time, the SRs reported, was a completely successful one-day action. The moral was clear.[36]

The last months of 1906 were dominated by the campaign for the workers' *curia* elections to the second Duma, which the SRs fought on the slogan 'Constituent Assembly and Land and Freedom'. Their respresentatives were elected in twenty enterprises and, while the SDs won in seventy, they had reasonable cause to be satisfied with their performance, signalling as it did the beginning of a breakthrough among the workers of the city.[37]

The SRs role in the strike by sailors of the Caspian Merchant Fleet will be discussed in due course.[38] It was symptomatic of their new-found assertiveness which was demonstrated again in the autumn when they successfully forestalled a Bolshevik initiative to launch a general strike. According to a later account 'from this time on nothing was undertaken by these workers without the leave of the SRs'.[39]

From the autumn of 1907 onwards the party was preoccupied with the 'conference campaign' – the government proposal to convene a state conference of workers and employers with the aim of negotiating a new labour contract (a move aimed at restoring industrial peace in the oil industry).[40] The revolutionary parties were sharply divided on the issue. While the Mensheviks favoured participation the Bolsheviks hesitated, eventually insisting on setting their own preconditions for entry. The SRs on the other hand (supported by the Dashnaktsutyun), called for an outright boycott of the conference, preferring straightforward industrial action as a way of guaranteeing the workers improved conditions.[41] The debate ebbed and flowed over a period of months. The initial proposal to call a conference had been made in May 1907. In January 1908 elections were held to a council of workers' representatives which was intended to present the labour case during the negotiations. The SRs, who contested the elections on the basis of boycotting the conference, took 8300 of the 35 000 votes cast (nearly 24 per cent).[42] It is difficult to tell whether this rather disappointing performance[43] indicates broad support for participation in the conference (Baku workers were known for their strong 'economistic' leanings) or whether it shows that mass support for the PSR was considerably weaker than its actual membership would lead one to believe. When the council finally voted on 26 April to participate in the conference the SRs and Dashnaks staged a walk-out, the latter calling instead for a general strike.[44] In the event, even before the conference was due to meet, the attitude of both government and employers had hardened and the previous conciliatory policy was replaced by one of unmitigated repression. Thereafter the labour movement in Baku quickly disintegrated. During the remainder of 1908 the number of work days lost through strikes fell dramatically. In 1909 there were only thirty strikes (involving 9771 workers) in the whole of the Caucasus and less than half that number in 1910.[45]

The Union of Oil Workers

Formed under Bolshevik auspices early in October 1906,[46] the Union of Oil Workers (UOW) was open to all those employed by the industry, irrespective of their role in the productive process. By mid-1908 there were 9000 members (approximately 18 per cent of the total workforce) though by no means all were up to date with their dues.[47] About half had been recruited during the previous six to nine months, a period which coincided with a remarkable increase in SR support within the union.

In the light of the available evidence (much of it admittedly biased towards the Social Democrats) SR influence within the UOW does not appear to have been exercised very constructively.[48] The party began to make its presence felt towards the end of 1907 when some of its supporters levelled accusations of corruption and financial mismanagement at the union board.[49] A broader 'opposition', including the Dashnaktsutyun membership, coalesced around the SR faction and continued to make trouble for the union leaders, who were naturally anxious to raise the cloud of suspicion which had descended on them at a uniquely inconvenient moment. At a general meeting held in January 1908 supporters of the board introduced a resolution absolving them from criminal liability and expressing the confidence of the membership. However, this was challenged by a counter-resolution which moved that the board be removed from office forthwith and that a new provisional body be elected in its place. The meeting ended in pandemonium (not for the first time) without anything being resolved.[50] This stalemate, and the attendant scandal, induced the board to dispense with general meetings altogether and to call instead for elections to a delegates' assembly.[51] An attempt by the SRs to introduce proportional representation in these elections (party influence in the union was said to extend to 'a little less than half' the total membership) was rejected. Thereupon SRs in the Bibi-Eibat district unilaterally voted to pull out of the union and encouraged other union members to follow suit, apparently with some success.[52] Meanwhile the majority of the opposition continued to attack the board relentlessly, with the aim of overthrowing the Bolshevik majority.

After months of persistent effort this strategy paid off. At a general meeting held in January 1909 the SR-led opposition finally gained majority control with only three members of the original board retaining their seats.[53] The victory proved to be a Pyrrhic one, however. Only the shell of the old organisation remained. The membership had deserted *en masse* and life within the union was described as 'empty and dull'; in any case, the SRs had too few activists to enable them to capitalise on their success and many party members were indifferent or even hostile to the trade union movement as it existed in Baku.[54]

The Union of the Caspian Merchant Fleet

In 1907 there were more than 6900 sailors in the Caspian Merchant Fleet, the vast majority of whom served on ships registered in Baku. The trade union catered predominantly for those employed in the shipment of oil, but membership included sailors working for the steamer lines which operated between Baku and the Caspian ports of Astrakhan, Krasnovodsk and Petrovsk. During 1907 there was a large influx of peasant migrants from the Volga region: 1500 arrived in the course of just three days in September.[55] Many of them were able to find employment only on board the schooners of the Caspian fleet, where they took the most menial jobs alongside the Azerbaijanis. Oil transportation was dominated by the same large firms which virtually monopolised the industry as a whole.

'A sailor in the Caspian Merchant Fleet [an article in *Pravda* once declared], is a living corpse, a piece of refuse of human life'.[56] Certainly, conditions of service in the fleet were extraordinarily harsh. Sailors rarely visited port and worked anything up to twenty hours out of the twenty-four for scandalously low pay. Refusal to work overtime resulted in instant dismissal – there was no shortage of labour in Baku, especially among the impoverished Persians and Volga Russians.

A trade union for sailors of the Caspian fleet was formed in 1907 and was dominated by the PSR more or less from its inception. The secretary of the union during 1907–8 was a Georgian student, K. T. Dzhavrishvili,[57] who also served on the Baku SR committee. Dzhavrishvili was twenty-one in 1907. As a student in Tiflis (his place of birth) he had joined the local SR troop organisation, but fled to Baku after arrest. In 1908 he emigrated to Paris but apparently maintained contact with the party. He returned to Baku in 1911 and worked for the SRs again until his final arrest in the summer of 1912.

The full extent of SR influence in the merchant fleet became apparent during the strike of March–April 1907.[58] Preparations had begun in February but the sailors only left their ships on 10 March. Their demands included a wage increase to compensate for rising prices, action to help the unemployed, canteen money, disability insurance and annual contractual agreements with the employers. A strike committee was formed and the PSR occupied seven of the eleven seats. The party also took charge of activity in the neighbouring port of Petrovsk. There were a number of mass meetings in Baku, during which SR resolutions were adopted. These called for the eight-hour day, all land to the toilers, a constituent assembly and an amnesty for political prisoners, in addition to the sailors' economic demands. Early on in the strike a minority of 'dark people' (that is, Persians) went back to work under police protection but the majority held firm. After a week both the police and the military raised the political temperature by intensifying searches, breaking-up public meetings and issuing threats. The SRs responded in kind by organising acts of terrorism: a nineteen-year-old Jewess, Khana Khitrik was responsible for an explosion at the Caucasus and Mercury steamship company for example.[59] After the end of the strike the *boevoi komitet* of the Baku organisation threated action if all the strikers were not taken back by the shipping firms.[60] Despite an ultimatum from General von Traube, threatening dire consequences if there was not a return to work by dawn on 13 April, the strike went on. A one-day sympathy strike was held in Baku on 17 April and normal working did not resume for another week. The outcome of the strike is unknown.

Unfortunately there is no further record of the union's activities until 1909, when the SRs still valued it highly enough to provide it with professional organisers, supported by a permanent party cell some thirty to forty strong.[61] The union was still quite a large and active organisation at that time: there were 1753 registered members in all, though admittedly only 274 were up to date with dues.[62] Apart from an interval of four or five months (October 1910–February 1911) the union continued to function, perhaps until the eve of the war. It was re-formed in March 1917 and again fell under the sway of the SRs, who maintained their control through the October revolution.[63]

The Armenian Section

The Armenian section of the Baku PSR was formed in May 1907 from 'young Dashnaks', dissident members of the Dashnaktsutyun party.[64] Workers whose ingrained nationalism had for the most part been tempered by, if not subordinated to, an emerging class consciousness, they had begun to gravitate towards the Russian socialist parties after 1905. By mid-1907 the SR organisation claimed the support of well over 600 former Dashnaks and there were still 400 organised Armenian workers in the party in the spring of 1909.[65] Russians and Armenians each constituted approximately 20 per cent of the labour force in Baku but the Russians, being considerably more literate, took a correspondingly higher share of the skilled jobs. Party reports convey the impression that the typical Armenian SR was unskilled and in receipt of very low wages. He probably worked for an Armenian oil firm, where he was subjected to considerable exploitation. Like most Armenians in the summer he returned to his family in the countryside. Being poorly educated, his politics were inclined to be partisan and unsophisticated, and he was more interested in wage bargaining than in conspiratorial activity.[66] Sympathisers among the more literate and skilled minority may have been the 'careerists' referred to by the Armenian delegate at the first party conference, who took advantage of educational opportunities (that is, propaganda circles?) not to assist in the transformation of their environment but to escape from it.[67]

Two prime objectives were pursued by the Armenian SRs. One was to eradicate chauvinism and stimulate class consciousness by 'bombarding' sympathisers with party propaganda. Ninety per cent of the organisation's budget, supplemented by contributions from the Caucasus Oblast' Committee, was devoted to this end.[68] The second, more ambitious objective was to promote liaison and co-operation with other nationalities via the legal organisations, primarily the trade unions. One problem here was that, unlike year-round workers, the Armenians were able to return to the countryside in time of unemployment or other hardship, and were therefore more reluctant to attach themselves permanently to urban labour organisations. In 1908 there were only about 140 unionised Armenian SRs in the Bibi-Eibat and Balakhany districts, and most of these could not have remained members for long.[69] The antagonism between Armenians and Azerbaijanis has already been commented on. As far as relations between Armenians and Russians were concerned the main difficulty was that of language, exacerbated by the custom for Armenian firms to employ exclusively Armenian labour.

Some Armenians seem to have become involved in terrorist activity. The history of SR terrorism in Baku is obscure,[70] but the involvement of Armenians is suggested by the fact that at the London conference in 1908 it was their delegate who fielded questions on the state of local combat work.[71] As the Dashnaktsutyun Party also included terror in its tactical armoury, it would not be surprising if ex-Dashnaks turned out to be an important source of recruitment for the PSR. The combat detachment itself was disbanded by 1908 and replaced by a smaller 'collective', but it is possible that former members of both SR and Dashnaktsutyun terrorist organisations had already turned instead to the nefarious but lucrative practice of extortion (*shantazh*) – in this case the extracting of money with menaces in the name of a political party or cause. Already rife throughout the Caucasus in 1907, extortion does not seem to have critically infected the Baku PSR until 1909.[72] In April of that year local party members felt that the situation had got out of hand and demanded action from the committee. An inquiry resulted in the overhaul of an entire *podraion* in the Balakhany district and the disbanding of a number of circles elsewhere.[73] There is no firm evidence implicating members of the Armenian section in extortion at this time, but as blame for similar activity had already been laid at the door of 'former Armenian detachments' and it is known that there were practitioners within the PSR itself, such an assumption appears plausible, even likely.[74]

The Armenian Organisation lost contact with the Baku Committee sometime towards the end of 1909. A report presented by the city executive committee to the Baku council in December mentions a 'recent' conference of Armenian SRs. This committee report called for the regularising of relations between the two organisations at the lower levels. Some delegates expressed the view that the language problem was a serious obstacle in the path of closer ties but this feeling was not shared by everyone (some Armenian SRs at least were able to speak Russian). Normal relations between the Russian and Armenian sections of the party were not restored until early 1912 and records cease shortly afterwards.[75]

THE SRs IN THE NORTH-WEST *OBLAST'*

Social and Economic Background

The North-Western *oblast'* of the PSR centred on Belorussia and Lithuania (see Map 4). In 1906 it was divided into twelve districts: Smolensk, Bryansk,[76] Vitebsk, Gomel', Minsk, Dvinsk, Vil'no, Grodno, Mogilev, Pinsk, Kovno and Novozybkov.[77] The region's boundaries coincided with the northern half of the Pale of Settlement,

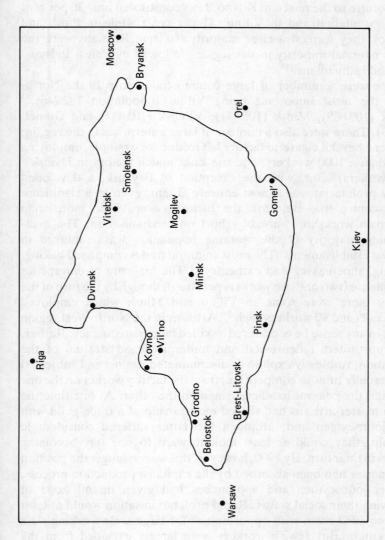

Map 4 The north-west oblast' of the PSR, 1906–07

since 1835 the prescribed place of residence for the Empire's Jewish population.[78] The distribution of Jews varied considerably from one urban centre to the next – in Kovno, Jews constituted only 36 per cent of the population and in Vil'no, 41 per cent; while in Pinsk and Belostok they formed a clear majority.[79] Great Russians were the largest national minority in the region, followed by Poles, Belorussians and Lithuanians.[80]

There were a number of large commercial centres in the North-West; the most important being Vil'no (population 192 746),[81] Dvinsk (109 689), Minsk (105 441), Vitebsk (103 411) and Gomel' (96 149). There were also a number of large enterprises in the region: the Shereshevskii cigarette factory in Grodno for example, employing more than a 1000 workers, and the Zaks match factory in Dvinsk[82] (800 workers). But, with the exception of Bryansk, a developed factory proletariat was almost entirely absent; even in a significant textile centre like Belostok the factories were little more than overgrown workshops, notably short on mechanisation. The overwhelming majority of the working population was employed in artisanal establishments. The most common trades comprised baking, tailoring, shoemaking and carpentry.[83] The majority of enterprises were minute (two or three workers per shop), though by the turn of the century there were some in Vil'no and Minsk which employed between 25 and 40 workers each.[84] Artisans in the North-West region cannot in any sense be considered a skilled labour aristocracy. Rather, they constituted a depressed and underprivileged stratum of the population; ruthlessly exploited, discriminated against and subjected to potentially ruinous competition, from the factory worker on the one hand and the peasant handicraftsman on the other. At one time the Jewish master-artisans had shared membership of a trade guild with their journeymen and, although the latter suffered considerable hardship, they could at least look forward to one day becoming masters in their turn. By 1900, however, this was no longer the position – the master had been absorbed by the capitalist production process, and his journeymen and apprentices had given up all hope of improving their social status. Rapid proletarianisation would at least have provided them with opportunities for large-scale working-class organisation. But Jewish workers were largely excluded from the factories – in Belostok, for example, the Poles 'regarded employment in the mechanised factories as their monopoly'.[85] In such circumstances, the sole alternative was emigration.

Special Characteristics of the North-West Oblast'

A number of features peculiar to the North-West *oblast'* posed special problems for the Russian revolutionary parties in general and for the PSR in particular.[86]

First, the policy of land socialisation was ill-suited to local social and economic conditions and was consequently less attractive to the inhabitants of the North-Western provinces. Agriculture here was not, for the most part, organised along communal lines – in 1892 fully 61 per cent of the land under peasant ownership in White Russia was in the hands of small property-holders; in some areas (Grodno and Minsk, for example) the *obshchina* was almost entirely lacking.[87] It was not easy, therefore, to convince the farmers of the region that their interests would best be served by a re-allocation of the land on egalitarian principles. In the towns, the PSR needed the support of Jewish workers if it was to have any real impact on local politics. But artisans with no rural ties and no direct interest in the repartitioning of the land were not easily converted to this particular cause.[88]

On a more practical level, the PSR had to contend with the intractable problem of raising money for party work. Financial difficulties were not, of course, unique to the North-West *oblast'*. However, the desperate poverty of the artisanal worker and the failure of the party to win the support of the local bourgeoisie placed it in an extreme position. Between October 1906 and February 1907, for example, the total income of the *oblast'* committee had stood at 1123 roubles, and 90 per cent of that sum had been contributed by the Central Committee! *Oblast'* officials complained about the 'give, give, give' attitude of local organisations, which 'bombarded' them with pleas for financial help. But the town committees were in no real position to put right this 'abnormal' state of affairs; most had a monthly income barely in excess of 200 roubles.[89]

The PSR was also desperately short of party activists. The Russian (and Polish) intelligentsia was said to be reactionary, or at best indifferent to revolutionary politics; while those who were willing to support the party were soon rounded up by the police.[90] The SRs had, therefore, to rely largely on defectors from the Bund, most of whom were extremely young; teenagers were to be found even on committees.[91]

Finally, the PSR in the North-West Region faced fierce competition from a plethora of political parties, including several more likely to appeal to the Jewish worker. The enormous choice was blamed for the notorious fickleness of the Jews:

> The appearance of an interesting reader, witty disputant [or] able speaker within the ranks of one or other party is immediately the cause of interest towards it, [leading to] an influx of new members, who will just as quickly hurry back, and with a change of circumstances move across to yet another's ranks.[92]

Clearly, for the average Jewish worker the PSR was no more than one of a number of staging posts on an interminable political journey.

1905–07 in the North-West Oblast'

Early History

SR activity in the North-West *oblast'* began in earnest during 1903. By the end of that year there were party organisations in Gomel', Vitebsk, Smolensk (and Bryansk).[93] In April 1904 these organisations, together with new groupings in Vil'no, Minsk and Dvinsk, became the constituent parts of a North-West *oblast'*, the first attempt by the party to co-ordinate the activities of an entire region.[94] As we saw in Chapter 1, Social-Revolutionism flowered here at a time when the majority of SR organisations had all but lapsed into silence. There is little ambiguity about the source of the party's attractiveness in Belorussia.

In 1902 Hirsch Lekkert, a member of the Bund, had made an unsuccessful attempt on the life of the Governor of Vil'no. His action had not been blessed with formal party approval, but it caused such a stir among rank-and-file workers that for a year or two afterwards the Bund wavered in its attitude to political terror. From that time on it began to lose the virtual monopoly of working-class support it had hitherto enjoyed. As early as 1902, a number of Bund members defected to form break-away pseudo-populist factions in Łódź and Belostok, with revolutionary terror high on the agenda.[95] For a time, the organisations of the new Russian SR party were able to ride on the crest of this wave of enthusiasm for the tactics of violence. But there was a high price to be paid for such easy-found support: the party was flooded with 'militant elements, dissatisfied with the slow progress of purely organisational work'.[96] This led to serious internal fissuring.

Terror

The year 1905 witnessed a rash of terrorist incidents in the northern Pale. *Pamyatnaya Knizhka* lists sixteen operations allegedly organised by the party during that year and a further ten carried out during 1906 and 1907.[97] In all but three of the twenty-six cases the assailants are described as members of armed detachments (*boevoe druzhiny*). The remainder were the work of the 'Flying Detachment of the North-West *oblast'*. In the latter organisation students and members of the intelligentsia seem to have predominated, whereas the local armed detachments consisted primarily of workers. Unfortunately, the age of the assailant is provided in only five cases: the youngest was eighteen, the oldest, twenty-three. The victims can be divided into the following categories:

(1) *civil police*: eleven officers and assistants, five city police chiefs and assistants and one inspector;
(2) *military police (Gendarmerie)*: one colonel, one sergeant-major and three captains; and
(3) *security division (Okhrana)*: head of Belostok district.

Only two of the known victims were provocateurs and there was only a single incident involving troops – a bomb attack on a group of cossacks in Gomel'. Slightly more of the casualties were wounded than were killed. Only a handful of the attacks were unsuccessful, but of course most of those nipped in the bud would not receive publicity in the revolutionary press. The most frequently-mentioned locations were Belostok (5), Minsk (4), Gomel' (4), Vitebsk (3) and Dvinsk (3).

One of the most active terrorists in the North-West Region was Moisei Davidovich Zakgeim (Zakheim). The details of his biography will help flesh out the statistical evidence just cited.[98]

Moisei Davidovich Zakgeim was born in Grodno province in 1885. A weaver by trade, he subsequently left the Grodno area to live and work in Belostok. Soon after joining the Bund in 1903, he transferred to the PSR, becoming a member of the local armed detachment. His career as a terrorist was properly launched in 1905. In February he participated in an unsuccessful attempt on the life of the head of the Belostok Okhrana. The following April he was involved in a shooting incident with a policeman and on 8 July took part in a bomb attack which wounded the local police chief, Pelënkin. In August he himself organised the shooting of another police officer, allegedly implicated in the Belostok pogrom. The actual assailant, a worker named Shlyakhter turned out to be a provocateur and Zakgeim was arrested. Amnestied in November, he returned to his former activities, but now as an SR Maximalist. In May 1906 he moved to Petersburg and began an association with the notorious terrorist, Sokolov. Five months later he participated in the celebrated Fonarnyi Alley bank raid which netted almost 600 000 roubles, but was arrested a month later and subsequently tried as one of the '44 Maximalists'. He was sentenced to fifteen years hard labour.

Maximalist and Anarchist Influences

Zakgeim was a typical example of the hot-headed, impulsive type of activist which the PSR found it all too easy to recruit. Like another native of Belostok, Aron Elin,[99] who subsequently became an Anarchist, Zakgeim was, no doubt, 'indifferent to delving into manifestos' and had primarily been attracted to the PSR because it had sanctioned terror. The SRs were not the only local advocates of this tactic, however. Anarchists had been operating in Belostok since 1903 and by mid-1906 had organised fifteen propaganda circles there. Their unrelenting attacks on the property and persons of the local textile bosses, unrestrained by party regulations or codes of conduct, captured the imagination of many in the revolutionary underworld. By the end of 1905 the SRs in Belostok had succumbed to the irresistible tide of extremism and gone over *en masse* to the Anarchists and Maximalists. The Maximalist movement soon degenerated into 'hooliganism' and quickly disappeared from Belostok. The Anarchists too were discredited, after terror had united rather than cowed the factory-owners. But the damage to the PSR had already been done. Furthermore, the corrosive influence of these movements could not be contained in Belostok. By the autumn of 1906 both Anarchism and Maximalism were to be found almost everywhere in the White Russian provinces.[100] Maximalists were almost invariably expelled from the official SR organisations, the exception being Smolensk, where the dissidents agreed to subordinate themselves to party discipline.[101] Both here and in Bryansk (and possibly elsewhere) it was not only Maximalist tactics which appealed to local workers – the demand for immediate socialisation of the factories was also attractive, implying as it did the possibility of a direct transition to the socialist utopia.[102]

In October 1906 the sixth *oblast'* congress passed a resolution tolerating Maximalism as an ideological course in party literature.[103] Factory terror was also looked on sympathetically in the North-West Region, as oppressive economic and political conditions pushed the regional organisations in an unorthodox direction. At a subsequent *oblast'* assembly in July 1907, delegates from Minsk, Dvinsk, Bryansk and Vitebsk all gave their approval to factory terror as the only effective response to lock-outs; only the representative from Smolensk dissented from the majority view.[104]

Dimensions and Content of SR Urban Work

It should be said at the outset that by April 1907, the PSR was already pessimistic about its chances of making a break-through in the North-West Region and was at the same time highly critical of its performance to date. Reports referred to the 'extreme weakness' of urban organisations and advice was given to the local parties that more time should be devoted to work in the countryside[105] (though the problems there were hardly less intractable than in the towns.)

Apart from Bryansk, the largest urban organisations in the North-West were Dvinsk[106] (maximum 900 organised workers in town and district), Vitebsk (570; 200 in seven suburban settlements) and Gomel' (about 100 in the town and 300–400 in the factory district of Dobrush'). Three others (Vil'no, Minsk and Pinsk) were more than 200 strong. The minor organisations (in descending order of size) were Grodno, Smolensk, Bobruisk and Novozybkov. Work in Belostok was exclusively confined to the local military garrison.

The majority of SR supporters in the North-West (almost 70 per cent of the Vitebsk organisation for example) were Jewish artisans.[107] In Dvisnk the entire urban party consisted of 'former Bundists'.[108] A variety of trades were represented: bakers and printers in Smolensk, tanners in Mogilev, matters in Gomel' and tailors in Minsk; leather workers, metalworkers, bookbinders, joiners and weavers also featured.[109] Outside Bryansk, factory work was more or less confined to Dvinsk and Gomel' (Dobrush'). In Dvinsk, work in the factory district began only in the spring of 1906; by October there were still only 93 party members there (all Russians). The Dobrush' settlement consisted of a large paper mill and a scattering of canvas, metal and rope enterprises.[110] Railway workers represented the largest non-artisan element in the North-West party. The SRs had significant support in Pinsk, Vitebsk, Dvinsk, Minsk and Smolensk, and there were circles, at least, in Vil'no and Gomel'.

A study of the biographies of nineteen urban party activists in PKS (Table 6.2) supported many of the points made in the first half of this profile. The overwhelming majoirty (16 out 19) were Jews of exceptional youth; the average age on entering the party was seventeen. Eight joined in 1904 and only three in 1905, suggesting a pattern of recruitment quite different from other organisations (Petersburg, for example). The majority were workers – the balance being made up by teachers, writers and students. Less than a third had received a secondary education. Only four of the nineteen are recorded as subsequently having become Maximalists or Anarchists.

Table 6.2 Urban party activists in the North-West region, c. 1905–07

Name	Nationality	Place of birth	Age of entry	Year of entry into N-W SR organisation and name of organisation	Occupation	Parental occupation	Education	Other later organisations
B. M. Diyakonov	Russian	Petersburg	18	1905 Grodno	?	worker	secondary	—
R. I. Erukhimovich	Jewish	Dvinsk	27	1904 Berdichev (Dvinsk)	leather worker	worker	home	—
A. S. Gel'fman-Zhukova	Jewish	Poltava	—	? Borisol (Minsk)	private teacher	?	trade school	—
Y. M. Grinshpan	Jewish	Kovno	19	1906 Kovno	worker	worker	primary	—
F. N. Gurcvich	Jewish	Minsk	17	1906 Minsk	dress maker	clerical worker	home	—
V. V. Kruglov-Deev	Russian	Roslavl'	19	1901 Roslavl	worker	worker	primary	—
M. M. Kuznctsov	Jewish	Mogilev	22	1904 Smolensk (Chernigov)	bookbinder	blacksmith	home	—
M. S. Matlin	Jewish	Vil'na	17	1906 Dvinsk	handicraftsman	unskilled worker	Jewish school	—
L. I. Murashko	Belorussian	Vitcbsk	?	1904 Vil'na (Smorgon)	writer	pharmaceutist	chem-tech school	—
L. B. Rivin	Jewish	Bobruisk	18	1906 Bobruisk	metal worker	chimney sweep	?	—
F. A. Rivkin	Jewish	Smolensk	15	1904 Smolensk	no occupation	dentist	home	Maximalist
A. I. Shapiro	Jewish	Vil'na	16	1904 Vil'na (Disensk)	?	private attorney	primary	—
M. L. Slutskaya	Jewish	Moscow gub.	13–14	? Vil'na	worker	worker	primary	Anarchist
Y. B. Solomonov	Jewish	Minsk	22	1905 Minsk	student	joiner	5 class/gymn	—
M. B. Shperling	Jewish	Grodno	17	1905 Grodno	leather worker	clerical worker	town school	—
E. V. Vasil'evich	Belorussian	Mogilev	18	1907 Smolensk	woodsman	joiner	trade school	Maximalist
S. S. Vol'fson	Jewish	Bobruisk	16	1904 Minsk	bookbinder	teacher	home	—
M. L. Volkind	Jewish	Discn (Disna?)	18	1904 Disna	joiner	joiner	home	Maximalist
M. D. Zakgcim	Jewish	Grodno	19	1904 Belostok	weaver	weaver	self-taught	Maximalist

Most organisations in the North-West were built on similar lines. Workers were grouped into circles, usually by trade. The membership then elected a 'representative assembly' (*predstavitel'naya skhodka*) which in turn chose a workers' union and committee. In Dvinsk and Vitebsk there were parallel organisations for Jewish and Russian workers. Two reasons were given for this. Firstly, that Russian workers tended to be less politically conscious than the Jews, being in the majority of cases only recent converts to the revolutionary cause. Secondly, that Jewish workers tended to have only a poor understanding of the Russian language, so that joint circle and agitational work was impractical.[111] The party was silent on another possible reason – racial antagonism.

The staple diet of the urban worker in the North-West Region was the propaganda circle. Agitational assemblies were held whenever possible, but frequency depended on the effectiveness and attitude of the police. The Minsk organisation claimed to have arranged twenty assemblies during 1906; in the same period, between seven and nine were held in Pinsk and only three in Novozybkov.[112] Only the Dvinsk organisation is known to have issued its own workers' newspaper – four issues of *Rabochii listok* had appeared by October 1906.

The PSR campaigned for seats in the second Duma, though a number of organisations (Vil'no, Kovno, Dvinsk and Bobruisk) had originally favoured a boycott.[113] The only creditable urban performance was in Minsk, where the PSR helped to form a co-ordinating bureau of all left-wing parties and trade union organisations, and issued a small quantity of propaganda material. In the 'progressive bloc' they were expected to deliver the votes of the railway workers and Post and Telegraph employees. As a reward for their endeavours they were allocated eight representatives in the workers' *curia*. Outside Minsk, the SRs were unable to make any appreciable impact on the election proceedings and at best managed a seat on the local coalitions of progressive parties.[114]

The SRs were involved only to a limited extent in trade union work. Not surprisingly they were most to the fore in the ARRU: in Minsk, for example, the party held half the seats on the committee of the Moscow–Brest railway workshops and over a third on the Libau–Romna line organisation. In Vitebsk, four-fifths of the union membership was said to be SR and in Dvinsk and Smolensk too the party was dominant on the railways. There is very little information concerning SR involvement in other trade unions. In Minsk, the party held six of the eleven seats on the controlling body of the union of tailors and in Smolensk there was a group of SR telegraphists; here however the committee felt unable to conduct formal union work because of a shortage of activists.[115] Generally speaking, the party's shortcomings in this field were probably less noticeable than in regions where there was a developed proletariat and strong union organisations.

It has been possible to confirm the continued existence of only five North-Western organisations after June 1907. In Minsk, no more than fifty Jewish artisans remained with the SRs by mid-summer, though the party was still involved in union work.[116] In Vil'no there were 100 workers in July and some propaganda circles continued to function.[117] Work recommenced in Vitebsk in the autumn of 1907 after two or three months disruption, but instead of 570 workers only ninety now remained in the workers' union.[118] The longest-known survivor in the North-West *oblast'* was the Dvinsk party. Here, the arrest of the committee and a large number of leading workers halted work completely in October 1907, but the arrival of a number of 'old hands' led to the election of a new *skhodka* and committee.[119] The subsequent history of the revived organisation is unknown. However, by the summer of 1908 there was evidently nothing more to be said about the PSR, either in Dvinsk or anywhere else in the region; the entire organisation had, to all intents and purposes, sunk without trace.

THE SRs IN THE MAL'TSEV INDUSTRIAL DISTRICT (BRYANSK)

Straddling the banks of the Bolva and Zhizdra rivers, (see Map 5) the Mal'tsev industrial district lies some 220 kms south-west of Moscow and to the north of the town of Bryansk.[120] In the early twentieth century this conglomeration of factories marked the confluence of three provinces – Orel, Kaluga and Smolensk. Several factors had contributed to making the Bryansk region one of Russia's oldest industrial centres. Though the local soil was rich in such minerals as coal, iron ore, phosphorite and quartz, it was also agriculturally unproductive, thereby guaranteeing a large supply of cheap, dependable labour for industry. Moreover, the entire region was dissected by an elaborate network of natural waterways, later superceded by a comprehensive railway system.

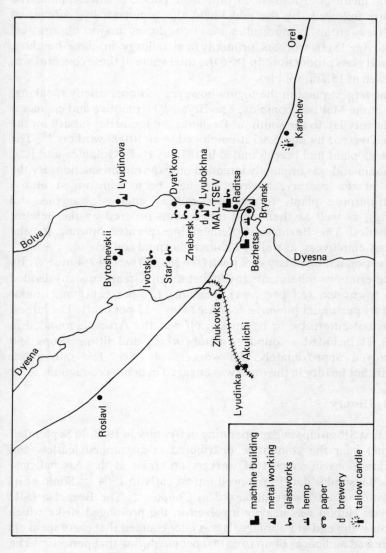

Map 5 Bryansk (Mal'tsev industrial district)

The first iron-ore works was built by E. Demidov at Lyudinova in 1755. Thirty years later, I. A. Mal'tsev established the first glass and crystal factories at Raditsa. A prolonged period of intense industrial activity followed. By the mid-1890s, the commercially-reorganised Mal'tsev group comprised some two dozen major enterprises, employing 15 000 workers, primarily in metallurgy, machine-building, rail and glass production. In 1886 the total value of these concerns was assessed at 15.7m. roubles.

The largest plant in the region however was not, strictly speaking, part of the Mal'tsev complex. The Bryansk locomotive and engineering factory lay to the south, at Bezhetsa, an industrial suburb on the river Dyesna; by late 1905 it employed over 10 000 workers.[121] The Bryansk plant had been founded in 1873 by B. F. Golub'ev and P. I. Gubonin and was originally intended only for rail production. By the turn of the century, however, it had been transformed into a multi-purpose plant, turning out railway engines, waggons and fittings, as well as shells and other items ordered by the defence ministries. The Bezhetsa settlement incorporated housing for the factory employees, as well as a church, hospital and school.

The population of Bryansk town (see Map 5) was 24 781 in 1897. By social estate its inhabitants (overwhelmingly Great Russian) divided into townsmen (58 per cent), peasants (21 per cent) and junior military personnel (*nizhnye voinskie chiny* – 13 per cent). The largest industrial enterprise in Bryansk itself was the Arsenal, founded in 1783. It included a foundry, metalworking and fitting shops and employed approximately 600 workers in 1905. The only other significant factory in the town was engaged in hemp production.

Early History

The first SR groups began operating in Bryansk in 1903. In September of that year the committee distributed hectographed leaflets and proclamations in support of workers on strike at the Arsenal, and played a similar part in renewed unrest early in 1904.[122] Some of its activities in 1905 were discussed in Chapter 1. The Bezhetsa (SR) workers' union was heavily involved in the prolonged strike which began at the end of February. It was later claimed that party speakers addressed audiences of up to 15 000 people during that period.[123] The SRs shared the platform with representatives of the RSDLP, who had begun formal work in the area in 1902. The Bolsheviks were the dominant Social Democrat faction in Bryansk.

When industrial trouble broke out again during the summer, the SRs were again to be found hectoring large crowds of strikers, on subjects such as Plehve and autocracy, armed rebellion, the nationalities question and political strikes. Their speeches were accompanied by the ring of revolver shots and the singing of the 'Marseillaise'. The Bezhetsa union of the PSR operated alongside the Bryansk committee. Its activities were not confined to the locomotive plant: leaflets were distributed at the Lyudinova metal factory for example, and local bricklayers were also assisted in elaborating their demands.[124]

In August, the Bryansk workers' union staged a major policial demonstration in protest against the Bulygin duma proposals – it was attended by workers from the station depot, the Arsenal and the Bezhetsa factory. A copy of the manifesto was ceremonially burnt, before the crowd was dispersed by troops and police.[125]

The accounts for the Bryansk workers' union and the Bezhetsa factory provide some clue as to the strength of the SR organisation during the first half of 1906.[126] The income of the Bryansk union increased, from 52.49 roubles in November 1905 to 119.45 roubles in March 1906. Contributions from two unnamed factories (probably the Arsenal and the hemp factory) average out at about 25–30 roubles per month, suggesting a membership of perhaps 150. Support for the party was much more significant, of course, in Bezhetsa, where the locomotive factory employed the equivalent of 40 per cent of the population of Bryansk town. Donations from workers here amounted to 87.52 roubles in May 1906 and reached 109.45 roubles in July; the workers' union as a whole operated on a monthly budget totalling well over 200 roubles. Contributions to party funds suggest that the PSR enjoyed the active support of between 400 and 500 workers in Bezhetsa, about 15 per cent of the total labour force. As in Petersburg and Sevastopol', the SRs drew sympathy from most sections of the plant as well as the office staff. The most regular contributors were the workers of the mechanical, shell, boiler and shrapnel shops, while the largest monthly donations came from the iron foundry (47.25 r. in July) and the shell shop (29.31 r. in May).

To find out about the composition of the party *aktiv* in Bryansk, recourse was made to the biographies in the handbook of the Society for Political Prisoners.[127] Information on twelve local activists was discovered there: the findings are presented in Table 6.3. All twelve activists were Russians and the overwhelming majority were natives of Orel province, in which Bryansk was situated. Two-thirds were between the ages of sixteen and eighteen in 1905, but less than half

Table 6.3 Urban party activists in Bryansk, c. 1905–07

Name	Nationality	Province of birth	Age in 1905	Year of entry into Bryansk PSR	Occupation	Father's occupation	Education	Subsequent involvement with other revolutionary organisations
Akimov, P. I.	Russian	Orel	18	1906	fitter	worker	trade school	1907: Bezhetsa SR Maximalist
Chistyakov, N. N.	Russian	Kursk	17	1904	fitter	worker	primary	1909–10 Bryansk and Moscow anarchists
Diyakhonov, B. M.	Russian	Petersburg	18	1907	?	?	secondary	1907: Bryansk SR Maximalist
Dvoryankin, A. I.	Russian	Orel	16	1905	worker	worker	trade school	1907: Bryansk SR Maximalist
Fateev, M. M.	Russian	Orel	25	1905	driller	worker	two classes	1906: Anarchist
Grinin, A. V.	Russian	Orel	?	1905	fitter	worker	trade school	
Grishin, I. S.	Russian	Orel	17	1904	joiner	worker	incomplete primary	1906: Bezhetsa SR Maximalist
Klimov, F. M.	Russian	Orel	16	1905	turner	worker	two years in ministry school	? : SR Maximalist
Kriger, V. A.	Russian	Orel	18	1905	joiner	worker	home	
Kruglov-Deev, V. V.	Russian	Smolensk	23	1901	worker	worker	primary	
Kuksin, I. N.	Russian	Orel	16	1906	factory clerk	peasant	two classes	
Zhirov, F. G.	Russian	Moscow	20	1904	turner	blacksmith/forge worker?	home	1906: Bezhetsa SR Maximalist

joined the party during the revolutionary year itself. There were three fitters in the sample, two turners and two joiners. At least nine of the twelve were second-generation workers. All had some education and five had attended trade, ministry or secondary schools. Over half subsequently defected to Maximalist or Anarchist organisations.

By October 1906, if not before, the Bryansk SRs were acknowledged to have the strongest organisation in the entire North-Western *oblast'*.[128] There were over 1000 in all: 460 in the Mal'tsev district (organised into nine independent workers' unions with a peasant group attached); 400 in Bezhetsa; and 100 in Bryansk town. There were smaller groups of railwaymen, handicraftsmen and teachers. Soldiers stationed in Bryansk were also leafleted, but there is no evidence of a formal troop organisation there. Both the major workers' unions possessed libraries, issued propaganda material and organised collections; in Mal'tsev at least, membership dues were obligatory.[129] The Bryansk organisations were said to function in an 'orderly manner' (*stroinyi*) and, remarkably, did not have to rely on outside financial assistance.[130] Relations between town and countryside were harmonious – 'The workers themselves conduct extensive peasant work, thanks to which there exists a close unity between the two sides of party activity...'.[131]

The SRs were formidable opponents for the Social Democrats – the latter were much the weaker at the Bryansk Arsenal, while 'in the Bezhetsa and Mal'tsev districts, influence is divided almost evenly between SR and SD'.[132] According to this report the SRs had struck deep roots among the workers of Bryansk, enabling them to withstand frequent 'blood-letting' and persecution by the police.

The Crisis from Within – Maximalism and Heterodoxy in Bryansk

Maximalism appeared comparatively late in Bryansk: there is no record of an independent organisation there before October 1906.[133] Originally, two workers had been expelled from the party for distributing a Maximalist brochure.[134] This action in itself produced only a small number of defections, but at the turn of the year the entire Bryansk organisation is said to have gone over to the outlawed organisation.[135] Whether or not this is an exaggeration, there can be no doubting the seriousness of the split. The PKS biographies give some idea of the scale – at least seven of the twelve SRs reviewed subsequently deserted either to the Maximalists or Anarchists. Disaffection with the mother party was probably strongest among members of the armed detachments. The reasons for such behaviour are manifold and complex. Doubtless many 'SRs' had originally joined the party mainly because it was known to practice terrorism. Such recruits were at best only superficially acquainted with the details of programme, tactics and ideology. Once they discovered that the party circumscribed the range of its terrorist activities, these 'emotional' elements were likely to seek more permissive alternatives.[136] It may also have been the case that the defection of a small number of respected, hence influential, workers was enough to trigger off large-scale desertions. Economic factors too played a role. The slump in the metalworking industry, which began during the last quarter of 1906, hit Bryansk with particular severity. The region was heavily dependent on metalworking and over 2700 jobs were lost at the Bezhetsa factory alone during this period.[137] Furthermore, the poverty of the surrounding countryside prevented it from adequately supporting the large numbers of returning unemployed. The essential attraction of Maximalism lay in its encouragement of uninhibited offensives against factory personnel and property. It presented the frustrated and despairing worker with an opportunity to strike directly at an enemy seemingly well-equipped to overcome more politically sophisticated forms of resistance.

As an effective and coherent opposition movement, Maximalism proved to be a short-lived phenomenon. As early as April 1907, a party activist writing from Smolensk felt able to assert that in Bryansk, Maximalism had 'withered without having even had time to bloom properly'.[138] Though Maximalist and Anarchist groups certainly existed well beyond that date, they no longer posed any direct threat to the survival of the PSR.[139] Yet the party continued to lean towards extremism, particularly on tactical issues. The summarised minutes of a local conference, held in December 1907, are interesting in this respect.[140] In the debate on economic terror (made topical by the recent murder of a member of the Bezhetsa factory management) even the *oblast'* delegate declared himself in favour, providing it was only used in response to lock-outs. The Bezhetsa representatives expressed no such reservations and only the Bryansk delegate held to the official party position. On the equally vexing question of private expropriations, the assembly did eventually come down in favour of the orthodox view, but only by the slender margin of six votes to four.

1907 in Bryansk

The SRs issued leaflets to mark the anniversary of Bloody Sunday, and to call for support in the second Duma election.[141] The May Day strike was a notable success for the party. All the major plants, the railways and a number of workshops downed tools, and in Bezhetsa at least the action was organised exclusively by the SRs.[142] Party support seems to have remained relatively stable, at least until the summer; a report dated July 1907 claimed 250–300 sympathisers in Bezhetsa (90 of whom were in circles), 95–100 in Bryansk and 495 in Mal'tsev (including 220 in Lyudinova, 230 in Star' and a small group at the Raditsa wagon works). There was also a thirty-strong troop section and a circle of 8–10 *intelligenty*.[143] The summer months brought the full force of political reaction in its wake. In July alone, 100 SRs were taken by the police; the provincial governor threatened fines for party meetings; and at the Bezhetsa plant, the penalty imposed for hanging a proclamation in one of the workshops was three months imprisonment for the individual and a fine of 500 roubles for the shop. Meanwhile, the succession of sackings and redudancies continued – 400 workers in the shell shop, for example.[144]

It was in this oppressive atmosphere that the SRs fought the election campaign for the third Duma. The party put up boycottist candidates, with mixed results. At the locomotive factory the SR suffered a narrow defeat at the hands of the Social Democrats, but the picture was brighter at the Raditsa factory and in the Mal'tsev district, where the party's candidates were returned.[145]

As autumn set in, the PSR in Bryansk sank into a painful and inexorable decline. By November, total support had shrunk to a little over 400, while at Bezhetsa only seventy sympathisers remained at the end of the year. The party had tried to revive its fortunes there by creating a new school of propagandists, but a combination of repression, unemployment and conscription quickly put pay to the idea. At Mal'tsev, meetings and *massovki* were held until October, when work was seriously interrupted owing to the lack of a propagandist. At Raditsa, there were still four workers' circles and fifty SR sympathisers at the end of the year, but the shortage of work at the factory meant that party collections were no longer taken. Finally, in Bryansk itself activity was confined to the distribution of literature. In November, the Workers' Union had been reconstituted after falling into abeyance, but here again straightened financial circumstances prevented any broadening of party work.[146]

The PSR was still active at the Bryansk Arsenal and the Bezhetsa factory at the time of the first party conference in July 1908, but thereafter records cease. There is no evidence of a revival before the First World War.[147]

THE SRs IN SEVASTOPOL'

Social and Economic Background

The port of Sevastopol' lies at the south-western tip of the Crimean peninsula. At the beginning of the century it served as a naval base for the Black Sea Fleet, and was defended by a substantial garrison. Troops in fact, comprised about a third of the total population of over 67 000 (1904).[148] An overwhelming majority of the town's inhabitants were of Great Russian nationality, but there were minorities of Jews (6.5 per cent), Poles (3.5 per cent), Tartars (1.5 per cent) and others.[149] Over 60 per cent of workers in Tauride *Guberniya* (where Sevastopol' was located) originated from outside the province.[150] In addition, the town itself attracted significant numbers of seasonal migrants.

Sevastopol' was essentially a trading, not an industrial centre. Its heyday was in the 1870s and 1880s, when a significant proportion of Russia's rapidly increasing grain exports passed through the town. However, this period of prosperity ended abruptly in 1894, when military considerations necessitated the diversion of commercial shipping to Theodossia.[151]

In 1900 there were only forty-two industrial enterprises in Sevastopol'.[152] By far the most important was the Lazarov Admiralty Shipyard which employed more than 3000 workers and dominated the port district.

Early History

The SRs made their first appearance in Sevastopol' in 1902.[153] They established contact with local workers and sailors but were unable to make much headway before 1905. During the summer of that year a newly-formed committee was issuing a regular stream of propaganda material, including a leaflet aimed at the troops, while an armed detachment had already been operating for several months. In spite of these efforts, the SRs remained very much in the shadow of the local Social-Democrat organisation (controlled by the Mensheviks) until November, when their fortunes took a remarkable upward turn. In that month Sevastopol', already seething with industrial unrest, became the centre of a rebellion staged by local sailors and troops, under the leadership of the famous Lieutenant Schmidt. While this drama was being played out the SRs began to make their presence felt at the daily agitational meetings. Their appearance had initially been greeted with cries of 'And where were you before 17 October?' from scornful Social Democrats. But the mass of workers responded favourably to the SR programme, especially, we are told, the sections dealing with the redistribution of the land, while the speakers' vociferous and uncompromising defence of armed rebellion also won popular approval. At the end of November the SRs created a three-man 'Workers' Centre' which, within two months, encompassed twenty agitators and 200 workers attending propaganda circles. Donations received by the town committee from sympathisers had meanwhile enabled the organisation to expand its publishing activities.[154]

The collapse of the naval mutiny in December brought swift retribution to all who had given it encouragement. For the SRs the situation worsened considerably after May, when the local combat detachment made an unsuccessful attempt on the life of General Neplyuev, the local divisional commander.[155] From then on military and police patrols scoured the streets and all revolutionaries were forced to lie low. The SRs survived, however, and began building again towards the end of the summer. Sevastopol' was blitzed with the party's leaflets, 60 000 of which appeared in the space of three months.[156] By February 1907 the PSR was indisputedly the dominant revolutionary force in the town, reckoning on up to 3000 organised workers, forty *intelligenty* activists and sixty worker-agitators. All the local trade unions (with the exception of the port workers), as well as the Council for the Unemployed had by now succumbed to the Party's ideological control. SR pre-eminence was underscored in the workers' *curia* elections to the second Duma when the party took 2000 votes to the Social Democrats' 80. The SRs could also boast one of the strongest troop organisations in the country and a highly successful combat detachment, which had begun contributing large sums of expropriated money to party funds.[157]

Social Location of Support

Clearly social-revolutionism in Sevastopol' had a very wide appeal, extending to soldiers, sailors and students, as well as workers. Nevertheless workers were indisputably an important component of the party's active membership. We will now identify the location of that support with a little more precision.

Like many other urban centres in this period, Sevastopol' attracted large numbers of seasonal migrants. In the spring and summer of each year, some 2000 bricklayers, stovemakers, carpenters and unskilled workers made their way to the town 'from Russia' in search of employment.[158] The SRs exerted influence over these workers via the 500 or so permanent artisans and handicraftsmen with whom they had already formed ties.

Within the town itself there were SR cells at the power station, among clerical and tramway workers and shop-assistants. The party had organised political/trade unions for the last two groups, and was in ideological if not formal control of local unions of woodworkers and metalworkers.

The SRs were predictably strong on the railways, claiming an organised membership of 300 (plus eight agitators) in the Sevastopol' workshops. Support for the party was solid among railwaymen – in the workers' *curia* elections to 1907 'all railway workers voted for the SRs; not one vote went to an SD candidate'.[159]

The party's power base in Sevastopol' was undoubtedly the port district, where workers, soldiers and sailors could all be found in close proximity. There were SR cells in a number of small factories: Stupin', Zigel', French and Black Sea; in addition the party received contributions from the port sentries and office workers and from the construction gangs on the 'Ochakov' and 'Ioann Zlatoust'. By far the most important enterprise in the district, however, was the Admiralty Shipyard, which employed up to 3500 workers in its eighteen workshops. Party accounts spread over the period December 1905 to July 1907 provide an interesting insight into the history and social composition of SR support at the factory and will therefore be examined in a little more detail.[160] Estimates based on monthly contributions to party funds suggest that the number of SR supporters at the shipyard ranged from a minimum of about 150 in December 1905 to a maximum of 600 towards the end of 1906 and in March to April 1907.[161] The first shops to be listed by name are sloop, forge, carpentry, paint and foundry. Of these all but the carpentry shop contributed unfailingly throughout the period. From the months October to December 1906 and March to July 1907 (for which the records are most complete), the following facts emerge: the numbers of shops contributing ranges from nine in April to May 1907 to sixteen in March to April (average 12–13 over six months of accounts). The highest contributions are recorded for October to November 1906 and March to April 1907; there is then a gradual falling off until the end of July, when the accounts cease altogether.

Table 6.4 Financial accounts of the Admiralty Shipyard (Sevastopol') October 1906–July 1907 (roubles)

		Oct.–Nov. 1906	Nov.–Dec.	March–Apr. 1907	April–May	May–June	June–July
1	Fitting and Assembly	23.76	20.83	13.87	33.24	14.50	6.83
2	Joinery	3.71	2.70	3.72	2.30	4.03	4.72
3	Paint		4.98	4.55	8.73	6.65	7.30
4	Repair			1.79		4.49	1.34
5	Rigging	8.38		8.46		14.67	2.13
6	Sloop		7.47	8.00	12.97	2.20	5.47
7	Beam			4.05			
8	Iron boiler	17.37		8.64		3.53	5.25
9	Copper boiler	12.15	12.69	3.37		2.05	2.59
10	Artillery		4.70	2.20			2.37
11	Carpentry	7.80	9.70	15.77			
12	Ship-building	24.29	7.22	6.77	11.27	8.21	7.14
13	Foundry		19.08	16.62	15.50	3.87	3.50
14	Forge	2.44	1.02	11.17	4.15	2.16	4.70
15	Mine	14.63	14.26	8.52	10.21	4.60	8.69
16	Compass			2.48	1.90	2.50	3.50
17	Sail	4.24	1.55				0.87
18	Pattern						
		118.77	106.20	119.98	100.27	73.46	66.4

The largest shop contributions come from: fitting and assembly (average 18.83 roubles over stated period), foundry (13.81), mine (10.15), sloop (7.41), shipbuilding (6.76), carpentry (5.94). The lowest contributions are recorded in the sail (0.14), beam (0.67), pattern (0.96) and artillery (1.15) shops. While average contributions are a fairly reliable indicator of the numerical distribution of SR support within the factory, they do not give an accurate picture of the proportion of SRs within a particular shop (a more accurate gauge of the party's popularity). For this we would need to know the total number of employees in each section. We could then compare this with estimates of support based on party contributions. Unfortunately it has not been possible to obtain detailed breakdowns of the distribution of the Admiralty workforce by shop. However, SR sources do inform us that there were 500 workers in the fitting-assembly shop, 400 in the iron-boiler section and 300 in shipbuilding. The accounts for 1906–7 would suggest average support in fitting-assembly of about 100 workers or about 20 per cent of the total. Similar calculations for the other two departments indicate that about 9 per cent of workers in the iron-boiler shop supported the PSR and about 14 per cent in the shipbuilding section. What of SR strength in the smaller shops? One or two very general approximations are possible if we make use of production-speciality figures from the Baltic shipbuilding factory in Petersburg.[162] At the Baltic, joiners comprised approximately 2.4 per cent of the total workforce. If this figure is applied to the Admiralty shipyard we find that although the joiners' section is low on the list of average monthly contributions, their monthly donation of 3.53 roubles represents about 20 per cent of workers in the shop. This would make the SRs as popular there as in the fitting-assembly section. A similarly based calculation for the paint shop suggests that party supporters there might represent over 30 per cent of all workers. The weak departments from the party's point of view were not those with the lowest average contributions but those contributing least regularly to the fund – that is, the sail and beam shops (one contribution each) and the pattern and artillery departments (two contributions). They represent a mixture of skilled and unskilled workers.

To sum up: at the height of its influence the PSR could claim the active support of up to 600 workers at the Admiralty shipyard, about 17 per cent of the total workforce. Support for the party was greatest towards the end of 1906 and in the early spring of 1907 and began to tail off from April to May onwards. This may initially have been due more to the impact of wage reductions and lay-offs than to police repression, which was almost certainly a major factor by July.

Finally, support for the PSR was distributed widely through the factory, among skilled and unskilled workers.

Terrorist Activity

The militancy of the Sevastopol' organisation is symbolised by the energy of its armed detachment.[163] Formed in the spring of 1905, it had carried out at least twenty-five operations by the end of 1906, the majority involving the ruthless pursuit of spies and provocateurs.[164] (It was probably the organisation's efficiency in this respect which did most to secure it against serious infiltration, although the SRs themselves also emphasised the care with which members of the combat units were chosen.) Notable victims in this period include the Commander of the Black Sea Fleet, Admiral Chukhin, an Okhrana official and the local head of Gendarmes.[165]

It will be recalled that in May 1906 an unsuccessful attempt was made on the life of the local divisional Commander, General Neplyuev. The intentions of the Sevastopol' committee, which sanctioned the attack, were unbeknown to the party's central Fighting Organisation. They had also sent a detachment to the town under Boris Savinkov, with the primary aim of killing not Neplyuev but Chukhin, who was to preside over a military review. Police agents had followed Savinkov and subsequently had him and his accomplices arrested. In the course of the same review, members of the Sevastopol' detachment hurled two bombs in the direction of General Neplyuev. The first failed to detonate but the second killed one of the terrorists (a sailor called Frolov), a policeman and six members of the public. Thirty-seven people were injured in the attack.[166] The detachment continued to operate beyond the end of 1906. Two of its later victims were military and naval quartermasters, two or three others, spies.[167] On 14 June a bomb attack was carried out on the offices of the Okhrana, killing the thrower (a worker named Ermolenko) and a policeman.[168]

Even as strongly-disciplined an organisation as the Sevastopol' detachment was not immune to internal dissension. In mid-1907 a group calling itself '*Svoboda vnutri nas*' ('freedom from within ourselves') broke away from the main detachment after an expropriation at the Post and Telegraph Office. It declared itself in favour of private expropriations and unrestrained terror, and was not prepared to submit to the authority of higher party organs. The reformed official detachment washed its hands of the rebel group, warning against the demanding of money with menaces for the sake of the party and the seeking of premature armed confrontation with the authorities.[169]

The Sevastopol' detachment consistently refrained from indulging in private expropriations but was active and successful in procuring money from the state. A total of 3319 roubles found its way into the party coffers in March and April 1907 by this route and a further 2000 roubles in May and June.[170] However, by that time the considerable sum of 17 981 roubles was being mentioned in party correspondence.[171] While the detachment seems to have been willing to share its spoils with other branches of the Sevastopol' organisation, it refused to hand over a percentage to the Central Committee, an attitude which stirred up a considerable amount of bitterness within the party's ranks.[172]

The Demise of the SR organisation

In the end the downfall of the PSR in Sevastopol' was partly of its own making. In June 1907, the committee had responded to the dissolution of the second Duma by issuing a defiant proclamation, declaring that the campaign for a constituent assembly would begin on the barricades and that local troops should be consulted about a plan for rebellion.[173] But, while both the Sevastopol' committee and the Workers' Centre ruled out any prospect of an uprising confined to the town itself, the local military bureau, with the blessing of the party Central Committee, was preparing just such an action. It was launched in September and ended, predictably, as an utter fiasco. Mass arrests, bitter recriminations and hostility towards the party were its fruits.[174]

The records of the Sevastopol' organisation fall ominously silent at this time and do not resume until the convening of the fifth party council in May 1909. By then, fear had paralysed *intelligenty* and workers alike, inducing the one to refuse to serve the party altogether and the other to shun any form of organised activity.[175] Despite further unrest among the sailors of the Black Sea Fleet in the years immediately preceding the war, there is no evidence of any attempt to revive the PSR in Sevastopol' before 1914. Social-Revolutionism was by no means finished in the Crimea however. In the local elections in the summer of 1917 the SRs took 70 per cent of the vote in Sevastopol'.[176] According to one historian of the party, at that time 'nowhere in Russia were the SRs stronger than the Tauride'.[177]

THE SRs IN THE URALS *OBLAST'*

Formed in February 1906, the Urals *oblast'* of the PSR incorporated the provinces of Ufa, Perm' and Vyatka. [178] For more than 100 years before the Emancipation, the Urals had been synonymous with Russian metallurgy; in 1860 76 per cent of the nation's pig-iron was produced there.[179] By 1900, however, a combination of factors, including diminishing coal reserves, primitive technology and poor communications had forced the Urals into second place,[180] behind the newly-emergent mining and steel towns of the Ukraine. The industrial slump at the beginning of the century only served to accentuate this trend, and although there was a partial recovery in the years immediately preceding the war, the Urals were unable to make up ground already lost to the foreign-financed centres of the Donbass (Krivoi Rog, Aleksandrovsk and Ekaterinoslav).

In the Urals *oblast'*, industry was not concentrated in the important towns (Ufa, population 99 614; Ekaterinburg, 70 000; and Perm', 61 000),[181] but unevenly dispersed in numerous factory and mining settlements.[182] The majority of iron-ore enterprises had originally been of the 'possessional' type, farmed out to merchants and worked by serfs transported from neighbouring (or distant) villages.[183]

After the Emancipation, peasants choosing to remain in the area were provided by their former owners with small allotments, intended both to supplement industrial wages, which were below the average, and to give the worker an incentive to stay loyal to the factory. The regular labour force was expanded by encouraging seasonal workers from the surrounding countryside. Most factories also employed large numbers of auxiliaries, mainly to assist in transporting ores and wood.[184] The majority of enterprises were of small or medium size; in 1900 for example, 65 per cent employed fewer than 500 workers.[185] There were a number of important exceptions however: the Motovilikha armaments plant near Perm', the Zlatoust armaments factory and the iron and steel works at Izhevsk and Votkinsk.

Izhevsk was one of the largest factories in the Urals (8000 workers in 1910).[186] Founded in 1760 by Count A. P. Shuvalov but later transferred into government hands, it was divided into two units, specailising respectively in iron and steel production and the

166

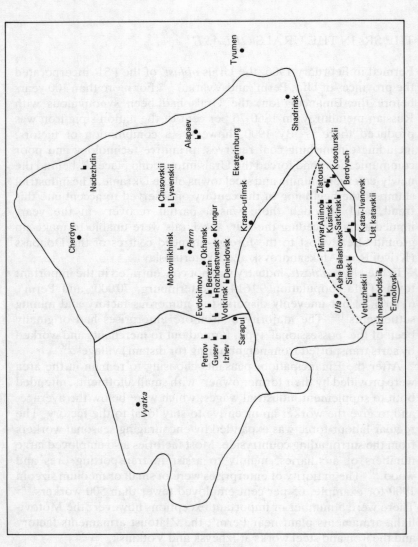

Map 6 Urals Oblast' of the PSR, c 1906–07

manufacture of firearms. Unlike many factories in the region, Izhevsk had been restructured and furnished with up-to-date machinery and equipment. As a result, output was relatively high and cost-effective, though there were problems in providing workers with the requisite skills. The bulk of the labour force was immediately to hand: the Izhevsk factory settlement had a population of 41 000 in 1905. Unfortunately this plant, like others in the region, was extremely vulnerable to fluctuations in demand and to seasonal interruptions (in winter, for example, it was sometimes impossible to carry raw materials and fuel along the Kama river). For most workers therefore factory employment was spasmodic and unreliable. Those out of work sought employment in handicraft production or in agricultural work. Allotments and kitchen-gardens could not in themselves provide a living for a worker and his family – to be exploited fully they required livestock and horses which most workers could ill-afford, particularly as the Izhevsk management were zealous in pursuing tax and rent arrears.

It will be apparent from what has just been said that the Urals *oblast'* was promising political territory for the PSR, even if the region's vast distances and poor communications made organisational work difficult. The short-term and long-term interests of workers here were more evenly divided between field and factory than in most other industrial regions. Factory employment went hand-in-hand with agricultural and handicraft work. Indeed, even when factory work was available, low wages compelled the worker to supplement his income with the produce from his allotment. Not surprisingly therefore, the struggle for material improvements centred on demands for additional land rather than on wage increases. As the Marxists noted, this was conducive to the development of 'petty-bourgeois illusions' about land-ownership which impeded the growth of proletarian consciousness.[187] Moreover, the struggle for land was to intensify in the years after 1905, when many factories were threatened with closure and their workers had to bargain for compensation in the form of larger allotments, improved pasture rights, and so on. Without doubt the SRs exploited the peculiar conditions in the Urals by pressing home their policy of land socialisation and appealing to the workers' dual outlook.[188]

Conditions in the Urals were also peculiarly conducive to the practice of terrorism. Mine-workers had access to dynamite and fuses and there were plenty of shops specialising in hunting rifles. Moreover, the sheer number of factories and settlements made the pursuit and capture of terrorists time-consuming, costly and hazardous. In sum, local conditions were ideal for the waging of guerilla war against the forces of law and order.

An historical Outline

Populist agitation in the Urals can be traced back to the end of the nineteenth century.[189] A Urals 'Union of Social Democrats and Socialist-Revolutionaries' was formed late in 1901 and continued to operate until the early months of 1903.[190] SR influence at the Motovilikha and Zlatoust factories was discussed in Chapter 1. Support for the SRs seems to have been slow to pick up during the first half of 1905, but later in the year the party played a prominent role in events in Zlatoust and Ufa.[191] SRs were also active in Perm', Ekaterinburg, Vyatka and Alapaev.[192] Evidence from a number of centres suggest that the popularity of the party increased steadily rather than dramatically during 1906. The founding congress of the Urals *oblast'* took place in February, and two more congresses were held in April and June. By the early months of 1907 the party had considerably expanded its activities and increased the number of its organisations. There were now groups in towns, like Tyumen, Cherdyn, Sarapul' and Kungur' as well as at twenty-five to thirty factories in the region, including Katav-Ivanovsk and Izhevsk as well as Motovilikha and Zlatoust. Although in stark numerical terms membership figures were not overly impressive (there were probably only 1400–1700 organised SR workers in the entire *oblast'*), supporters in the Urals tended to be more committed and self-sufficient than elsewhere.

The Urals *oblast'* voted in favour of participating in the (second) Duma election campaign, but by a comparatively narrow margin.[193] In the event, the SRs scored a number of successes. The best results were recorded at the Zlatoust, Katav-Ivanovsk and Izhevsk factories (where the SRs scored something of a landslide in the workers' *curia*) and at Ufa; in fourteen smaller factories in the region support was evenly divided between SRs and SDs. The PSR performed less well in Perm', Vyatka and Ekaterinburg, where it probably received most votes from railway workers.[194]

In common with revolutionary organisations throughout the country, the SRs in the Urals were confronted with a crisis in party work after the dissolution of the Duma in June 1907, a crisis caused by the combined effects of political repression and industrial decline.

During the summer and autumn of that year the party lost some of its best activists while at the same time, growing unemployment seriously depleted its finances and weakened morale.[195] Propaganda circles were reduced in number and agitational activity became virtually impossible. At the same time, some SR detachments (particularly in the Perm' area) came under the influence of Maximalist groups and began to break free of party control, terrorising the locality and causing grave embarassment to party leaders and considerable disruption to their organisations.[196] Nevertheless, many centres emerged from these trying times more or less intact; indeed, a number of new groups were formed during 1908. The main reason for this was the remoteness of many Urals factories and the self-reliance of party organisations there. As Chernov recalled at the first party conference in July 1908;

> In the Urals I saw a whole series of workers' organisations which made do with their own resources, there not being any *intelligenty*. They set up a press themselves and wrote proclamations – true, sometimes not very grammatically, but in terms of spirit there was much life in them.[197]

There were more arrests in the Urals towards the end of 1908, but a conference held in December was able to elect a new *oblast'* committee. This body successfully convened one more congress, in March 1909. Reports presented to delegates at the fifth party council in May suggest that there was still a considerable amount of worker activity in a number of centres, including Izhevsk, Votkinsk, Perm', Lysva, Motovilikha and Zlatoust.[198]

Although the Urals was cited as an important centre of worker-agitation in reports to the Socialist International in Copenhagen (1910) and Vienna (1914),[199] no details of the party's activities in the region are supplied – most probably the emigration was relying on outdated information and had actually lost contact with local organisations.

Perm' Province

Propaganda material alone testifies to the existence of SR activity in Perm' during November and December 1905.[200] Accounts for the period April–July 1906 show an income of little more than 100 roubles per month, suggesting an active membership of between 100 and 140 workers. Much of the organisation's expenses went on books and propaganda. By the spring of 1907, there were said to be between 200 and 300 SR sympathisers but only 30 or 40 actual members.[201] Activity focused on a number of local enterprises, including the Lyubimov boat-building plant to the south of the town, the Kama factory, the power station, two printing works and a number of artisan shops. The party had some support too in the railway workshops, but the Social Democrats were firmly in control of the union there. The SRs did, however, lead a 'professional-political' union at the state liquor depot. The party's best work had apparently been done in the summer of 1906. Fifteen *massovki* were held during that period, attracting audiences of up to 150 workers, while the presence of a dozen or so propagandists meant that circle work too was able to flourish. The Perm' organisation supplemented its income a little with the proceeds of state expropriations. There was later to be some impatience with the official party line on this question – half the delegates at a local assembly voted in favour of sanctioning private expropriations. Workers in one of the nearby factories would soon take the matter into their own hands.[202]

The Perm' organisation was broken up in the summer of 1907 and had still not regathered its strength by October. Indeed, the SRs there were largely ineffective until the end of 1908 when fresh attempts were made at revival. By the spring of 1909 propaganda had resumed in the railway workshops and extended to local shop assistants and the employees of a vodka distillery.[203] There is no record of an organisation in Perm' beyond that date.

The Motovilikha armaments factory (about 6000–8000 workers) was situated a short distance from Perm', above the banks of the Kama river. SR propaganda had begun there in 1903, but progress appears to have been slow. By March 1907 there were about 100 active supporters in the cannon, shell and turning shops of the factory and in April the organisation began publishing its own workers' newspaper, *Bor'ba*.[204] The shop-based trade union was controlled by the Social Democrats, though the SRs claimed that their demand to politicise it was well received in certain sections of the plant.[205] In the summer of 1907 the Motovilikha organisation was rent apart by the exploits of the notorious terrorist, L'bov.[206] An artilleryman during the Russo-Japanese war, L'bov worked at the factory and had formed an armed detachment there, originally to defend party meetings from troops. Eventually the band defected from the party and, from bases in the surrounding hills, carried out a series of robberies and armed attacks. In August, L'bov and his *lesnye brat'ya* were held responsible for the murder of the director of the Nadezhdinsk rail factory. This incident, which included the death of an innocent by-stander, led to the closing of the plant and consequently to a decline in L'bov's prestige. His ultimate fate is unknown. The L'bov episode seriously reduced SR influence at the Motovilikha factory, but there was still a party committee there in the spring of 1909.[207]

In the course of its activities, the Motovilikha organisation had formed links with a number of factories in the vicinity, namely those at Chusovaya, Verkhne-Kamsk and Lys'va. The last-mentioned was still flourishing in 1909 and was said to be stronger than Perm' itself.[208]

The only other important centre of SR activity in the province was Ekaterinburg. In October 1906, more than 300 supporters were attending propaganda circles here and the PSR was the guiding influence in the local branch of the ARRU.[209] By the autumn of 1907 however, the party had been reduced to about a third of its former size.[210] Nothing was heard from Ekaterinburg for much of 1908. A report presented to the fifth party council (May 1909) reported activity among shop assistants and in a few local factories.

Vyatka Province

The town of Vyatka (population 24 780 – 1897) was a small but prosperous commerical centre lying near the confluence of the Cheptsa and Vyatka rivers. There were only fifty-seven industrial enterprises in the town, predominantly tanneries, candle-works and distilleries.[211] The SRs were influential here during the 'Days of Freedom', but Vyatka was never to become a party stronghold. In February 1907 there were 173 fully-organised workers, attending eleven circles. Several factories were propagandised and the party were also active in the railway workshops.[212] However by the autumn, party workers had shifted their attention to the surrounding countryside. The organisation was by then seriously weakened – the number of circles was 'insignificant', the armed detachment had no weapons and there was neither an apartment nor a printing press.[213] Vyatka did not report to the first party conférence in July 1908 but a representative did attend a regional conference in December. At the time of the fifth party council, a small and penurious band of enthusiasts continued to propagandise local workers, students and soldiers.[214]

The most important workers' organisation in Vyatka *guberniya* was at the Izhevsk factory. The SRs had individual supporters here from at least 1904,[215] but for a long time the party was unable to make an impact on what was very much a Social-Democrat stronghold. The breakthrough came in sensational style early in 1907.[216] The arrival of a professional activist provoked immediate interest on a wholly unlooked for scale. At one time the SRs were propagandising 500 workers in several dozen circles and they quickly established links with three private factories – Petrov, Evdokimov and Berezin. The Izhevsk organisation had up to sixty agitators at its disposal and a committee, independent of Vyatka but sometimes drawing on it for assistance.[217] The huge influx of party members meant healthy finances – the Izhevsk organisation took 200–500 roubles per month in dues alone. Many of the new converts were defectors from the Social-Democrats, some even former committee members. There was great enthusiasm for the SRs' agrarian programme and tactics, and it was suggested that the erstwhile popularity of the SDs at the factory was due primarily to the absence of competition. The PSR swept the board in the second Duma elections, taking fully 60 per cent of the vote and leaving the SDs with only 15 per cent. Over the following months the SRs consolidated their position. Though actual membership had stabilised at the 150–200 mark by the autumn, the organisation had a large income at its disposal and was able to publish a workers' newspaper, *Izhevskii rabochii*. There was also an armed detachment at the factory. In addition, ties had been formed with the Votkinsk steelworks across the provincial border. Here, however, the PSR had arrived too late to make the decisive breakthrough it had achieved in Izhevsk. The SDs remained firmly in control and SR influence in the factory as a whole was admitted to be 'insignficant', being confined to a group of forty workers.[218] Whether in spite or because of the trying political and economic conditions, the Izhevsk organisation continued to thrive when many SR organisations up and down the country had fallen dormant. Financial accounts for the second half of February and the first half of June 1908[219] record contributions from nearly a dozen shops in the armaments section (including instrument, pattern, fitting and repair) and five or six shops in the steel division, where the less skilled workers were concentrated. The size of contributions suggests the active support of about 200 workers in all, about the same number as in the autumn of 1907. Donations at the Votkinsk factory in June and July 1908 amounted to 14.64 roubles, received from nine shops, a sum which suggests that the party had been unable to extend its influence there.

Reports presented to the first party conference and the fifth party council testify to the continuing vitality and durability of SR work in Izhevsk.[220] In the summer of 1908, the party could still draw between 250 and 300 workers into its circles and call on funds of almost 200 roubles, some of which was assigned to help workers in need. The organisation continued to publish its own material in hectographed form. In May 1909 the Izhevsk PSR was described as 'one of the most energetic in the *oblast'*'. There was a printing press, and propaganda inroads had even been made among the regimental armaments craftsmen who gave technical instruction to workers in defence factories. The number of SR sympathisers at the factory was said to equal the total complement of workers. Ties had not been lost with the Votkinsk plant, which operated entirely without the help of *intelligenty*. In return for financial support, the factory was supplied with literature from Izhevsk.

The only other centre of SR activity in Vyatka province was Sarapul' (population 21 395 – 1897). Industry in Sarapul' specialised in leather goods, especially shoes.[221] Early in 1907 the SRs had the support of 100 workers at nine factories in the town, and had issued 50 000 leaflets.[222] By the autumn, the number of organised supporters had doubled, but this expansion was to be short-lived.[223] In fact, nothing more was heard of the SRs in Sarapul' until 1909, by which time they were focusing their attention on the peasantry.[224]

Ufa Province

As most of the factories in this province were propagandised from Zlatoust, the first part of this section will be concerned exclusively with Ufa town.

In 1900 there were almost 800 commercial enterprises in Ufa, but only ninety-four factories: breweries, saw-mills and candle-works for the most part.[225]

The SRs began working in Ufa in 1903 and benefited from the stir caused by the assassination of the governor, Bogdanovich. In 1905 the party again made its impact via terrorism, with the wounding of governor Sokolovskii in May of that year.[226] During the spring and summer months, both SRs and SDs arranged regular *massovki* and eventually combined to form a voluntary militia. Up until then, party membership may have been more or less confined to *intelligenty*; a Workers' Union was not formed until October. The SRs were involved in clashes with troops during the railway strike in December.[227]

Party accounts suggest a slow but steady expansion during 1906 – by the end of the year the Workers' Union disposed of a monthly income in excess of 100 roubles.[228] Nine factory committees united over 300 workers, while another four enterprises were considered to be under SR influence. Organisational work centred on a dozen or so propaganda circles, and the publication of a workers' newspaper: *Sotsialist'*. Before the summer of 1906 *massovki* had been held weekly, attracting audiences of between 100 and 300, but by 1907 all forms of agitational activity had more or less ceased. The SRs were also absent from the trade unions. Terror was in the hands of a twelve-man detachment, responsible for the expropriation of 2000 roubles from a state enterprise in the summer, and for a bomb attack on a sentry post later in the year. This attack, which killed three guards and injured four others was in retaliation for the death of a party agitator, known as 'Anton'.[229] Like so many other SR organisations, Ufa now began to drift towards extremism. A report, dated October 1907, detailed a weakening of the PSR as a number of activitists defected to the Anarchists and approval grew for factory terror and private expropriations. The Workers' Union shrunk to a third of its former size.[230] Nevertheless, the party survived these difficult times. At the first party conference, the Ufa delegate was able to report some successes, particularly in the publishing sphere. Operating now on a monthly budget of 500 roubles, the Ufa SRs were issuing a number of newspapers and flysheets, including *Znamya Urala*, *Krest'yanin i rabochii* and a bulletin for the railway workers. The SRs seem to have focused their attention on the peasantry: only eighty of the 350–400 party members were workers.[231] Arrests shortly after the conference put pay to any further expansion and seriously debilitated the efforts of those remaining. Security remained the chief worry into 1909, when work among the proletariat was deliberately kept to a minimum.[232]

Zlatoust District

For the SRs, Zlatoust was synonymous with the armaments factory situated some four or five miles outside the town. The part played by the party during the disturbances of 1903 was described in Chapter 3. By 1905, Zlatoust was undoubtedly the most important workers' organisation in the Urals and the SRs were more influential there than the Social Democrats.[233] The party was led by a Jewish agitator called

Hollander, who led negotiations with the factory management during a strike in November and toured the surrounding countryside in search of support, instilling a militant spirit into the local workers. The railway strike in December brought matters in Zlatoust to a head. There was talk of seizing the factory finance office and of organising resistance to an expected cossack attack. A major demonstration duly brought the troops in and they succeeded in restoring order. The revolutionary movement subsided, but the foundations of a powerful SR organisation had been laid. During the summer of 1906 the party drew crowds of 250–300 to their *massovki* and the Workers' Union was financially secure. By the end of the year there were at least 100 organised workers and probably many more; income from membership dues was in excess of 150 roubles per month. The party had also established links with workers at the neighbouring Kusa and Satka iron-works, and its widespread popularity was demonstrated convincingly in the second Duma elections, when the PSR won landslide victories at the Zlatoust and Katav-Ivanovsk factories.[234] Zlatoust also had an active terrorist organisation. There were twenty-three members of the armed detachment at the beginning of 1907. Between April and July over 100 roubles were expended on military equipment, such as Brownings and cartridges, which were supplemented by the expropriation of knives, rifles, percussion caps, slow-matches and dynamite. Terrorist actions included the bombing of a sentry post and the robbery of a post-office on the outskirts of Zlatoust.[235]

By the spring of 1907, the SRs had established new organisations at more distant factories: Katav-Ivanovsk, Ermolovsk, Vetluzhsk and Nizhne-Zavodsk. The Zlatoust SRs emerged from the repression following the dissolution of the second Duma relatively unscathed, even though unemployment had a serious impact on party finances. There were still between 130 and 150 members of the central organisation in September 1907 and an additional 180 in the surrounding district, which now included three new enterprises, the Ust'-Katav and Demidov factories and the Kuvashinsk mine.[236] In flat contradiction of the prevailing trend elsewhere in Russia, the Zlatoust organisation continued to thrive there well into 1908. At the time of the first party conference there were 450 organised workers in the district, which now included a further six factories: Ailino, Berdyash, Asha-Balashovsk, Kosotursk, Simsk and Min'yar. Circles met regularly, and there were even occasional *massovki*. The main threat was posed not by the police, but by continuing industrial decline. Zlatoust now had to manage on a monthly income of 60 roubles, half of which was allocated to workers in need. Propagandists found it difficult to afford the cost of the constant journeyings from one factory to another. Furthermore, the threatened closure of the Belosel'sk-Belozersk group of factories (Ust'-Katav, Katav-Ivanovsk, and Yurazan-Ivanovsk) came as a great blow to many local workers. The SRs launched a campaign on their behalf, but were unable to persuade the authorities to concede more than half the land allotment they had originally recommended.[237] Signs of strain now began to show at last. A district conference, held in November 1908, registered a substantial decline in membership and a halving of income.[238] The spirit of party members was beginning to wilt as the fruits of revolution appeared ever more remote and the scope for activity was continually reduced. By the time of the fifth party council, in May 1909, a core of the most dedicated activists ran a small but disciplined conspirational organisation. A conference of factory representatives was convened monthly and Zlatoust still disposed of two printing presses. The main problem continued to be the financial one; although the mass of local workers continued to be sympathetic to the party, they could no longer afford to maintain it.[239]

7 The SRs and the Trade Union Movement

INTRODUCTION: THE SRs AND THE 'WORKERS' QUESTION' AFTER 1905

Before 1905 the SRs paid relatively little attention to labour questions in general and the workers section of the party programme in particular. Of more than ninety pamphlets and brochures produced by the Central Committee during 1902–3, for example, only two were on subjects of direct concern to the urban worker.[1] The same trend is discernible in the party's official organ *Revolyutsionnaya Rossiya*, even if there the shortfall is less obvious. Analysis of labour affairs was sparse and confined largely to exposing the motives behind police socialism and to discussing the place of political strikes and demonstrations in revolutionary strategy. Questions relating to the party programme and to working conditions were left to the propaganda sections of the local committees. One does not have to look too far for explanations of this neglect. In the three short years before the revolution SR policy-makers were preoccupied with elaborating and refining the details of their agrarian programme, the party's most distinctive contribution to the revolutionary movement. The bias in favour of the peasant seemed fully justified in view of the serious disturbances which erupted in the Ukranian provinces less than twelve months after the party's formation. Even had the SRs wanted to devote more attention to the urban movement, however, their leaders' lack of expertise in labour affairs would have proved a considerable hindrance. B. N. Lebedev, the party's leading specialist in the field after 1905, acquired his practical experience only in the course of the revolution itself when he stood at the head of the Narva district organisation in Petersburg. Of the founding fathers, Gershuni perhaps

177

had the best credentials,[2] but he was fully occupied with the affairs of
the Fighting Organisation before his premature death in 1908. In the
short term the party's weaknesses in the urban sphere were not too
damaging. Political conditions ruled out any possibility of large-scale
organisation and local activists could concentrate on recruiting
workers who returned annually for seasonal work in the countryside
and who therefore retained a direct interest in the solution of the
agrarian problem. Even factory workers more firmly rooted in the city
might be persuaded that it was pointless becoming absorbed in the
economic demands of the minimum programme while basic democratic freedoms remained to be won. As we have seen, the momentous
events of 1905 radically altered the perspective. Pressure from the
working class, in make-shift alliance with other dissatisfied sections of
the population, compelled the government to retreat from its
absolutist principles and to concede at least some of the trappings of
Western democracy. In the process the PSR was transformed from a
tiny and largely ineffectual conspiratorial organisation into a mass
political party measuring its membership in thousands and its
sympathisers in tens of thousands. Inevitably these developments gave
added urgency to the workers' question, especially as the SRs'
best-organised support was located in the towns. Suddenly the party
was confronted with a host of newly-emergent and emerging
organisations – soviets, factory committees, trade unions, co-operatives, cultural – enlightenment societies, and so on. It had to formulate
a considered response to a wide variety of issues such as collective
bargaining, lock-outs, the eight-hour day, as well as to new government proposals on trade unions and social insurance. The fate of
labour issues at top-level party gatherings after 1905 nicely illustrates
the extent to which the party failed to measure up to these formidable
challenges and allowed itself to be overtaken by events. It is to this
subject therefore that we now turn our attention.

   It was unfortunate for SR activists in the urban movement that the
party's founding congress did not take place until after the collapse of
the great proletarian offensive of October–December 1905, by which
time all eyes were turning once again towards the peasantry as the
likely source of future resistance.[3] This tendency partly accounts at
least for the fact that only two issues of immediate concern to the urban
worker (factory socialisation and economic terror) were discussed at
the first congress.[4] The trade union question was deferred, pending
discussion at local committee level.[5] There is no evidence of any
properly organised review ever taking place, however, and the first

two party councils passed without any further mention of this or any other related subject.

Working-class interests did not fare much better at the second (extraordinary) congress of the party in February 1907. Early on in the proceedings delegates from Vil'no and Petersburg suggested a number of urban-related matters for debate – including lock-outs, trade unions and economic terror.[6] From the start there was little prospect of these issues being properly aired; the main purpose of the congress was to debate the party's attitude to participation in the Duma, the most pressing and weighty question of the day and one which was bound to consume much of the participants' time and energy. When time did indeed appear to be running short 'Petrov', representing the Moscow organisation, intervened to urge that the trade unions at least should be discussed and not relegated to a commission, on the grounds that this issue was 'so close to those of us working in the large cities'.

This proposal was rejected after a vote.[7] With the exception of expropriations, which of course were of relevance to delegates representing peasant as well as worker constituencies, labour issues were consigned, as anticipated, to a commission. Worse still, there was insufficient time for the commission to present its report. Rather piously the delegates approved instead a resolution to summon at the earliest opportunity an all-Russian conference of party workers involved in the trade union and labour movement.[8] Needless to say, no such body ever met. It was not until July 1907, in fact, that the third party council finally got round to promulgating resolutions on the trade union question. There is no evidence either that the matter was properly aired at local level beforehand or that the party hierarchy was aware of the practical difficulties inherent in its chosen approach. The same council proposed to create a special bureau on trade union affairs 'for supporting and directing work in the localities' and as a school of theory and practice for activists intending to specialise in the field.[9] The chances of such a venture succeeding were remote. Witness the fate of an earlier project, recalled by Chernov at the first party conference:

We tried [in the spring of 1907] to create a professional bureau of specialists on questions relating to the workers' movement. It even began to function: one issue of 'Trade Union Movement' appeared and with great effort material for a number two was collected, but it perished. Because of police conditions, the people who made up the bureau had to disperse. This was especially regrettable as we have very few party workers with practical experience of the trade union movement, able for example to occupy the post of secretary, editor of a trade union journal, etc. The bureau must be revived.[10]

Evidently the bureau had not been revived by the summer of 1907, nor is there any indication that the proposal of the third council was ever put into operation. The speeches of delegates to the first party conference, held in August 1908, confirm that even at that late stage no serious attempt had been made to correct the party's wayward course on the Workers' Question. For example, the North-West *oblast'* delegate regretted that 'our literature on the workers and on workers' questions is also almost non-existent',[11] while 'Fedotov', representing Baku (arguably the strongest SR urban organisation at the time) felt the need to insist that:

> serious attention be paid to the lack of literature on the trade union movement and on co-operatives, and added that in a large centre like Baku there was no one competent to turn to for advice in difficult cases.[12]

In the end this conference went the way of all the other major gatherings, contenting itself with issuing resolutions framed in the most generalised and obscure terms and unaccompanied by any practical guidelines.[13] In any case by the summer of 1908 the party's mass support had all but evaporated.

The frustations of being an urban activist in the PSR are well-illustrated by the experiences of Lebedev at the fifth party council in May 1909. The council was (again) to urge that a workers' commission be attached to the Central Committee to direct work among the proletariat and to elaborate the labour section of the party programme.[14] Yet Lebedev's report on the workers' question (typically missing from the stenograph record of the proceedings) was not discussed until the closing sessions of the council, and then in short order. As he bitterly complained the party 'always put the question of the workers somewhere at the end of the list'.[15]

THE TRADE UNIONS AND THE SRs

Trade unions, or associations analogous to them were by no means unknown in Russia before 1905.[16] It was only in the course of that year however that they became in any real sense mass organisations, able to function on similar lines to those of their Western counterparts. During the unprecedently relaxed atmosphere of the 'days of freedom' trade unions sprouted 'like mushrooms after rain', to borrow the Russian expression. By the end of the year there were close to 100 in Moscow and Petersburg alone,[17] representing workers as occupationally diverse as printers, bakers, ribbon-weavers, metal-craftsmen, watchmakers and shop assistants. Though employees from the artisan trades predominated at first, industrial workers followed closely in their wake: major unions of metalworkers and textile-workers were formed during the first half of 1906 for example. The second trade union conference, held in Petersburg in February of that year was able to draw delegates from ten cities representing 200 000 members.[18]

By that time unfortunately, the hot-house atmosphere of political liberalisation which had accounted for the rapid growth of the movement had all but evaporated. Government and employers resumed the offensive after successfully riding the storms of the previous year. The embryonic unions of the October days were among their earliest victims. As labour resistance collapsed the pressure on the authorities eased and they were able drastically to revise the liberal union legislation tentatively prepared the previous spring. The law of 4 March 1906 was at best ungenerous and at worst an outright repressive measure, which among other things demanded formal registration for all unions, forbade amalgamation, made no mention of the right to strike and entirely excluded certain categories of workers from its provisions.[19] The revolutionary parties were now faced with a dilemma: whether to refuse to comply with the new regulations and risk annihilating the movement or to accept all the petty restrictions and encumbrances and in so doing rob the unions of much of their class and political significance. The majority of activists reluctantly came round to the idea that it was preferable to work at least nominally within the law than to be forced to abandon the masses completely and return underground. After all, the very existence of trade union legislation betokened an advance on the pre-1905 situation.[20]

By early 1907, despite continual harassment the union movement was able to claim close to a quarter of a million members. Over 100 newspapers and journals were published, welfare funds were distributed and lectures organised. And although the unions were no longer able to win material benefits for their members, they did at least provide workers with an opportunity to view the politics of confrontation and class interest from a new vantage point.[21] Admittedly, after the *coup de main* of 3 June 1907, the few trade unions which survived were forced to eke out an unrelievedly meagre existence, subjected to continual disruption and persecution by the police and cold-shouldered by the overwhelming majority of workers.[22] That being said, it must also be borne in mind that as far as the working class was concerned other forms of political activity were circumscribed just as narrowly and enforced with equal rigour. At the very least unions were able to serve as front organisations for illegal activity and as useful training grounds for party cadres, who would eventually have the oportunity to turn their experience to good account.[23]

The SRs' response to the developments described above was confused and hesitant. In July 1905 the Petersburg organisation had advised workers against participating in trade unions while the basic political freedom had not been achieved.[24] Presumably this view was close to the general tenor of party thinking on the issue, though early SR prominence in the All-Russian Railway Union suggests ambiguity or, more probably, uncertainty as to the correct approach to adopt. With the publication of the October manifesto the party apparently decided that its basic political requirements were sufficiently met. A declaration in the SR newspaper *Syn Otechestvo* in November 1905 called for the 'creation of open organisations enveloping the masses as broadly as possible'.[25] Professional organisations were included in this instruction. Yet there is no evidence that the party took the opportunity to clarify its position on the trade unions, at least in any detailed, authoritative and comprehensive form. In fact, signs that the question was beginning seriously to attract the attention of the SRs are not readily detectable until early in 1907. A report by Chernov on the proceedings of the third congress of the railway union, published in the January issue of *Partiinye Izvestiya*,[26] contained an exposition which closely resembled the party's eventual approach. The following month a conference of SR activists representing twenty-three Petersburg unions regretted the absence of a policy statement on the subject and called for urgent action at the next congress.[27] This was followed by an article in *Trud* which set out some basic principles.[28] The trade union issue was given added relevance in March when the SR Duma group issued a set of draft proposals on union legislation.[29] However, it was not until the summer that the long-awaited clarification of the party's position appeared. A major article by Chernov in the second number of *Znamya Truda*[30] coincided with the publication of the third party council resolutions in July. These expositions were loyally taken up by the regional press, which had begun to publish a flurry of articles on trade unions early in the summer.[31] There would be no further elaboration of SR policy on the subject until the convening of the fourth party council in August 1908. Its resolutions included a paragraph on the aims of trade unions omitted from earlier statements.[32] The fifth party council (May 1909) issued a new set of practical guidelines,[33] but the party's basic position remained unchanged.

SR policy on the trade unions reflected an attempt to steer a distinctive course between three existing approaches, outlined by Chernov in the following terms.[34]

At one end of the spectrum were the 'trade unionists',[35] who rejected any notion of social revolution and conceived union tasks solely in terms of winning material concessions for workers within the framework of the existing political and social order. Radically different from this position was the stance of the 'orthodox social democrats'.[36] In their view social revolution was inevitable but would be achieved only under the leadership of the appropriate political party. Trade unions were assigned a subordinate role: to struggle for specific material improvements within the existing capitalist order. At the other end of the spectrum the 'revolutionary syndicalists' viewed the trade unions as the legitimate organ of the social revolution and as the centrepiece of a future socialist society organised on corporatist lines. Their scenario excluded the political parties entirely, thus rejecting any notion of trade union subordination.

For the Socialist-Revolutionaries[37] (as for the Social Democrats) the guiding principle of any trade union organisation was that it should be an instrument of class struggle, embracing 'all workers exploited by capital, whatever the level of their class understanding, their political consciousness, their revolutionary temperament'.[38] The sole criterion for entry should be a determination to engage in active struggle for working interests. The need for struggle implied that relations between workers and employers and between workers and government were conceivable only in antagonistic, adversarial terms: the interests of capital cannot 'but be hostile to the interests of labour'.[39]

The SRs interpreted the field of action of trade unions in broad terms. They existed to secure the 'legal' and 'spiritual' as well as the material interests of their members.[40] Even the struggle for material advances had wider implications, however. Concessions won were more than mere palliatives; they helped to undermine the very foundations of the capitalist structure and to roll back permanently the frontiers of exploitation. In the process the trade unions became 'schools of consciousness', compelling workers to confront their class enemies, thereby increasing their understanding of class relations and contributing to the radicalisation of union demands:

> the individual membership defines those demands and aspirations which are the essence of the unions. But just as those strata of the population are united by their class position in irreconcilable enmity towards the bourgeois strata, so the activity of the trade unions will develop according to this predetermined direction.[41]

Unlike the Social Democrats, Chernov argued, the SRs did not refuse to contemplate the role of trade unions beyond the confines of the capitalist order. On the contrary, they were ready to assign them a 'historic mission', as 'agents in the transition to a new social order and as natural organisations of the future socialist economy'.[42] In other words, having paved the way for the complete emancipation of labour, the unions were to assume the management of industrial production. At that point they would cease to be 'militant workers' organisations of today' and become 'everyday organisations of the new order'.[43]

Trade Unions were to achieve their goals by a variety of means: by 'mutual assistance' and economic struggle, in the form of strikes, boycotts and other types of protest; by using parliamentary and other democratic means to defend the interests of the working class against the encroachments of their enemies; by securing greater participation in the internal regulation of industrial enterprises and by playing an active role in municipal government.[44]

It should be clear from what has already been said that the SRs drew no line of demarcation between the political and economic spheres of revolutionary activity: 'Class struggle is, first and foremost political struggle'.[45] This did not imply that the trade unions had been allowed to usurp territory traditionally occupied by the political parties. It did mean that, unlike the Social Democrats, the PSR conceived the relationship between the revolutionary party and the unions as one of equal partnership in autonomy. Both forms of organisation were considered 'equally valuable, equally necessary'.[46] They were 'the two detachments of one and the same revolutionary army of labour'.[47] They both embarked from an identical standpoint; that the existing order must be changed, and converged on the same goal, the socialist society. The differences lay only in their approach, in the means by which they reached their destination. Chernov summed up these differences in the following terms: the trade union was a 'school of life' rather than a 'school of thought'. It progressed not by adhering to a 'scientifically-based programme', but by accumulating experience provided by the day-to-day 'lessons of life'. The trade union not only recruited the fully conscious minority but everyone awakened to class struggle. The role of the party was to illumine the experience of the trade unions, to anticipate and explain their mission and to embody their aims.[48]

Further to their view on the relationship between party and unions the SRs asserted the principle of trade union 'neutrality' (*bezpartiinost'*). In doing so they claimed the support not only of eminent European socialists such as Karl Kautsky, but the authority of the Socialist International itself.[49] In Russia, the same principle had been adopted by the Menshevik Social Democrats. According to Kautsky, neutrality was particularly suitable in countries where there was more than one socialist party. It would (so it was argued) protect the trade unions from becoming the mouthpiece of any one political organisation and so prevent them being turned into battlegrounds for 'all kinds of factional squabbles'. The SRs hoped (rather unrealistically) that neutrality would facilitate 'co-ordination of the forces of both parties [that is, Social Democrats and Socialist–Revolutionaries] and co-operation by one and the other inside trade unions'.[50] For the SRs neutrality also implied respect for the independent role of the unions in the struggle for the achievement of socialism. It was not intended to sanction 'political indifferentism', to insulate the unions from the impact of party ideology.[51] In fact, it was in order to facilitate its own influence that the PSR issued a number of confusing and naïve (or disingenuous) guidelines to members on appropriate party behaviour towards the unions.[52] These insisted first of all that every party member join his/her respective trade union. Once in, SRs were on no account to conduct party propaganda collectively but they were expected to attempt to influence union thinking as individuals in the spirit of the SR approach and even to encourage others to join the party. Moreover, while there was to be no concerted attempt to interfere with the internal regulation of union affairs and procedures, party members were instructed to form cells outside for discussion purposes. These cells, grouped by profession, were to elect representatives on to local bureaux who would in turn elect delegates to a regional party conference.

More controversial than trade union neutrality, was the notion of the 'political platform'. This idea (always exclusive to the SRs)[53] originated in the draft rules elaborated by V. N. Pereverzev for the ARRU in the spring of 1905.[54] It was argued there that all union member should be prepared to accept a broad statement of political principle as a condition of entry into the union. As one SR representative later put it: 'Once it was decided that the union takes part in political struggle, than the boundaries of that participation must be indicated.'[55]

The political platform was conceived as expressing both the necessary synthesis of economic and political goals within the union and the mutual interests of union and party. It would also (so the argument went) proclaim the basic truth that under Russian conditions no material improvements could be guaranteed until the political freedoms enjoyed elsewhere in the west were introduced. In addition, of course, it reminded railway workers of the strategically sensitive nature of their work. As later experience would indeed illustrate, industrial action on the railways was bound to be construed as political and would therefore be met with force. The SRs in the railway industry continued to promote the political platform after the revolution and it was successfully defended, in the face of stiff Social-Democrat opposition, at the third congress of the ARRU in December 1906. Interestingly enough, however, the statement was not contained in the opening paragraph of the union statute which defined the union's aims, but was appended to the list of demands which followed. The text is as follows:

> In view of the fact that all the above-stated [demands] can be achieved and secured in full for railwaymen only within a democratic system, it is essential to fight for a sovereign constituent assembly summoned on the basis of general, equal, direct and secret suffrage, without distinction of sex, religion and nationality, for the elaboration of new fundamental laws for the country in the interests of the toiling classes.[56]

The concept of the political platform was not confined to SRs in the railway industry. The conference of union activists in Petersburg (referred to earlier) called in more general terms for a 'special political platform' as something 'wholly admissible and desirable'.[57] More revealing, however, are the views of the SR delegate to the first All-Russian conference of print-workers.[58] He argued for a platform which included not only demands for the basic freedoms and for the summoning of a constituent assembly (the democratic republic was considered too much for all workers to stomach), but for 'the transfer of the land to the people', on the grounds that without a solution to the agrarian question there could be 'no movement forward'. This seemed to be sailing very close to the wind as far as the preservation of trade union neutrality was concerned. Not surprisingly, the Menshevik-dominated assembly rejected the resolution. As Grinevich puts it, in the desire to find a statement of principle which would be acceptable to all workers, the delegate had substituted a 'bourgeois-democratic political programme' for the socialist programme of the PSR![59]

Given the difficulties inherent in the platform idea, revealed in experiences such as those described above, it is not perhaps surprising that there is no mention of a political platform as such either in Chernov's policy statement on the trade unions, or in the text of the third party council resolutions. The council does seem to imply a rejection of the idea when it speaks out against including in the union rules 'any kind of out-and-out specific minimum political demands as conditions of acceptance into the union'. Their aim, according to the same party statute, must instead be expressed in more general terms, as the 'struggle for the material, legal and spiritual interests of workers'. The council says nothing, however, about appending a political platform to its list of formalised union demands in the fashion of the ARRU statute. This would have injected the political element without necessarily being construed as a condition of entry. Perhaps this is what Grinevich had in mind when he described this section of the Third Council resolution as 'ambiguous'.[60]

Now that our exposition of SR policy towards the trade unions is complete, we can turn our attention to a second, related issue, namely the extent to which theory which could be related to practice. A useful starting point in this respect is the history of the Russian railwaymen's union, one of the few important labour organisations in which the PSR was able to exert a proponderant influence.

THE ALL-RUSSIAN RAILWAY UNION

The All-Russian Railway Union was formed in Moscow in April 1905.[61] From the moment of its inception the SRs were the largest single grouping on the ruling bureau; the union chairman, V. N. Pereverzev, was himself a member of the party. While it is true, as the Social Democrats never tired of pointing out, that the ARRU was built initially on white-collar foundations, SR influence was by no means confined to the clerical and administrative echelons of the labour force. The party had a number of strong bases in urban repair and maintenance shops, for example: on the Kazan' line in Moscow, and the Warsaw line in Petersburg; in Sevastopol', Ekaterinoslav and Baku. Furthermore, evidence from the capital[62] suggests that line personnel – engine-drivers, stokers, pointsmen, and so on – were also a significant element in SR support. It is worth mentioning in this respect that when the going got rough for the union after 1905 and many white-collar members deserted, the changing balance in favour of the proletariat did little to shake the party's hold on the union. That being said, the rural context of much of the network, and the strong ties retained by many railwaymen in the countryside, were undoubtedly factors in the SRs' success.[63] It was no accident that the ARRU maintained the closest of links with the All-Russian Peasant Union, also in the hands of the Socialist-Revolutionaries.

The ARRU was spared little time to bask in the glories of its role in the October strike movement. In December 1905 the government imposed martial law on the railways and a period of extreme repression followed. According to SR calculations, by the end of 1906 over 250 railwaymen had been executed and 15 000 had lost their jobs.[64] Never again would the ARRU be prepared to serve in the vanguard of a political strike movement.[65] Weakened by persecution, the union also had to contend with the secession of a number of its branches, as many members saw no future in a politicised railway union.[66] Yet despite these setbacks the ARRU managed to recover some of its former ground. By the time of its third congress (December 1906) the union was organised on twenty-nine lines throughout the Empire with a total membership of nearly 15 000.[67] Finances ran to maintaining a system of roving agents and to publishing a number of railway newspapers: *Zheleznodorozhnyi Soyuz* (the official union journal), *Izvestiya* (Moscow *oblast'*), *Chugunka* (Petersburg), *Signal* (Polessia), *Gudok* (Ryazan'-Urals), for example.[68] The third congress marked the highpoint of the union revival, however. During 1907 membership declined dramatically for the familiar reasons. According to a Menshevik source, the south-eastern railway, with 33 000 employees, had only 553 union members (one-third of whom were white-collar workers); the Libau–Romna line had 100 unionised members and the Polessia only thirty-six.[69] Membership was more substantial in the workshops of the urban junctions; nevertheless the general trend remained the same. By 1908 the ARRU was fighting for its life, and in October had to turn to the PSR as the last resort for financial help.[70] By the end of the year most of the union's effective activity was confined to the peripheral regions; there were still 2300 members on the Orenburg–Tashkent line, for example. Elsewhere in

Russia the ARRU gradually lapsed into silence.[71] An article in the final issue of *Znamya Truda* (April 1914) commenting on the growing industrial unrest in the country remarked: 'We are not hearing anything from the railway union …'.[72]

SR influence within the ARRU in general and the imposition of the political platform in particular were the reasons for it becoming one of the key battlegrounds in a war for union control which no revolutionary party could realistically hope to evade. Here more than anywhere SR concern that the trade unions should not become the scene of incessant fractional squabbling could never be anything more than a pious hope. The Social Democrats resorted to a number of different strategies in order to breach this particular SR stronghold. Their initial response was to form breakaway organisations under SD (usually Menshevik) auspices which concentrated on winning material benefits for their members. Even during 1905, for example, the important south-western (Odessa) railway had disaffiliated from the ARRU.[73] Subsequently there were a number of further defections: on part of the Moscow and Riga networks, on the Khar'kov–Kursk–Sevastopol' line and on the Baltic section of the Petersburg junction. The majority of these enterprises were not notably successful. The SDs then resorted to a different tactic: campaigning within the union to have the detested political platform removed. There was never any real prospect of this while the SRs exerted such a strong influence. There were fierce arguments on the subject in the course of the third congress but the outcome was a near total triumph for the PSR, sixteen lines voting in favour of the platform and only one against (there were two abstentions).[74] Within the Petersburg network only the Baltic railway favoured the Social Democratic position.[75] A refinement of this SD tactic was to attempt to persuade railwaymen to vote for a full political programme, a move which, if successful, would have transformed the ARRU into a political party and so made a nonsense of the SR position. Such an attempt was made at a conference of the Moscow–Yaroslavl'–Arkhangel'sk line in December 1906 but again without success.[76] The SDs also tried to have the union divided into separate proletarian and white-collar sections but this idea too failed to meet with any favour.[77]

Although the PSR generally came out on top from these interminable wrangles, the political platform caused them considerble difficulty and embarassment and may have been the decisive factor in the leadership's apparent change of heart on the subject at the time of the third party council. The railway bureau wasted considerable time in trying to come up with solutions for union members who claimed to suffer from the dilemma of dual allegiance – to the ARRU on the one hand and the Social-Democratic party on the other. In May 1906 the bureau issued elaborate guidelines based on notional conflicts which might arise: a union strike call considered inopportune by the party, for example. At the same time it was pointed out that similar divergences of interest could arise even without the political platform. The only solution, the bureau argued, was regular discussion between the parties and the ARRU on matters of potential diagreement.[78] In the world of abstractions nothing should have been easier, of course; after all, trade union autonomy had been designed to facilitate comradely co-operation among the socialist parties. The problem was that in the eyes of the Social Democrats the PSR was not a revolutionary socialist party at all but a (revolutionary-democratic) party of the petty-bourgeoisie. Following this logic no proletarian union could be allowed to fall under its sway. Furthermore the Social Democrats argued that autonomy in the ARRU was nothing more than a convenient front for SR wire-pulling behind the scenes. That party (they maintained) had taken over the union for its own ends and had transformed it into a political organisation. The SRs were, it was claimed, indifferent to the material position of railwaymen and cared only for political conspiracy.[79] These accusations were vehemently denied by Chernov at the third railway congress.[80] The ARRU, he declared, was not an SR organisation – it had specifically rejected calls for affiliation to the party. As proof of the SRs' scrupulousness in observing the neutrality principle he cited the union's advice to its members to vote for socialist and not specifically SR candidates in the second Duma elections. This self-denying ordinance was, he claimed, in direct contrast to the behaviour of the Moscow Social Democrats whose 'neutral' trade unions instructed their membership to vote only for Social Democrats![81] Chernov also cited economic concessions won by the union to refute the accusation that it had become overly politicised.

Clearly then, SR claims that the neutrality principle would protect the unions from the deleterious effects of party internecine warfare hardly stood the test of reality. Indeed, signs of unrest over the idea appeared even among the ranks of the SRs themselves. Interesting in this respect is a party conference of union activists in the Tauride held during August 1907.[82] Here, local workers and their committee expressed the view that questions of neutrality or affiliation should be decided according to individual circumstances and not set out as a matter of principle. In their opinion no SR could remain politically neutral within a trade union. However, it was not necessary to bind the union legally to the party, only to expose it to unfettered ideological influence.[83] There is no way of telling how extensive and widespread these views were. It would be surprising, however, if there was not considerable unrest among SR members, especially in those (admittedly few) unions where the party had a chance of exercising control. The Bolsheviks had already rejected the principle of union neutrality and, as far as the PSR was concerned, the Mensheviks only played lip service to it, calling for neutrality in unions where they formed the minority but effectively removing political opponents from all key positions in unions where they were predominant. The Menshevik tactic, the SRs argued was 'seizure of power' from above (that is, the central bureau). Kerch was cited as one town where the SD bureau did not even allow the minority SRs consultative rights.[84] This was of course one of the consequences of the SRs' failure to gain a foothold within the union movement in the period of its formation. One might argue, indeed, that neutrality was the only option open to the party, the only means of ensuring that its voice was heard at all. Everywhere the SRs complained of foul play. At the Moscow conference of trade unions in February 1906, they alleged, attempts had been made (unsuccessfully) to exclude the party entirely; the final verdict on the proceedings was that it had been 'more a conference of Social–Democrat activists in the trade unions than a trade union conference'.[85] Such examples could be multiplied many times, as the SRs were faced with opponents who 'unswervingly and energetically' conducted campaigns aimed at winning hegemony over the trade union movement. All in all there were few opportunities for the PSR to see its trade union policy translated into practice. Of the important national organisations only the ARRU and the Post and Telegraph union were entirely in SR hands, while at the provincial level the Volga shipping union had been of an SR orientation from its inception.[86] Generally speaking the SRs did best in those few towns where the tide in their favour was sufficiently strong to exclude the Social Democrats entirely: SR trade union activity was notable, for example, in Astrakhan', Tsaritsyn and Sevastopol'. In the major industrial centres the party was largely unsuccessful. True, there was a considerable measure of support on the ground in Petersburg and Baku, but no real breakthrough was recorded; the SRs remained a small minority on the all-important central bureaux. Even some *prima-facie* successes were in fact illusory. The SRs owed short-lived advances in the Petersburg metal union and the Baku union of oil-workers to sudden (and temporary) influxes of migrant workers and young militants previously involved in factory-centred labour organisations which had been disbanded in the 1907–8 period.[87] In the other major cities the SR record was embarassing, especially in view of the fact that the party called incessantly for active involvement in the trade unions. In Moscow, for example, where the SRs had been influential in a number of small unions late in 1905, the party was entirely unrepresented on the city bureau by the summer of 1907.[88] Elsewhere 'SR' unions turn out for the most part to be the small, strategically unimportant and least glamorous artisanal unions which the Social Democrats were not generally interested in controlling: shop-assistants, bakers and joiners in Simferopol', clerks in Saratov, tailors in Penza and Minsk, sawyers in Arkhangel'sk, shoemakers and seamstresses in Tula, bookbinders and bricklayers in Vologda, and so on. There were whole regions (the Urals and the Ukraine, for example) where SR influence on the trade union movement appears to have been almost non-existent.

There were many reasons why SR union practice failed to live up to the expectations of the party policy-makers, some of which will by now be apparent. The SRs were 'badly prepared' and 'caught unawares' by the explosion of union activity in 1905.[89] The party leadership was never able to eradicate the 'very harmful prejudice' towards work in the legal labour movement, a result of the party's inbred abhorrence of 'economism' and its earlier myopic obsession with armed rebellion. This led to the 'boycotting' of the unions by SR activists and sympathisers alike; to the stubborn preference of the Sevastopol' delegate for armed rebellion,[90] to the widespread distaste for union work in Baku and to the indifference registered in Khar'kov, Kiev and the Caucasus.[91] Because of their lack of experience of union affairs and owing to a pitiful dearth of party literature on the subject, the SRs were left with a shortage of effective union activists. For this reason, unions with a large SR membership came to be represented almost solely by Social Democrats as elected SR officials gradually drifted away from their union duties or proved incompetent, or dishonest in exercising them.[92] Finally, in cases where the SRs were unimpeded by their opponents in attempting to form their own unions they failed, for the most part, to build on solid foundations. Lebedev cites the case of unions of bakery and leather-workers in southern Russia by way of example.[93] Here the SRs would form a union, copy out a set of rules from elsewhere and summon two or three meetings of activists poorly-equipped to influence their fellow-workers. Inevitably the union disintegrated with the first instance of repression, and the SRs' reputation with it.

Epilogue

In May 1909 the fifth party council met to discuss the implications of the Azef affair, the most serious and damaging internal crisis in the short history of the PSR. The astonishing, wellnigh scandalous revelations could not have surfaced at a worse time, with local reports testifying to a further deterioration in the fortunes of party organisations at grassroots level. Indeed, there were now only three properly functioning urban centres in the whole of Russia – Baku, in many respects the leading SR organisation; Petersburg, where limited progress was constantly being checked by ruthlessly efficient police containment, and the Urals. Here, because of the physical remoteness of factory organisations and the remarkable determination and perseverance of their activists, party life had retained at least something of its old vitality. Elsewhere, however, there was an awesome silence, permeated by no more than the occasional signal from a handful of lesser centres – Arkhangel'sk, Riga, Voronezh, Poltava, Kiev, Khar'kov and Sevastopol'. There was to be no substantial improvement in this situation before the outbreak of the First World War, despite a significant upturn in labour unrest between 1912 and 1914. Information presented to the Socialist International at Copenhagen in 1910 and Vienna in 1914, taken together with press and archival evidence, strongly suggests that appreciable SR activity was still confined to Petersburg, Baku and the Urals. Though attempts were made to revive party organisations in Odessa (1910 and 1912), Moscow (1913) and Kiev (1912–13), all were quickly stifled by the police.

The SRs seem to have been generally unable to capitalise on the marked revival of industrial unrest between 1912 and the war. Nevertheless, one must take into consideration the hopelessly fragmentary nature of the evidence for this period. *Znamya Truda*, the central party newspaper, ceased to appear in April 1914; and the

193

information it carried from Russia was already well out of date. The report presented to the International at Vienna on the eve of war makes it clear that the *émigrés* had very little idea of the strength or distribution of their forces inside Russia, or of their activities, and the sparseness of material in the party archive confirms that communications with Russia were tenuous to say the least. Whatever the truth of the matter, the party leadership was itself demoralised and divided on the eve of the First World War. The agrarian section of the SR programme had been seriously damaged by the impact of the Stolypin reforms in the Russian countryside.[1] The party's tactics appeared to many to be outmoded and ineffective – especially terror, which was now exclusively confined to the rhetoric of the propagandists.[2] The revelations about the arch-traitor Azef, able for so long to operate at the very centre of the party, had cast a long shadow over the leadership and raised serious questions as to its credibility and trustworthiness. A group of 'neo-Maximalists' broke away from the party during 1908–9,[3] and by 1910 a much more dangerous 'right opposition' had begun to develop. This faction, led by B. N. Lebedev, I. I. Fundaminskii and N. D. Avksent'ev and grouped around the journal *Pochin*, was the SR equivalent of the Menshevik 'liquidationists'. The 'Pochinists' argued that changing conditions in Russia had rendered the old conspiratorial organisations obsolete and demanded revitalised and more or less exclusive work in the legal labour movement. They also believed that the PSR had been wrong to continue its boycott of the Duma after the elections of 1912.[4] There is evidence of Pochinist influence in Petersburg and it may well have been the case that there was a considerable amount of SR work in the legal labour organisations which went unrecorded in the party press precisely because it was led by 'deviationists'. As far as the traditional conspiratorial organisations were concerned, unrelenting persecution must be advanced as the single most important reason for the party's apparent weakness in the cities. It is surely significant that when legalised activity became possible in 1917 the PSR quickly became the most popular of the revolutionary parties, in both town and countryside.[5]

Conclusion

Let us begin with a summary of our findings.

The formative years of the PSR (1902–5) saw the emergence of about fifty urban groups and committees, widely dispersed over European Russia. In sheer numerical terms membership of these organisations was miniscule. Outside the largest cities and industrial centres, only fifty or so workers regularly attended party propaganda circles at any one time, with perhaps a hundred turning up to occasional meetings or rallies in the woods and fields on the outskirts of town. The local leadership of these organisations was drawn almost exclusively from the ranks of the intelligentsia. The SRs, however, relied much more heavily on the student element than their Social-Democrat rivals and seem to have suffered more seriously from a shortfall in active cadres. Several reasons can be advanced for this: the party's commitment to work equally among peasants and workers itself made insupportable demands on their slender resources; the SRs' active involvment with terror earned them 'most wanted' status in the eyes of the police, subjecting them to more frequent raids and disruptions than other parties and frightening off faint-hearted but possibly wealthy and influential sympathisers. Finally, in the view of one old hand at least,[1] the Social Democrats had been able to draw on a capital of intelligentsia support accumulated in the years preceding the formation of the PSR. In the opinion of the present writer it was this dearth of activists rather than any inherent inability to convert mobilised into organised support (as Manfred Hildermeier has suggested) which was primarily responsible for the failure of the SRs to overtake their Social-Democrat rivals in the cities. If the student intelligentsia formed the vanguard of most SR organisations before 1905, there is evidence to suggest that workers already constituted a significant minority of the core membership.

Analysis of the propaganda output of the Moscow and Petersburg committees revealed that workers were addressed most frequently in SR party proclamations and that worker-related issues received the

195

greatest attention. Although there was probably some variation in the propaganda content of other urban organisations up and down the country there seems no reason to doubt that SR groups were as much concerned with the local workers as were the RSLDP and should certainly not be regarded as mere distribution centres for peasant-orientated propaganda.[2] Leaflets commemorating or encouraging a sympathetic response to acts of terror appeared no more frequently than those criticising government policy in general and the war with Japan in particular.

There can be little doubt that the infant SR organisations only rarely made the acquaintance of the working masses during this period. The demarcation line drawn by the populists of the 1890s to stake themselves off from the Social Democrat 'economists' remained intact long after the formation of the PSR; indeed, the party's suspicion of economically motivated activity frequently bordered on prejudice. As a rule, when the SRs did become involved in leading or influencing the course of strikes it was with the aim of steering them in a political and confrontational direction. The party's interest in 'armed demonstrations' (rarely realised) was again symptomatic of its militant and uncompromising stance. Given the popularity of police socialism in the years leading up to 1905 and the overt hostility of most workers to political agitators of all kinds, this sort of appeal must, more often than not, have fallen on deaf ears. On the other hand, when the working class did become more radicalised and politicised during the revolution the SRs may well have benefited from being most closely associated with the prevailing mood. Even when enjoying surges of popularity, however, the SRs' numerical inferiority *vis-à-vis* the Social Democrats usually put them in the invidious position of relying on the acquiescence if not the active support of that party (or one or other of its factions) before embarking on initiatives of their own. Such support was rarely forthcoming; on the contrary, the parties were continually at loggerheads, preferring to highlight rather than disguise their ideological differences. If the SRs sometimes appeared the more conciliatory in this respect, it was probably a case of magnanimity born of weakness. The erstwhile co-operation between Social Democrats and Socialist-Revolutionaries in the Urals can be considered as the exception proving the rule.

The SRs' appeal to Russia's urban working class was based on the sound assumption that a proletariat in Marx's sense of the word constituted as yet only a small minority of the total labour force. The majority of workers, even in the more advanced industrial centres, continued to retain socio-cultural if not direct economic ties with the countryside and an appropriately dichotomous self-image. There was some variation in the strategy adopted by local committees towards the workers, dictated in part by the nature of the individual centre and its industrial composition. In some places (Kiev and Odessa, for example) the local activists appear to have focused their attention on seasonal migrants, whom they considered (as did the party leadership) most suitable for channelling the discontent of both urban and rural communities at the same time as the messages and exhortations of the revolutionaries. The impression one gains is that this strategy enjoyed only limited success, though admittedly measurement is difficult. Organising and maintaining regular contact with migrants shuttling backward and forwards between town and village must surely have presented formidable difficulties. Opinion on the behaviour of seasonal migrants seems to divide between those who, like Robert Johnson,[3] believe that there was a traffic in radical ideas between town and village and those, like Eugen Weber, whose study of nineteenth-century French workers[4] suggests that migrant communities remained homogenous, largely impervious to the urban influences lapping around them and remote from the mainsprings of industrial life. Wherever the truth lies, the SRs worked more effectively in the large, mechanised factories of the major industrial concentrations. Here the party *aktiv* began building permanent cells among the more secure, skilled and literate migrant workers who, while remaining factory-based, continued to retain substantial ties with the land and were perhaps willing to distribute political propaganda in their home villages during the holidays. The success of this strategy was demonstrated after 1905: the Obukhov, Pipe and Nevskii shipbuilding plants in Petersburg, the Prokhorov textile mill in Moscow, the Bryansk engineering works in Ekaterinoslav and the Urals factories of Motovilikha and Zlatoust all became SR strongholds in the course of the revolution and remained party bastions in 1917, when the SRs found themselves at the centre of the political stage.

In the year and a half between the promulgation of the October Manifesto and the convening of the second Duma, the PSR became, by Russian standards at least, a mass party, counting on about 50 000 members and 300 000 sympathisers. My own estimates of the party's organised support (based largely on archival evidence) confirm the findings of Hildermeier and Perrie, namely that workers comprised about half the total, or more than any other single segment of the population. The SRs found their most numerous following in

Petersburg, Baku, Sevastopol', Moscow, the Bryansk and Urals regions and a number of smaller provincial centres, the most prominent being Astrakhan' and Tsaritsyn. Impressionistic evidence suggests that Khar'kov, Odessa, Nikolaev and, perhaps Ekaterinoslav were also important party bases at one time or another. On the other hand, there were noticeable areas of weakness: the Baltic region, the Donbass and the Central Textile District being the most significant examples. The relative absence of communal land tenure or land shortage was probably one factory operating against the SRs in these areas. In the Donbass, management had been forced by 1905 to settle workers permanently with their families in specially constructed industrial settlements – a move which would certainly have weakened rural ties there.[5] The relatively late arrival of the PSR on the political scene may also have been a more telling impediment in some areas than others. The overall geographical distribution of urban support suggests a pattern quite distinct from that prevailing in the country-side. Radkey's assertion[6] that the SR support 'remained primarily a phenomenon of the Black-earth and Volga regions' must therefore be rejected as far as the urban worker is concerned. In terms of national composition the PSR continued to be a predominantly Russian organisation though there were significant minorities of Ukrainians and Jews; and Armenians formed an important constituent of the Baku organisation. Jewish workers were particularly important in the North-West Region: indeed it may not be much of an exaggeration to suggest that there the PSR was more a Jewish than a Russian party, drawing much of its core support from renegades from the Bund. Undoubtedly the chief reason for the party's popularity in the Pale of Settlement was its advocacy of terror; the land policy held no attraction for Jewish handicraftsmen.

Occupationally speaking, the PSR recruited a wide spectrum of workers during the revolutionary period: seasonal labourers, artisans and service-sector employees as well as industrial workers. Certain patterns do emerge, however. The party seems to have enjoyed most support among workers in the larger enterprises, particularly those employed in the metalworking and engineering industries. This impression, noticeable over a number of centres, contradicts the findings of Diane Koenker[7] for the Moscow municipal elections of 1917 that 'metalworkers least of all cast their votes for the hugely popular peasant-oriented Socialist-Revolutionary Party'. Unfortunately there is very little archival evidence on the sources of SR support in Moscow during the 1905–7 period. Laura Engelstein's study of workers in that city[8] mentions a variety of enterprises passing SR resolutions during the October to December (1905) period, including a number of textile firms but not many metalworking firms. The industrial structure of Moscow affords part of the explanation. In contrast to Petersburg, only 16 per cent of Moscow workers were employed in metalworking and they were concentrated in rather smaller plants than in the capital. Only four (Belgian Electric, Guzhon, Bromlei and Zhako), for example, accounted for more than 1000 workers each, whereas in Petersburg the large number of truly giant plants formed the cornerstone of the SR organisation there. A less unexpected finding was that, almost everywhere, the PSR was very strongly represented among railway workers – repair shop employees and line personnel, however, as well as clerical staff. Social-Democrat inferences that SR support in this industry was essentially white-collar-based must, therefore, be dismissed. By way of contrast, little evidence was found to support the inference of Pankratova[9] and other Soviet authors to the effect that the PSR was closely associated with the raw peasant workers of the textile industry. As has already been remarked, the SRs were unable to compete with the Bolsheviks in the textile belt around Ivanovo and, while textile workers did vote for the PSR in considerable numbers in the Petersburg workers' *curia* elections in 1907, they received slightly less support than the Mensheviks. Furthermore, the Petersburg factory index confirms that SRs there were much more dependent on metalworkers than textile workers. Koenker produces evidence to confirm this impression in her study of the Moscow municipal elections of 1917 and suggests that the SRs' celebrated connection with the Prokhorov mill may have been something of an exception.[10]

More predictably, the PSR was found to have enjoyed only weak support in the printing industry, that most proletarian of occupations. Modest followings in Petersburg and Moscow appear to have been transient and may have been rooted among the apprentices of the less technologically sophisticated enterprises. Nevertheless, it ought not to go unrecorded that PKS does include lithographers and compositors among its lists of Socialist-Revolutionary activists before the First World War so the party was evidently not without its attractions even for these workers.

Several other points about the party during the 1905–7 period are worthy of note. For one, Lenin's description of the SRs as 'stormy petrels', 'incapable of solid and persistent work among the proletariat' and disappearing from the working-class suburbs at the slightest change in the workers' mood[11] is not borne out by the evidence, especially (but not only) where Petersburg is concerned. Time and again the ebb and flow of party activity was found to have been regulated, not by the disposition of the workers but by the intervention of the police. Similar, if not identical, patterns are readily discernible among Social-Democratic organisations. The SRs also merit some defence from the perennial charge of poor organisation, at the local level at least. The electoral campaign preceding the second Duma elections in Petersburg might be cited as the star witness in this respect but the party was capable of campaigning with reasonable effectiveness elsewhere. Moreover, ground-level organisations in the places I have been able to examine were found to have been built on the same principles as those of the Social Democrats and to have operated with a comparable degree of efficiency, always allowing for the constant disruptions caused by the police. Organisational structures, though inevitably fragile and incomplete, are not mere chimeras or fictions; the evidence records sessions of councils, assemblies and *raion* and factory committees discussing party policy and other issues in much the same way as the SDs. That being said, certain differences remained between the activities of the two rival parties. At the local level the PSR retained a heavy bias towards purely political activity, the wishes of the party hierarchy notwithstanding. SR weakness in the soviets can be partly attributed to the fact that the party was not yet sufficiently established and influential to compete with the SDs, but the failure to make telling inroads among the trade unions, the councils for the unemployed, the factory commissions, the co-operatives and the cultural enlightenment societies in part reflects the old prejudice towards 'economistic' forms of activity. Even where local party organisations loyally repeated the injuctions and exhortations of their superiors and urged their membership to become active in the trade unions, their appeals seem largely to have fallen on deaf ears. This was partly because the SR leadership was guilty of neglecting its urban wing but presumably it also reflected the social composition of the party in the towns: workers with ongoing ties in the countryside had an alternative source of security and support to the trade unions and could see no use for them, especially during the Reaction. No doubt there was also frustration at the stranglehold maintained by the Social Democrats over the controlling bodies of these organisations. SR activity between 1905 and 1907 focused, then, on the direct politicisation of the workers – the composing and disseminating of labour newspapers and other revolutionary literature, the encouraging of protest strikes, organising propaganda circles and lecture sessions, agitating at the factory gates, campaigning on key labour issues and, of course, most distinctively, preparing acts of terror against representatives of the State. However, while terror certainly claimed a significant share of SR activity during the revolutionary period, Soviet claims[12] that the party was more or less exclusively concerned with that mode of operations must be rejected. The spectactular assassinations carried out by the SR Fighting Organisation were undoubtedly popular among the workers, and there can be little doubt that the removal of hated police officials and tyrannical or vindictive factory personnel by the local detachments were similarly well-received. Nevertheless the PSR had to pay a heavy price for arousing publicity and support through these methods. Indeed, in some respects the local combat units can be seen as the Achilles heel of the party. They brought down on its fledgling shoulders the full wrath of the authorities and placed its members under the strictest surveillance. The lax conditions of entry and almost complete operational independence left the detachments wide open to infiltration by provocateurs, Maximalist and Anarchist groups and a whole range of muddled hot-heads unfamiliar with or disinterested in coherent programmes and philosophies of any kind. The cost to the urban organisations was prohibitive in another respect – probably the majority of operations were nipped in the bud and group members (and other compromised persons), weapons and ammunition seized. Finally, when discipline disintegrated entirely during the early months of 1907 the PSR inevitably received the blame for all kinds of acts which it had neither authorised nor approved – the plague of petty private 'expropriations', for example, which often amounted to nothing more than criminal theft. Yet despite the militancy of the PSR and its unequivocal espousal of political terror, it would be a mistake to see the party wholly in the colours painted so often by Soviet authors – as the reckless, adventurist and irresponsible wing of the revolution, always anxious to provoke the working class into suicidal confrontations on the barricades, hopeless rebellions and empty but costly gestures of defiance. On the contrary, the party's long-held belief that no urban-centred insurrection could succeed without the active support of the peasantry, led it to adopt tactical positions which must often have appeared more cautious, certainly, than those of the Bolsheviks. Take as examples the SRs reluctance to back the Petersburg Soviet's campaign for the eight-hour day towards the end of 1905; the counselling of a breathing space to allow for organisation and consolidation in the early months of 1906, and

opposition to the abortive Bolshevik-inspired general strike in July of
that year. Finally, with the exception of the military rebellion in
Sevastopol' in the summer of 1907, the SRs resisted the temptation
(despite the bravado of their propaganda) to commit themselves to
desperate revolutionary heroics following the dissolution of the second
Duma, upon realising that there was no ground-swell of support. And
even in Sevastopol', the rebellion went ahead in the face of opposition,
both from the local committee and the workers themselves.

The considerable success enjoyed by the PSR (the party of the
peasantry) in recruiting and organising urban-based and, more
particularly, factory-based support during the revolution of 1905–7,
together with the party's evident popularity in Russia's towns and cities
during the first half of 1917,[13] leads one to reflect on a number of
questions relevant to the nature of the working class in general and the
migrant or peasant-worker in particular.[14] These include: the relative
resistance or receptivity of migrants to the processes of urban
acculturation and proletarianisation, the formation and characteristics
of peasant-worker 'class' and party consciousness, and the implications
of what Robert Johnson has described as the 'symbiotic' relationship of
town and countryside for our understanding of the revolutionary
dynamics operating in Russia during the early part of the twentieth
century.
It is important at the outset to arrive at a correct evaluation of the
attitudes and motivation of migrant workers on their arrival in the city
and of the circumstances in which they become acclimatised to the
urban and industrial environments. Here we are presented with two
contrasting typologies. One suggests that integration was a painful and
protracted process:

> Migrants are assumed to be uprooted, isolated and therefore anomic,
> that is, unrestrained by binding norms of behaviour. In rural areas,
> established institutions guide political attitudes and actions, instilling
> habits of deference and passivity. Migrants are uprooted from this
> centre and plunged into a bewildering, harsh, impersonal environ-
> ment where traditional controls are absent while effective, alterna-
> tive forms of control have not been established.[15]

The supposed reaction of these reluctant and uprooted migrants has
been described by a number of historians, sociologists and political

scientists. In a justly celebrated article of the 1960s,[16] Leopold
Haimson drew a direct connection between the enormous influx of
migrant labour to Petersburg in the years immediately preceding the
First World War and the appearance during the general strike of 1914
of ill-disciplined and extremist tendencies in the labour movement,
which resulted in premature calls for an immediate armed uprising.
More recently, Daniel Brower[17] has instanced a number of official
reports on outbreaks of violence and disorder in Russian towns during
the 1890s which were also attributed, at least in part, to migrant
workers. Or take this modern Italian example:

> Inherent in the urbanization process is also a certain potential for
> anomic movements, rioting and disorder. Of the thousand people
> arrested in Turin during the riots of the summer of 1962 over
> two-thirds were southern immigrants, most of them very young,
> many of them barely able to speak Italian.[18]

It would be wrong, of course, to deny either that such events occured
in Russia during the early years of the present century or that migrants
were sometimes participants. I would suggest, however, that this was
hardly a form of behaviour peculiar to migrant workers – disgruntled
artisans and 'unconscious' factory proletarians were surely prone to
act in a similar way. Also, this model does not account for the evidence
of this study, to the effect that the PSR, which was heavily reliant on
the active support of young, migrant, peasant-workers was capable of
organised, disciplined and systematic political activity which
demanded at least a measure of restraint, commitment and ideological
conviction from its core membership.

Recent research on migrant behaviour, both for Russia and for the
contemporary developing world, has yielded an impressive body of
evidence which confounds, or at least challenges, the traditional view
and which seems more consistent with my own findings concerning the
worker constituent of the Socialist-Revolutionary party. This alternative model suggests that migrants were drawn to the city by a variety of
positive or 'pull' factors such as better wages and employment
opportunities, in addition to the more negative factors such as
over-population and economic need; that they tended to be youthful
and ambitious, rating urban forms of work and life-styles above those
on offer in the countryside; and that they originated among the literate
and middle-income strata of the peasantry. As Johnson has demonstrated in the case of Moscow workers, migrants adjusted to the city by
means of an elaborate, supportive network of kin and neighbour

association rooted in the village (*zemlyachestvo*). As we have seen, the *zemlyachestvo* system operated on a number of levels to facilitate the transition from one mode of existence to another: in establishing contact with the city, in locating accomodation, in finding work, in providing information on urban conditions and services, in fostering migrant children and in facilitating the common defence of interests in the work-place. This typology suggests a fairly rapid, comprehensive and relatively untraumatic acclimatisation to the urban environment but one which tended to preserve rather than dissolve peasant ties. Thus, a young peasant-worker might conceivably become involved in organised urban politics at an early stage without necessarily losing his former identity. Here it is important to emphasise the word 'might', for radical politics embraced only a fraction of the industrial population directly during this period and a smaller proportion still of service-sector or seasonal workers. In Petersburg, for example, the organised membership of the two major revolutionary parties (RSDRP and PSR) combined, amounted to about 15 000: 10 per cent of industrial workers but only 2–3 per cent of the total labour-force. Of course, the significance of the membership cannot be measured in numerical terms alone; equally, it must be said that much larger numbers of workers were reached indirectly: at agitational meetings, through the medium of revolutionary leaflets and newsheets or via participation in strikes or factory elections. Nevertheless, even among the best educated and most highly skilled workers there was widespread antipathy towards the revolutionary parties, if not towards revolutionary policies as such. In the Petersburg workers' *curia* elections in 1907, for example, nearly 17 per cent of voters chose 'non-party' candidates, while the printers, acknowledged to be the leading stratum of the city's proletariat, apparently elected to put up their own independent representatives. Much more typical were the unskilled or overburdened factory workers who, worn out by the strenuous conditions of the work-place, preferred to seek escape from serious issues through diversions such as drink, card-playing or fist-fights in the little leisure time available to them. Such attitudes were prevalent among settled as well as migrant workers. As far as the peasant-worker in particular is concerned, it may be recalled how the manager of the Baltic shipyard described land-holding workers as 'the most conservative and independent' element of his labour-force.[19] It has been suggested that the financial obligations incurred in maintaining an extended family in the countryside, together with the running costs of the allotment, itself made peasant-workers extremely reluctant to risk dismissal by becoming involved in revolutionary politics.[20] Other peasant-workers were probably more concerned with political issues 'back home' than with those attracting the attention of the fully-urbanised worker.

On the other hand, there were factors operating in favour of urban-based political involvement. Robert Johnson has reversed the argument about the 'conservative' worker-landholder by pointing out that, in contrast to the urban wage worker, the peasant-worker had less to lose from political involvement, being always able to fall back on his plot of land – his 'social security' in the countryside – where, of course, he could always return during periods of unemployment.[21] One must also bear in mind that, unlike some modernising societies which make a considerable effort to mobilise workers in support of the regime and to provide opportunities for political participation in neighbourhood or local politics at least,[22] the Russian government remained uncertain about how to treat its working class, seeing it more often than not in negative terms as a potentially destabilising force. This indecisiveness allowed the revolutionary parties to fill the void and to create a situation ultimately perilous for the regime. As Victoria Bonnell puts it: 'radical solutions most readily gain acceptance by workers in a political environment that nurtures hope for amelioration on the one hand and suppresses genuine progress on the other'.[23] The concessions of 1905 increased the already growing sense of frustration, as newly-created opportunities for political articulation were increasingly denied to the masses in general and the working class in particular. There is neither reason to believe, nor evidence to suggest, that this sense of frustration was confined to the cadre proletariat of the cities.

If an 'advanced' stratum of peasant-workers did become involved in radical politics, how then did they meet its acquaintance? A number of subjective influences can be identified. By 1905, some second-generation migrants may have been following the allegiance of parents or elder brothers, already influenced by populist or Marxist circles of one kind or another. More often, a newly-arrived apprentice would take his lead from the fellow *zemlyak* who accomodated him, or the foreman who found him his job. The local environment was also important in determining political attitudes. Factors such as the density of migrants in a particular district, or the presence of a large factory traditionally associated with one or other of the parties, might influence a newcomer; while bad relations with local police or administrative officials could create a more radical and restive frame of mind among the inhabitants of one neighbourhood than the next. Even chance acquaintance could play a role in determining political allegiance. Like the modern Santiago woman who voted communist because members of that party came to her assistance during a squatter 'invasion' by the authorities,[24] so too might a young worker who received a sympathetic or attentive hearing from an SR or Social Democrat later come to side with that party. Of course, initial acquaintance did not necessarily lead far in the direction of political consciousness. Many workers wore their party allegiance like a badge, to mark them off from others more than to symbolise deeply held ideological convictions.

Generally speaking, one might guess that the initial level of understanding was low – not too far removed from the Moscow worker in 1917 who understood 'Bolshevik' to signify 'large' or 'well-to-do' person,[25] or the Italian peasants of the 1960s who voted Christian Democrat, thinking the party name signified a 'symbol or shield with a cross' or a 'particular person'.[26] (The identification of parties with individuals or the preference for individuals over parties was often remarked on in revolutionary Russia.)[27] However, by 1907 many workers must have become familiar at least with the outline of party policies and interests. The PSR, easily identified with the slogan 'land and freedom' was obviously the party of the peasant interest and of workers with a perceived stake in the solution of the land question. Similarly, political terror was closely associated with the SRs, winning them popularity as well as a considerable notoriety – even the legal press attributed acts of terrorism to 'SRs', whether that party was actually responsible or not. Finally, by stressing time and again the common origin of workers and peasants, their interdependence of interest and their 'brotherly solidarity', the PSR was bound to appeal to the peasant-worker, whose symbiotic or dichotomous status these slogans and appeals encapsulated. Having won the ear and sympathy of the mass of workers, the SRs were then able to recruit a small but influential corps of better-informed activists – mostly young, skilled or semi-skilled and literate.

As the SRs themselves readily acknowledged, their advance during the revolution of 1905–7 (generally underplayed or dismissed by Soviet historians for ideological reasons) was largely due to the fact that a genuine 'cadre' or wholly wage-dependent urban proletariat still constituted a minority of workers in all but a handful of industrial centres. Not only had large numbers of factory and mill-workers retained economic or at least socio-cultural ties with the countryside, it is my guess that those ties were often continued in one form or another long after Soviet statisticians and historians have generally been prepared to admit. The Kabo investigations conducted in Moscow during the early 1920s attest to the persistence of these rural habits and influences. Take the smelter who had settled permanently with his wife in the city, yet continued to tend a cow, birds and a sucking-pig on an urban allotment in his spare time; the joiner and filer who had worked full-time as an urban craftsman from the age of 16, yet twenty years later still maintained part of his family in the countryside; the weaver at the Prokhorov mill who worked there from 1900 yet kept up the allotment acquired by his wife through her first husband and visited the countryside himself, primed with gifts for his relatives; the printing worker who, despite having been resident in Moscow since about 1907 bought an allotment during the famine of 1921 and considered settling again in the countryside. Finally, and perhaps most instructively, the metalworker at the Guzhon plant who left his home village at the age of twelve to become an apprentice and rose rapidly through the factory ranks, yet was content after thirteen years to acquire and maintain land and property in his native province. (The same worker continued, even in the 1920s, to keep half his family in the countryside while his wife moved seasonally between the two homes.)[28] The peasant-worker was, then, by no means necessarily a transitory phenomenon. Furthermore, the memoir evidence suggests that the presence of an advanced cadre element in the machine-building plants of the major cities may have served, not to advance and disseminate proletarian consciousness but, on the contrary to reinforce the distinction between urban workers and peasant-workers, bound together by *zemlyachestvo* ties. Not only did workers in the major factories divide according to a hierarchy based on skill; even those employed in the skilled shops, we are told, split broadly into 'workers' and 'peasants', the former treating the latter with disdain. Admittedly, there was a 'leakage' of talented young peasant apprentices into the cadre proletariat yet can we necessarily assume that this kind of social mobility was widespread, or that many workers were not actually content with their dual status, positively preferring to associate with fellow-*zemlyaki*? Even for the most ambitious peasant-worker, standing in awe of the highly skilled, mature and sophisticated cadres, the transition from one camp to another was not an easy one[29] – for the majority it was unthinkable. They would continue, for a prolonged period at least, to retain much of their peasant cast of mind, together with a direct interest in the future of both town and countryside. It was the PSR, the party of 'land and freedom' which most clearly articulated that interest.

Appendix

Politicheskaya Katorga i ssylka: biograficheskii spravochnik chlenov obshchestva politkatorzhan i ssyl'no-poselentsev (2nd edn, Moscow, 1934)

The Society of Political Prisoners was open to all Soviet citizens who had endured imprisonment or administrative exile for political offences under the tsarist regime and was active during the period 1921–34, at which point it was closed by order of Stalin. The second edition of the directory contains several thousand biographies in all, more than a thousand of which are of former SRs. The data has already been extensively researched by Maureen Perrie and Manfred Hildermeier and an evaluation of its usefulness as a source will be found on pp. 18–24 of the Perrie thesis (see Bibliography). I myself used it primarily in order to obtain information about the social profile of local party activists, particularly in Petersburg, and the findings can be found on pp. 177–88 of my doctoral thesis. In the present work, however, I have used the directory rather more sparingly, mainly as a source of information about individual members of local SR organisations.

Notes and References

Introduction

1. M. P. Perrie, *The Agrarian Policy of the Russian Socialist-Revolutionary Party from its Origins through the Revolution of 1905–1907* (Cambridge, 1976).
2. Manfred Hildermeier, *Die Sozialrevolutionäre Partei Russlands: Agrarsozialismus und Modernisierung im Zarenreich (1900–1914)* (Böhlau: Cologne and Vienna, 1978).
3. The present book is a substantially reduced version of my doctoral thesis: 'The Socialist-Revolutionary Party and the Urban Working Class in Russia, 1902–1914', PhD thesis, University of Birmingham, 1984.
4. '[The] process by which societies have been and are being transformed under the impact of the scientific and technological revolution', C. E. Black, Levy Jansen, *et al.*, *The Modernization of Japan and Russia* (Laven: Macmillan, 1975) here p.3.

1 The Social and Industrial Context: Post-Reform Russia, c. 1861–1910

1. This section is based on the following works:
A. Gerschenkron, 'Agrarian Policies and Industrialization: Russia 1861–1917', in *Cambridge Economic History of Europe (CEHE)*, vol. 6 (Cambridge, 1966), pp. 706–800; A. Gerschenkron, *Economic Backwardness in Historical Perspective* (Cambridge, MA, 1962); A. Gerschenkon, 'Problems and Patterns of Russian Economic Development', in C. E. Black (ed.), *The Transformation of Russian Society* (Cambridge, MA, 1960); A. Gerschenkron, *Europe in the Russian Mirror* (Cambridge, MA, 1970); R. Portal, 'The Industrialisation of Russia', in *CEHE*, vol vi, pp. 801–72; O. Crisp, *Studies in the Russian Economy before 1914* (London, 1976); O. Crisp, 'Labour and Industrialization in Russia', in *CEHE*, vol. vii, pt 2, pp. 308–416; W. L. Blackwell, *The Industrialization of Russia: An Historical Perspective*, 2nd edn (Arlington Heights, 1982); T. H. Von Laue, *Sergei Witte and the Industrialization of Russia* (New York and London, 1963); M. Falkus, *The Industrialization of Russia: 1700–1914* (London, 1972); R. W. Goldsmith, 'The Economic Growth of Tsarist Russia, 1860–1913',

209

in *Economic Development and Cultural Change*, 9 (1961), pp. 441–75; P. Gregory, 'Economic Growth and Structural Change in Tsarist Russia: A Case of Modern Economic Growth?', in *Soviet Studies*, vol. 23, no. 3 (1972), pp. 418–35; P. I. Lyashchenko, *History of the National Economy of Russia to the 1917 Revolution* (New York, 1949; 2nd edn, 1970), pp. 408–692; V. I. Lenin, *The Development of Capitalism in Russia* (Works, English edn vol. 3, 1977); P. A. Khromov, *Ekonomika Rossii perioda promyshlennogo kapitalizma* (Moscow, 1963); P. A. Khromov, *Ekonomicheskaya istoriya SSSR period promyshlennogo i monopolisticheskogo kapitalizma v Rossii*, (Moscow, 1982); M. Tugan-Baranovskii, *Russkaya fabrika v proshlom i nastoyashchem*, vol. ı, 3rd edn (Petersburg, 1907).

2. Gershenkron, 'Agrarian Policies and Industrialization', *CEHE*, vol. vı, pp. 706 ff.

3. Notably, Crisp, 'The Pattern of Industrialization in Russia, 1700–1914', in *Studies in the Russian Economy before 1914*, p. 5; and 'Labour and Industrialization in Russia', *CEHE* vol. vıı, pt 2, pp. 323–9.

4. The best treatment of economic developments and their implications in the first half of the nineteenth century is W. L. Blackwell, *The Beginnings of Russian Industrialization 1800–1860* (Princeton University Press, 1968).

5. Von Laue, *Sergei Witte*, p. 12.

6. A. G. Rashin, *Formirovanie rabochego klassa Rossii* – hereafter *Formirovanie* (Moscow, 1958), p. 117. Between 1860 and 1890 the number of railway workers increased from 11 100 to 248 300.

7. Crisp, 'The Pattern of Industrialization', p. 21.

8. For Witte and the economic policies of his predecessors, see Von Laue, *Sergie Witte and the Industrialization of Russia*; R. Portal in *CEHE*, vol 6, pp. 824 ff. Also Gerschenkron, *Economic Backwardness in Historical Perspective*.

9. Von Laue, *Sergei Witte*, p. 107.

10. Crisp, 'The Pattern of Industrialization', p. 26. By the end of Witte's term, direct taxes accounted for only 17 per cent of budgetary revenue; the figure declined to 12 per cent in 1910 (ibid., p. 27).

11. Crisp, 'The Pattern of Industrialization', p. 26. The length of the railway network increased by 46 per cent between 1892 and 1902 (Von Laue, *Sergei Witte*, p. 265).

12. Crisp, 'The Pattern of Industrialization', pp. 29 for a valuable case study of foreign intervention in Russian industry, see J. P. McKay, *Pioneers for Profit: Foreign Entrepreneurship and Russian Industrialization 1885–1913* (Chicago, 1970).

13. Von Laue, *Sergei Witte*, p. 100.

14. Gerschenkron, 'Russia: Patterns and Problems of Economic Development, 1861–1958', in *Economic Backwardness*, p. 129.

15. Crisp, 'The Pattern of Industrialization', p. 32.

16. For production statistics, and so on, see Lyashchenko, *History of the National Economy of Russia*, pp. 527–8; Khromov, *Ekonomika Rossii*, pp. 102–58.

17. T. S. Fedor, *Patterns of Urban Growth in the Russian Empire during the Nineteenth Century* (Chicago, 1975), p. 35. The overall urban share of the population increased from 5.7 per cent in 1858 to 12.6 per cent in 1897 (Lyashchenko, *History of the National Economy of Russia*, p. 503). For individual urban populations, see Table 100 in Rashin, *Formirovanie*, p. 353 (figures for 1863, 1897, 1914).

18. Lyashchenko, *History of the National Economy of Russia*, pp. 503–8.

19. Von Laue, *Sergei Witte*, p. 188 and *passim*.

20. Rashin, *Formirovanie*, p. 352; Blackwell, *The Industrialization of Russia*, p. 46.

21. Rashin, *Formirovanie*, p. 171, Table 50.

22. Ibid., p. 64, Table 21.

23. Ibid., p. 218, Table 68.

24. Ibid., p. 280, Table 84.

25. Ibid., pp. 275, 276.

26. Between 1863 and 1913 the population of Baku increased 16.7 times, that of Ivanovo-Voznesensk 13.4 times and that of Ekaterinoslav 10.6 times (Rashin, *Formirovanie*, p. 353, Table 100). Before the end of the nineteenth century at least, most of that growth was attributable to immigration rather than natural increase – J. Bater, 'Transience, Residential Persistence and Mobility in Moscow and St Petersburg, 1900–1914', *Slavic Review*, no. 2, 39 (June 1980), p. 240. Of a sample of nearly two million workers surveyed by Pogozhev in 1902, an average of 52.4 per cent were migrants, ranging from 3.4 per cent (Pskov province) to 90.5 per cent (Petersburg) and 90.5 per cent (Moscow city): A. V. Pogozhev, *Uchet chislennosti i sostava rabochikh v Rossii (materialy po statistike truda)* (Petersburg, 1906), p. 93. See also Von Laue, 'Russian Peasants in the Factory, 1892–1904', in *Journal of Economic History*, 21 (1961), pp. 61–80; Von Laue, 'Russian Labour between Field and Factory', *California Slavic Studies*, 3 (1964), pp. 33–65; Richard H. Rowland, 'Urban In-migration in Late Nineteenth-Century Russia' in Michael F. Hamm (ed.), *The City in Russian History* (University of Kentucky, 1976), pp. 115–25.

27. Rashin, *Formirovanie*, p. 514, Table 119; Bater, 'Transience, Residential Persistence and Mobility', p. 241.

28. E. E. Kruze and D. G. Kutsentov, 'Naselenie Peterburga', in *Ocherki Istorii Leningrada*, vol. III, p. 105 (Akademiya Nauk SSSR, 1956).

29. Less than 28 per cent of Moscow's population, according to the 1902 census, were native born and nearly one-third had lived in the city for five years or less. (Bater, 'Transience, Residential Persistence and Mobility', p. 241) In 1912 only 10 per cent of the working population of Moscow had been born there (Diane Koenker, *Moscow Workers in the 1917 Revolution* (Princeton, 1981), p. 47) The most recent and detailed study of migrant workers in Moscow is Joseph Bradley, *Muzhik and Muscovite. Urbanization in Late Imperial Russia* (University of California Press, 1985).

30. Rashin, *Formirovanie*, p. 515.

31. In Khar'kov, for example, more than two-thirds of residents in 1912 had been born in rural areas: Crisp, *CEHE*, vol. vii, pt 2, p. 365. Even in the highly industrialised city of Riga, two-thirds of residents in 1912 had been born elsewhere. See also Rashin, *Formirovanie*, pp. 365–7, Table 101; Pogozhev, *Uchet chislennosti i sostava rabochikh v Rossii*, pp. 95–6.

32. See the article by R. Munting, 'Outside Earnings in the Russian Peasant Farm – the Case of the Tula Province 1900–1917', *Journal of Peasant Studies*, 3 (1976), pp. 428–47. Recent research has indicated the link between heavy areas of emigration and the presence of the following factors: (a) high levels of literacy; (b) accessibility of suitable urban centre; (c) home environment geared to factory and other seasonal wage-labour opportunities providing familiarity with conditions approximating to those prevailing in urban centres. (See Anderson, below, n. 64).

33. 'Probably not more than one-third of the factory labour force, even by 1913, was fully committed to industrial employment in the sense of total severance from farming and a corresponding self-identification' – Crisp, *CEHE*, vol. vii, pt 2, p. 414.

34. M. F. Desjeans, 'The Common Experience of the Russian Working Class: The Case of St. Petersburg, 1892–1904', PhD thesis, Duke University, 1979, p. 55. To enforce the year-round discipline, employers used the carrot (bonuses for staying on over summer or higher wages) and stick methods (long-terms stipulated in contracts, sacking for leaving between April and October, and so on). There were still plenty of opportunities to visit the countryside, however: the average number of working days during the 1890s was around 260 – Crisp, *CEHE*, vol. vii, pt 2, pp. 378, 381.

35. Koenker, *Moscow Workers*, p. 52, n. 33.

36. Rashin, *Formirovanie*, p. 565, Table 136.

37. U. A. Shuster, *Peterburgskie rabochie v 1905–1907gg* (Moscow, 1976), p. 30.

38. S. A. Smith, 'The Russian Revolution and the Factories of Petrograd, Feb 1917 to June 1918', PhD thesis, University of Birmingham, 1980, p. 25.

39. See below, p. 116.

40. Rashin, *Formirovanie*, p. 573, table 142.

41. See n. 17, above.

42. Smith, 'The Russian Revolution and the Factories of Petrograd', p. 26.

43. Ibid., p. 26; Shuster, *Peterburgskie rabochie v 1905–1907*gg, pp. 30–1.

44. V. E. Bonnell, 'The Politics of Labour in Pre-Revolutionary Russia: Moscow Workers' Organisations 1905–1914', PhD thesis, Harvard University, 1975.

45. Smith, 'The Russian Revolution and the Factories of Petrograd', p. 32.

46. Cited by Crisp, *CEHE*, vol. vii, pt 2, p. 372. Note her reservations about the original source, however.

47. Cited by Koenker, *Moscow Workers*, p. 51.

48. Crisp, *CEHE*, vol. vii, pt 2, p. 382; Smith, 'The Russian Revolution and the Factories of Petrograd', p. 33. A survey of Petersburg metalworkers in 1908 found that 53.3 per cent of those employed in plants

with more than 1000 workers each had more than five years experience at their factory (Rashin, *Formirovanie*, p. 505).

49. Smith, 'The Russian Revolution and the Factories of Petrograd', p. 35.
50. See in particular the excellent review of the subject in Smith, 'The Russian Revolution and the Factories of Petrograd', based on memoir material. Also, the discussion of Moscow's Working Class in Koenker, *Moscow Workers*, p. 25 ff.
51. A. Buzinov, *Za Nevskoi Zastavoi – zapiski rabochego Alekseya Buzinova*, p. 21.
52. After loyalty to the shop, 'factory patriotism' was another factor militating against working-class unity. See, for example, the recently published supplement to the memoirs of P. A. Garvi, *Zapiski Sotsial Demokrata (1906–1921)* (Newtonville, MA, 1982), p. 88.
53. See, for example, the survey of Moscow workers conducted during the 1920s by E. O. Kabo, *Ocherki rabochego byta – opyt monograficheskogo issledovaniya domashnego rabochego byta*, vol. ɪ (Moscow, 1928).
54. There is an ever-growing literature on this subject. See, for example: Bradley, *Muzhik and Muscovite. Urbanisation in Late Imperial Russia*; Barbara A. Anderson, 'Internal Migration During Modernization in Late Nineteenth Century Russia', PhD thesis, Columbia University; Jerzy G. Gliksman, 'The Russian Urban Worker', in C. E. Black (ed.), *Transformation of Russian Society*; Bater, 'Transience, Residential Persistence and Mobility'; and *St Petersburg – Industrialization and Change* (London, 1976), pp. 146–9, 302–7 and *passim*; R. E. Johnson, *Peasant and Proletarian – The Working Class of Moscow in the Late Nineteenth Century* (New Brunswick: Rutgers, 1979). On France in the nineteenth Century: E. Weber, *Peasants into Frenchmen – the modernization of rural France 1870–1914* (London, 1977). On Italy in the nineteenth Century: Tilly, Louise, 'The Working Class of Milan 1881–1911', PhD thesis, Toronto, 1974; and 'Italy', in C. L. and R. Tilly, *The Rebellious Century (1830–1930)* (London, 1975). On the Contemporary Third World: Joan M. Nelson, *Migrants, Urban Poverty and Instability in Developing Nations* (Cambridge, MA, 1969); and *Access to Power in Politics and the Urban Poor in Developing Nations* (Princeton, NJ, 1979); Pauline H. Baker, *Urbanization and Political Change: The Politics of Lagos, 1917–1967* (University of California Press, 1974).
55. Tugan-Baranovskii, *Russkaya fabrika*, pp. 513–14.
56. In saying all this one must remember that not only 'pull' factors (for example, better wages, employment opportunities) operated in the migration process. There were also 'push' factors (under-employment, poverty, family conflict, and so on). Thus, in Russia, migration to Siberia was promoted more by the latter; similarly (in all probability) the migrations to Baku from the Volga and Persian regions. One must bear in mind the stubbornly seasonal migration of, for instance, construction workers which tended to remain relatively impervious to urban influences.
57. Shuster, *Peterburgskie rabochie*, p. 24.

58.	Kabo, *Ocherki*, p. 103. Generally the younger generations were heavily over-represented in the populations of many of Russia's cities. See the table in Crisp comparing Moscow and St Petersburg with Berlin in this respect (*CEHE*, vol. vii, pt 2, p. 365).

59.	See Kabo, *Ocherki*; Johnson, *Peasant and Proletarian*; Koenker, *Moscow Workers*. The settling by a worker of his family in the city is seen as an important stage on the road to proletarianisation. Before it could be contemplated, however, workers needed a sizeable income of the kind usually obtainable only in specialised industries such as printing and engineering. According to Semanov, at the turn of the century in Peterburg 38 per cent of married printers, 31 per cent of metalworkers but only 13 per cent of workers employed in textiles lived with their families – S. N. Semanov, *Peterburgskie rabochie nakanune pervoi russkoi revolyutsii* (Akademiya Nauk SSSR: Moscow, 1966), p. 49.

60.	A. Buiko, *Put' rabochego-zapiski starogo bol'shevika* (Moscow, 1934), p. 10. Buiko's isolation is at least partly explained by his place of origin. Vil'no was only the eleventh most common place of origin of Petersburg workers in 1910 (see Table III in Rashin, p. 438) and the traditions and social patterns associated with the Russian commune were weak there – see Francis M. Watters, 'The Peasant and the Village Commune', in W. S. Vucinich (ed.), *The Peasant in Nineteenth Century Russia* (Stanford, 1968), p. 146.

61.	See Leopold Haimson, 'The Problem of Social Stability in Urban Russia, 1905–17', pt. 1: *Slavic Review*, no. 23 (1964), pp. 619–42; pt. 2: no. 24 (1965). Haimson at one point quotes Martov: 'As they [that is, the migrant workers] face the hardships, the darkness of city life, they hold on to their dream of returning to a patch of land and their own cow and chickens ... and they respond to the slogans of those who promise them the fulfilment of this dream'. The nature and social stability of the peasant workers has been recently discussed at length in the debate on labour violence conducted through the medium of the *Slavic Review*. See especially the essay by Daniel R. Brower, 'Labour Violence in Russia in the Late Nineteenth Century', *Slavic Review*, winter 1982, pp. 417–31. Also Johnson, *Peasant and Proletarian*, especially pp. 121 ff.

62.	The manager of the Baltic shipbuilding works in Petersburg, for example, found that peasant workers with a *nadel* were 'the most conservative and independent' element of the workforce. By contrast, workers from the 'townsmen' (*meshchane*) and artisan segments of the population were 'the most restive and ill-disciplined': *Arkhiv Istorii Truda v Rossii* (Petrograd, 1921), pp. 80–1 (the evidence relates to the turn of the century). See also Crisp, *CEHE*, vol. vii, p. 378, on the impact of financial constraints of the peasant worker.

63.	For a full discussion of *zemlyachestvo*, see the works by Johnson and Koenker already cited. The contemporary equivalents in the developing world are treated illuminatingly by Nelson in *Access to Power*, pp. 49–126.

64.	*Ocherki*, pp. 103–11.

65. Shuster, *Peterburgskie rabochie*, p. 22.
66. Johnson, *Peasant and Proletarian*, p. 70.
67. See, for example, the Moscow weaver cited by Kabo, who began work as a sweep at the municipal Duma before being found a job at the Trekhgornyi mill by relatives (*Ocherki*, p. 55). The practice of beginning work in non-factory employment was a common one.
68. Johnson, *Peasant and Proletarian*, p. 69.
69. See Shuster, *Peterburgskie rabochie*, pp. 20–2.
70. Johnson, *Peasant and Proletarian*, pp. 72–7; Koenker, *Moscow Workers*, p. 49.
71. James D. White in his article: 'The Sormovo-Nikolaev Zemlyachestvo in the February Revolution', *Soviet Studies*, XXXI, no. 4 (October 1979), pp. 475–502, makes the point that *zemlyachestvo* was a flexible social institution which had formerly tended to insulate peasant-workers from the industrial environment rather than helping them to come to terms with it. It remains a matter of controversy, however, as to how much *zemlyachestvo* worked against rather than in favour of proletarianisation and urban acculturation.
72. Crisp, 'The Pattern of Industrialization', p. 44.
73. Garvi, *Zapiski Sotsial Demokrata*, p. 71.

2   A New Party and a New Programme

1. Sletov, 'Ocherki', p. 19. For the intellectual history of populism, see the following: A. Walicki, *A History of Russian Thought from the Enlightenment to Marxism* (Stanford, CA, 1979), chs 10–13 and 18; and by the same author, *The Controversy over Capitalism: Studies in the Social Philosophy of the Populists* (Oxford, 1969); F. Venturi, *Roots of Revolution. A History of the Populist and Socialist Movements in Nineteenth Century Russia* (New York, 1966); R. Wortman, *The Crisis of Russian Populism* (Cambridge, 1967); P. Pomper, *The Russian Revolutionary Intelligentsia* (New York, 1970); also Hildermeier, *Die Sozialrevolutionäre Partei*, ch. 1; C. J. Rice, 'The Socialist-Revolutionary Party and the Urban Working Class in Russia, 1902–1914' pp. 30–37.
2. For the rural movement in this period see M. P. Perrie, *The Agrarian Policy of the Socialist-Revolutionary Party*.
3. For biographical sketches of Breshkovskaya and of all other leading actors in the SR movement, see Hildermeier, *Die Sozialrevolutionäre Partei*, pp. 404–12.
4. Sletov, 'Ocherki', pp. 37–8. For the economist trend in Russian Marxism see J. H. L. Keep. *The Rise of Social Democracy in Russia* (Oxford, 1963), especially pp. 54 ff.; A. K. Wildman, *The Making of a Workers' Revolution – Russian Social Democracy, 1891–1903* (Chicago and London, 1967).
5. The following is based on Sletov, 'Ocherki', pp. 30–101; Spiridovitch, *Histoire du terrorisme Russe 1886–1917* (Paris, 1930), pp. 35–108. See also A. Argunov, 'Iz proshlogo partii sotsialistov-revolyutsionerov', in

Byloe no. 10/22 (1907), pp. 94–112; Hildermeier, *Die Sozialrevolutionäre Partei*, pp. 35–57; R. H. Eiter, 'Organisational Growth and Revolutionary Tactics; Unity and Discord in the Socialist-Revolutionary Party, 1901–7', PhD thesis, University of Pittsburg, 1978, pp. 14–53.

6.   For later developments in Petersburg see below, ch. 5, pp. 74–80.
7.   Sletov, 'Ocherki', p. 46.
8.   Specifically on the Ryazan'–Urals railway, at the Sergeev paper mill and the Kruger machine-building plant.
9.   Sletov, 'Ocherki', pp. 55–70; Spiridovitch, *Histoire du terrorisme Russe*, pp. 61 ff.; Hildermeier, *Die Sozialrevolutionäre Partei*, pp. 38–41.
10.   Sletov, 'Ocherki', pp. 70 ff.; Spiridovitch, *Histoire du terrorisme Russe*, pp. 91 ff.; Hildermeier, *Die Sozialrevolutionäre Partei*, pp. 41–3.
11.   Sletov, 'Ocherki', pp. 87–93; Hildermeier, *Die Sozialrevolutionäre Partei*, pp. 43–5.
12.   For details on the League, see Perrie, *The Agrarian Policy of the Russian Socialist-Revolutionary Party*, pp. 24–34.
13.   Sletov, 'Ocherki', pp. 95–101; Spiridovitch, *Histoire du terrorisme Russe* pp. 101–7; Hildermeier, *Die Sozialrevolutionäre Partei* pp. 46–57; Eiter, 'Organisational Growth and Revolutionary Tactics', pp. 40 ff.
14.   On terror and the PSR see: Hildermeier, *Die Sozialrevolutionäre Partei*, pp. 58–68, 358–94; also Hildermeier, 'The Terrorist Strategies of the Socialist-Revolutionary Party in Russia, 1900–1914', in W. J. Mommsen and G. Hirschfeld, *Social Protest, Violence and Terror in Nineteenth and Twentieth Century Europe* (London, 1982), pp. 80–7; Spiridovitch, *Histoire du terrorisme Russe*, ch. 7 and passim; M. P. Perrie (ed.), *Protokoly pervogo* (Introduction); also Perrie, 'Political and Economic Terror in the Tactics of the Russian Socialist-Revolutionary Party before 1914', in Mommsen and Hirschfeld, *Social Protest, Violence and Terror*; B. Savinkov, *Memoirs of a Terrorist* (New York, 1931). For Azef, see Hildermeier, *Die Sozialrevolutionäre Partei*, pp. 380–7 and *passim*.
15.   Savinkov, *Memoirs of a Terrorist*, p. 198.
16.   *Trud* no. 6, Dec 1906, p. 14.
17.   V. M. Zenzinov, *Perezhitoe* (New York, 1953), p. 108.
18.   Details in 'Statistika terroristicheskikh aktov', in *Pamyatnaya knizhka sotsialista-revolyutsionera*, issue 2 (Paris, 1914). (Oblenskii was wounded).
19.   See the propaganda brochure, consisting of two letters by Kachur and a party gloss, in Archive 431.
20.   Savinkov, *Memoirs of a Terrorist*, p. 170.
21.   Acts of local terror continued without obvious interruption.
22.   For Zil'berberg see Hildermeier, *Die Sozialrevolutionäre Partei*, pp. 374ff.
23.   The following summary is based on articles in *Revolyutsionnaya Rossiya*: 'Terroristicheskii element v nashei programme', no. 7 (Jun 1902), pp. 2–6; 'Kak otvechat' na pravitel'stvennyya zverstva', no. 12 (October 1902), pp. 1–3; 'Yuzhnyi rabochii' o sotsialistakh-re-

volyutsionerakh', no. 22 (April 1903), pp. 2–5; 'Terror i massovoe dvizhenie', no. 24 (May 1903), pp. 1–3; 'Po povodu godovshchiny vystrela i kazni G. Lekerta', no. 25 (June 1903), pp. 4–6; 'Nashi zadachi i ikh formuilirovka (zamechaniya na proekt programmy PS-R)', no. 67, supplement (May 1905), pp. 2–3.

24. On the background and history of the first congress see Perrie (ed.), *Protokoly pervogo* (especially Introduction). For the text of the party programme: Perrie, pp. 355–66. The draft can be found in *Revolyutsionnaya Rossiya* (*RR*) no. 46, (May 1904), pp. 1–3.

25. 'The minimum programme is the sum of the partial revolutionary gains [which are] practically advantageous and useful even before the complete removal of the bourgeoisie from the helm of the state' – Victor Chernov, 'Novyya sobytiya i starye voprosy', in *RR*, no. 74 (September 1905), pp. 1–6, here p. 5. There was considerable disagreement over this separation of tasks. See Perrie (ed.), *Protokoly pervogo* (Introduction).

26. *Protokoly 1906*, p. 136 (quoted in O. H. Radkey, *The Agrarian Foes of Bolshevism: Promise and Default of the Russian Socialist-Revolutionaries, February to October 1917* (New York, 1958), p. 45). For a Soviet critique of the SR programme see A. N. Stepanov, 'Kritika V. I. Leninym programmy i taktiki eserov v period novogo revolyutsionnogo pod"ema (1910–1914gg), in *Bolsheviki v bor'be protiv melkoburzhuaznykh partii v Rossii* (Moscow, 1969), pp. 5ff. Also K. V. Gusev, *Partiya eserov: ot melkoburzhuaznogo revolyutsionarizma k kontrrevolyutsii*, ch. 1 (Moscow: Istoricheskii ocherk, 1975).

27. See n. 1 above.

28. Chernov, 'K voprosu o teoreticheskom obosnovanii sotsializma', *RR*, no. 36 (November 1903), pp. 1–5.

29. Ibid., p. 3.

30. On the role of the radical intelligentsia see 'Rabochee dvizhenie i revolyutsionnaya intelligentsiya', in *Vestnik Russkoi Revolyutsii*, no. 2 (February 1902), pp. 211–31. Also Hildermeier, *Die Sozialrevolutionäre Partei*, p. 69.

31. *Protokoly 1906*, p. 136.

32. Workers and peasants, that is. The revolutionary intelligentsia were held to occupy a 'supra class' position, but one favourably disposed to the working class (Hildermeier, *Die Sozialrevolutionäre Partei*, p. 69). The broad use of the term 'working class' caused some disquiet among delegates at the founding congress. See, for example, the speech by 'Rozhdestvenskii' (V. A. Myakotin), *Protokoly 1906*, p. 87. Also B. V. Levanov, *Iz istorii bor'by bol'shevistskoi partii protiv eserov v gody pervoi russkoi revolyutsii* (Leningrad, 1974), pp. 53 ff.

33. 'Sotsial' demokraty i Sotsialisty-Revolyutsionery', *RR*, no. 16 (January 1903), pp. 1–2.

34. 'The entire burden of the struggle with tsarism, despite the presence of a liberal-democratic opposition... falls on the proletariat, the toiling peasantry and the revolutionary-socialist intelligentsia', 'Programma partii', *Protokoly 1906*, p. 360.

35. Ibid., pp. 359–60.

36. See for example, 'Nasushchnye voprosy sovremennoi revolyutsionnoi strategii' in *RR*, no. 50 (August 1904), p. 8.

37. The SRs rarely made any distinction between Bolshevik and Menshevik lines of argument when discussing points of disagreement with the Social Democrats.

38. *RR*, no. 32 (September 1903), p. 5.

39. 'Programma Partii', *Protokoly 1906*, p. 363. For discussion of the agrarian programme of the PSR, see Perrie, *The Agrarian Policy of the Russian Socialist-Revolutionary Party, passim*; Hildermeier, *Die Sozialrevolutionäre Partei*, pp. 83–99; V. N. Ginev, *Agrarnyi vopros i melkoburzhuaznye partii v Rossii v 1917g* (Leningrad, 1977), ch. 1. For the Social Democrat alternatives see M. Loizou, 'The Development of the Agrarian Programme of the Russian Social-Democratic Labour Party', MPhil thesis, University of Birmingham, 1982; A. Hussain and K. Tribe, *Marxism and the Agrarian Question*, vol. II, *Russian Marxism and the Peasantry, 1861–1930* (London, 1982); G. T. Robinson, *Rural Russia Under the Old Regime* (New York, 1949).

40. Quoted by M. P. Perrie, 'The Socialist Revolutionaries on Permanent Revolution', in *Soviet Studies*, 24 (1972–3), p. 411.

41. *RR*, no. 74, (September 1905), p. 5.

42. 'Programma Partii', pp. 361–2.

43. Ibid., pp. 362–3. The Social Democrats did not include a demand for a minimum wage, nor did they mention the possibility of a working day shorter than eight hours. (*Second Congress of the Russian Social Democratic Labour Party*, New Park Publications, 1978, pp. 7–8).

44. Perrie (ed.), *Protokoly pervogo* (Introduction).

45. See below, pp. 64–5.

46. *Protokoly 1906*, p. 106.

47. Ibid., p. 107.

48. Ibid., p. 114.

49. Ibid., p. 102.

50. Ibid., pp. 116–17, 154.

51. Ibid., pp. 115, 119.

52. Ibid., p. 121. The general strike in Novorossiisk lasted from 8 to 25 December 1905.

53. Ibid., pp. 122–3.

54. The relevant portion of Chernov's address can be found in ibid., pp. 147–52.

55. Ibid., p. 150.

56. For the very real complexities confronted in this field during the revolution see E. H. Carr, *The Bolshevik Revolution 1917–23*, vol. II: *The Economic Order* (London, 1952).

57. 'Postanovleniya III s"ezda oblastnoi Ural'skoi organizatsii PSR' (25 June 1906), in *Partiinyya Izvestiya* (*PI*) no. 1 (October 1906), pp. 22–3.

58. 'Zakavkazskaya oblast'. Iz doklada upolnomochennogo Ts.K. o rabote v zakavkazskoi oblasti', in *PI*, no. 9 (May 1907), pp. 12–13; here p. 12 (emphasis in the original).

59. For Sokolov and his Geneva-based group, see below pp. 64–5.

60. See the article 'Anarkhizm v Rossii' in *Sotsialist-Revolyutioner*, no. 3 (1911), pp. 75–94. Also P. Avrich, *The Russian Anarchists* (Princeton, 1967).
61. *Protokoly 1906*, pp. 332–8.
62. Ibid., pp. 334, 337
63. For examples, see the chapters on local organisations in this study.

3 First Acquaintance with the Workers. Propaganda and Agitational Activity on the Ground, 1902–5

1. For general party developments during this period see Hildermeier, *Die Sozialrevolutionäre Partei*, pp. 109–25.
2. See O. H. Radkey, *The Agrarian Foes of Bolshevism*, p. 49.
3. One might add that the SRs found it easier to recruit intelligentsia cadres as a result of the renewal of student disorder at the turn of the century. For the importance of students in the PSR see Hildermeier, *Die Sozialrevolutionäre Partei*, p. 117.
4. Calculations based on information in A. Spiridovitch, *Histoire du terrorisme Russe*, pp. 121, 168, 197–8, 214; though most of his data on the subject can be confirmed from *Revolyutsionnaya Rossiya*, specifically the 'Iz partiinoi deyatel'nosti' section.
5. *RR*, no. 51 (August 1904), p. 23 (North-West); *RR*, no. 59 (February 1905), p. 22 (Siberia); *RR*, no. 63 (April 1905), p. 15 (Volga); *RR*, no. 67 (May 1905), p. 12 (Caucasus).
6. The PSR Peasant Union was the organisation chiefly responsible for revolutionary work in the countryside. It established its own local committees wherever they were needed. But the urban committees and the workers affiliated to them also played a role, both in distributing propaganda and agitating in the rural localities. Comment will be made on this later. See also M. Perrie, *The Agrarian Policy of the Russian Socialist-Revolutionary Party*, p. 70.
7. *RR*, no. 13 (November 1902), pp. 22–3.
8. Ibid. no. 33 (October 1903), p. 20.
9. Ibid. no. 39 (January 1904), p. 39.
10. A survey of material in *RR* revealed specific mention of at least thirteen such bodies which were given a variety of names (Centre, Union, Organisation or Council). They were in Petersburg, Moscow, Odessa, Kiev, Ekaterinoslav, Saratov, Khar'kov, Kishinev, Penza, Vitebsk, Bryansk, Nizhnii-Novgorod and Poltava. Spiridovitch, *Histoire du terrorisme Russe*, has a much smaller list but also mentions Samara and Vil'no. No doubt there were others.
11. The source for the structure of the Odessa committee is a report which appeared in *RR*, no. 73 (August 1905), pp. 21–4. See also Spiridovitch, *Histoire du terrorisme Russe*, p. 218.
12. See the description of the 'typical' party structure described in 'Proekt instruktsii o podgotovitel'noi rabote i boevoi taktike PSR' (*RR*, no. 67, supplement, p. 2).
13. Moscow: *RR*, no. 55 (November 1904), p. 22; Kishinev: *RR*, no. 71

(July 1905), p. 15; Penza: *RR*, no. 73 (August 1905), p. 27. Rules for the fund as opposed to the organisation itself are also available for Kiev: *RR*, no. 19 (March 1903), p. 20; and Saratov: *RR*, no. 14 (December 1902), p. 21.

14. The SRs emphasised that the funds were established first and foremost to advance the political struggle. There may well have been other mutual-help funds to deal with the unemployed, the sick, and so on.

15. The Ekaterinsolav workers' centre was consulted in this way during the general strike of August 1903 (*RR*, no. 33, pp. 12–18), and again in July 1905 (*RR*, no. 73 [August 1905], p. 18]. Also in August 1905 the Bryansk workers' union 'decided to hold a demonstration' (*RR*, no. 74 [September 1905], p. 16).

16. *RR*, no. 61 (March 1905), p. 20; *RR*, no. 67 (May 1905), p. 24; *RR*, no. 68 (June 1905), p. 24; *RR*, no. 75 (September 1905), p. 20.

17. Precision is difficult here because of the term '*tekhnicheskie raskhody*' which sometimes includes printing expenditure. As outlay on this is covered by other entries in this account, '*tekhnicheskie raskhody*' have been omitted from the calculation. If included, 178r must be added to Table 3.1.

18. D. Lane, *The Roots of Russian Communism: A Social and Historical Study of Russian Social Democracy, 1898–1907* (Assen, 1969), p. 106.

19. *RR*, no. 33; *RR*, no. 45, p. 21; *RR*, no. 48, p. 22; *RR*, no. 65, p. 16; *RR*, no. 72, supplement, p. 8; *RR*, no. 72; p. 28; *RR*, no. 75, p. 20.

20. *RR*, no. 45, p. 21.

21. This impression is strengthened by evidence in Hildermeier, *Die Sozialrevolutsionäre Partei*, p. 111, where it is recorded that in the summer of 1902 Azef used Petersburg as a 'distribution centre' for illegal SR literature from abroad.

22. The lists appeared in the 'iz partiinoi deyatel'nosti' sections of the paper.

23. None fit the category 'labour issues'. This is partly because some relevant material is contained in the newspapers issued by the workers' union. This has been included in the first category, but on the basis of one paper counting equal to one proclamation. In addition, of course, many proclamations addressed directly to the workers would have been on 'labour issues'.

24. The others were Belostok, Kiev, Smolensk and Ekaterinoslav. Many produced workers' newspapers during 1906–7.

25. See *RR*, no. 74 (August 1905), p. 27. Also Archive 333.

26. The Governor of Moscow, killed by the SR, Kulikovskii, on 28 June 1905.

27. Discussion now includes titles published by committees and groups outside Moscow and Petersburg.

28. See *RR*, no. 56, p. 18.

29. D. S. Lane (*The Roots of Russian Communism*, p. 83) has pointed to the most noticeable differences, that is, the use of the term *zemskii sobor* for the Constituent Assembly and the call for communal ownership of the land.

30. *RR*, no. 35 (November 1903), pp. 20–2.

31. Kachur, a member of an SR workers' circle in Ekaterinoslav, made an attempt on the life of the Governor of Khar'kov, Prince Obolenskii, in 1902.
32. V. M. Zenzinov, *Perezhitoe*, p. 112.
33. 'Programma zanyatii v rabochikh kruzhkakh', *RR*, no. 28 (July 1903), pp. 21–3.
34. Ibid. p. 21.
35. It was explained that most workers attending the circles would be familiar with both kinds.
36. A comparison of the amount of space consumed in describing the two stages provides an idea of how much more expansive; the first was described in 29 lines, the second took 117.
37. 'Propagandist, k voprosu o zanyatiyakh v rabochikh kruzhkakh', in *RR*, no. 49 (July 1904), pp. 7–10. The material which follows also draws on two later contributions from Kiev; a programme for elementary circles (*RR*, no. 53, supplement (September 1904), pp. 11–12) and another for 'flying' circles, *RR*, no. 65 (April 1905), p. 15. See also: Programma dlya zanyatii sredi rabochikh v 1906g, Archive 478 and Programma chteniya (issued by Vyatka student group, 1906), Archive 548.
38. It was stressed that the content should be kept flexible, and be dependent to an extent, on the response of the workers themselves.
39. The picture has been vividly drawn by an SR propagandist in Moscow: Mark V. Vishnyak, *Dan' proshlomu* (New York, 1954), pp. 101–2.
40. See Hildermeier, *Die Sozialrevolutionäre Partei*, p. 225,
41. It was common practice for organisations with their own printing press to produce literature for others. The Ekaterinoslav group, for example, used literature produced in Saratov and Kiev, while an Ekaterinoslav activist later drew up and helped distribute proclamations for the SRs in Belostok (Eiter, 'Organisational Growth', p. 99).
42. *RR*, no. 29 (August 1903), p. 16.
43. *RR*, no. 12 (October 1902), p. 12. A Social-Democrat report acknowledged that this demonstration was called 'on the initiative of the SR group' (*Iskra*, no. 18 [February 1902], p. 2). See also J. Schneiderman, *Sergei Zubatov and Revolutionary Marxism. The Struggle for the Working Class in Tsarist Russia* (Ithaca and London, 1976), p. 296.
44. Schneiderman, *Sergei Zubatov*, p. 296.
45. *Iskra*, no. 34 (December 1902), p. 6.
46. *RR*, no. 25 (June 1903), pp. 22–3; *Iskra*, no. 42 (May 1903), p. 7.
47. *RR*, no. 29 (August 1903), p. 4. For the SD account of events see *Iskra*, no. 47 (September 1903), p. 8.
48. *RR*, no. 36 (November 1903), p. 17. This was the third printing press, at least, to have been seized by the Odessa police during 1903 (Eiter, 'Organisational Growth', p. 78.
49. *RR*, no. 4 (February 1902), pp. 22–3. A Social-Democrat report acknowledges SR involvement in the distribution of leaflets: *Iskra*, no. 17 (February 1902), pp. 2–4.
50. *Iskra*, no. 19 (March 1903), p. 13.

51.	The PSR placed a high value on this form of activity during 1903–4. See Perrie, *Agrarian Policy*, pp. 88–90.

52.	*RR*, no. 23 (May 1903), pp. 10–12.

53.	*RR*, no. 33 (October 1903), pp. 19–20; *Iskra*, no. 47 (September 1903), pp. 6–7. The SDs claimed to have originally been against a demonstration but to have later changed their minds. The reason for the failure, they argued, was the fact that leaflets announcing the event only appeared two hours before it was due to take place.

54.	The following account is based on: *RR*, no. 31 (September 1903), pp. 17–19; *RR*, no. 33 (October 1903), pp. 12–18; and *Iskra*, no. 47 (September 1903), pp. 7–8.

55.	The SDs claim initially to have agreed on a common date, but admitted that in the event they failed to provide adequate notice of their intention to begin the strike on 7 August rather than 4 August.

56.	The *Iskra* account mentions some stone-throwing at the Tube factory and records that the manager there appeared at the gates with a revolver.

57.	The *Iskra* source makes clear that the SDs were anxious to avoid giving the strike a political complexion.

58.	*RR*, no. 42 (March 1904), p. 18.

59.	The report of the PSR to the Socialist International in Amsterdam (August 1904) provides little information to supplement that already available in *Revolyutsionnaya Rossiya*. See: *Rapport du Parti Socialiste Revolutionnaire de Russie au Congrès Socialiste International d'Amsterdam* (Paris, 1904). Also Hildermeier, on a conference of the SR Foreign Organisation in July of the same year in *Die Sozialrevolutionäre Partei*, pp. 117–18.

60.	*RR*, no. 9 (July 1902), pp. 12–13.

61.	Archive 474. See below, p. 1630.

62.	*RR*, no. 21 (April 1903), pp. 9–10. In May 1903 the Fighting Organisation took revenge on behalf of the workers by assassinating the Governor (Bogdanovich).

63.	*RR*, no. 18 (February 1903), p. 15; no. 21 (April 1903), p. 12.

64.	D. Lane, *The Roots of Russian Communism*, p. 165.

65.	*RR*, no. 37 (December 1903), p. 20.

66.	Ibid.

67.	*RR*, no. 39 (January 1904), p. 14.

68.	*RR*, no. 42 (March 1904), p. 18.

69.	Spiridovitch, *Histoire du terrorisme Russe*, p. 203.

70.	*RR*, no. 52 (September 1904), p. 22.

71.	*RR*, no. 46 (March 1904), p. 16.

72.	*RR*, no. 40 (January 1904), p. 19; no. 46 (May 1904), p. 22.

73.	*RR*, no. 39 (January 1904), p. 14.

74.	*RR*, no. 56, supplement (December 1904), p. 24.

75.	*RR*, no. 50 (August 1904), p. 18.

76.	*RR*, no. 38 (December 1903), p. 15.

77.	Apart from *RR* these sources include: V. Zenzinov, *Perezhitoe*, chs 4–7; M. V. Vishnyak, *Dan' proshlomu*, ch. 3; *Rapport du parti Socialiste-Revolutionnaire de Russie au Congrès Socialiste Inter-*

national de Stuttgart (Ghent, 1907; hereafter, *Rapport 1907*), pp. 53–63;
Ocherki rabot v tsentral'noi oblasti, Archive 676; and Hildermeier, *Die
Sozialrevolutionäre Partei*, pp. 251–7.

78. *RR*, no. 30 (August 1903), p. 22; no. 55 (November 1904), p. 22.
79. Zenzinov was followed shortly afterwards by another, subsequently
distinguished figure in the party, V. V. Rudnev. For biographical
sketches of both, see Hildermeier, *Die Sozialrevolutionäre Partei*, p.
410 (Rudnev) and p. 412 (Zenzinov).
80. Already in February, in fact, 'almost all members of the group' had
been arrested. This was the opportunity for a younger, more energetic
element to take over (*Rapport 1907*, p. 54). The activists in the party at
that time consisted of two-thirds students; teachers, medical orderlies,
several workers and two or three women from solid bourgeois families
(Hildermeier, *Die Sozialrevolutionäre Partei*, p. 253).
81. *RR*, no. 46 (May 1904), p. 18.
82. Zenzinov, *Perezhitoe*, p. 131.
83. *RR*, no. 58 (January 1905), pp. 14–15; *Rapport 1907*, p. 55. I could find
only eleven biographies of Moscow workers in PKS (for details of this
source, see Appendix). They comprised: one compositor, one
draughtsman, one painter, one baker, one fitter, one smelter, one
'factory worker', one 'worker', one blacksmith and two workers
identified as belonging to the Prokhorov textile mill. Both I. M.
Kukleev and S. O. Komissarov were members of the Moscow Soviet in
1905. Komissarov (aged 25 in 1905) also served on the revolutionary
council during the December uprising.
84. *RR*, no. 57 (December 1904), p. 17.

4 The SRs and the Revolution of 1905–7: An Overview

1. Hildermeier, *Die Sozialrevolutionäre Partei*, p. 254.
2. *RR*, no. 58 (January 1905), p. 15.
3. *RR*, no. 67 (May 1905), pp. 11–12; no. 68 (June 1905), p. 20. The
former report provides some indication of the type of workers attracted
to the PSR in Moscow. Party agitators preferred operating in the
countryside because they considered themselves to be essentially
village people. Many SRs here demanded weapons.
4. *RR*, no. 74 (September 1905), p. 26; *Rapport 1907*, p. 58.
5. Spiridovitch, *Histoire du terrorisme Russe*, pp. 216–17.
6. *RR*, no. 61 (March 1905), p. 13; *Iskra*, no. 93 (February 1905), p. 7
claims that the 'revolutionary committee (from which the SD's
disassociated themselves) sent a letter threatening terror if their
demands were not met'.
7. *RR*, no. 64 (April 1905), p. 12. See also *Chemu uchit Saratovskaya
zabastovka*, Archive 521/II, and *Iskra*, no. 86 (January 1905), p. 5.
8. *RR*, no. 69 (June 1905), p. 19. *Iskra*, no. 90 (January 1905), p. 5.
9. *RR*, no. 59 (February 1905), pp. 15–16; *Iskra*, no. 86 (January 1905), p.
5. There were fierce disagreements between SRs and SDs about the aim
and direction of this strike.

224   *Notes and References to pp. 60–4*

10. *RR*, no. 63 (April 1905), p. 13.
11. *RR*, no. 70 (July 1905), p. 19.
12. *RR*, no. 69 (June 1905), p. 19; no. 66 (May 1905), p. 14.
13. *RR*, no. 68 (June 1905), p. 21.
14. What follows is based on two reports in *RR*: no. 73 (August 1905), p. 21 and no. 74 (September 1905), p. 16. The biographies of eleven workers in the Odessa PSR were discovered in the PKS source. They comprised one merchant seaman, one joiner, one typographer, one railway technician, one fitter/boiler-maker, one builder, one pattern-maker, one shop-assistant, one 'unskilled worker' and two 'workers'. Six of the sample were Jewish, two Ukrainian.
15. See Spiridovitch, *Histoire du terrorisme Russe*, pp. 218–20.
16. *RR*, no. 72 (August 1905), p. 18.
17. Riga: *RR*, no. 75 (September 1905), p. 13; Kiev: *RR*, no. 75 (September 1905), p. 13; Bryansk: *RR*, no. 74 (September 1905), p. 19; Novozyb-kov: *RR*, no. 72 (August 1905), p. 19.
18. For the following see *Rapport 1907*. Contemporary accounts of SR activity during the October–December period in particular are almost wholly lacking. *Revolyutsionnaya Rossiya* ceased to appear after 15 October 1905 and its successor, *Syn Otechestva* was a legal paper with only a general populist direction and as such devoted little space to specific party activity. Recourse has therefore had to be made to a variety of retrospective accounts.
19. *Rapport 1907, passim*, pp. 216–17, 226, 234, 236, 249–50.
20. These are based on a survey of thirty-six urban and regional organisations. They tend to confirm the findings of Hildermeier and Perrie (see Bibliography) on the social composition of the party, namely that urban worker activists comprised about half the total in the party as a whole.
21. These included Dvinsk, Vitebsk, Khar'kov, Tiflis and Zlatoust. The Stuttgart report included Nikolaev and Ekaterinoslav in its list of strong urban organisations, but there is no information on member-ship figures for these two centres (*Rapport 1907*, p. 242). The term 'organised' workers was generally used by the SRs to imply something broader than 'members' but more precise than 'sympathisers'. Membership was often limited to leading cadres and to the participants in propaganda circles. Caution is in any case appropriate where membership figures are concerned. There was considerable disagree-ment and confusion over what precise qualifications the party required for membership – some organisations appear to have made only the vaguest demands. (The same was undoubtedly the case with the other revolutionary parties.) For further information on this question, see the debates in *Protokoly 1906*, pp. 294–301; *Protokol 1907*, pp. 109–32.
22. The information on arrests is in Spiridovitch, *Histoire du terrorisme Russe*, pp. 502–3. For a further revealing and comprehensive account of the party's disintegration see *Protokoly pervoi obshche-partiinoi konferentsii PSR* (Paris, 1908; hereafter *Protokoly 1908*). On the later history of the party, see pp. 275–86 of my doctoral thesis.

23. That is, the group of 'legal populists' who worked on the journal of that name. Three of its most prominent members, N. F. Annenskii, V. A. Myakotin and A. F. Peshekhonov, later collaborated on the SR legal newspaper *Syn Otechestva* in 1905 and attended the founding congress of the party. The legal populists established themselves as an independent Party of Popular Socialists in the spring of 1906, but never gained a mass following. For further details see Perrie, *The Agrarian Policy of the Russian Socialist-Revolutionary Party*, pp. 160–7; Hildermeier, *Die Sozialrevolutionäre Partei*, pp. 145–50; also A. F. Peshekhonov, *Pochemu my togda ushli* (Petrograd, 1918).

24. For a full bibliography and discussion of Maximalism see Hildermeier, *Die Sozialrevolutionäre Partei*, pp. 126–41. Also Perrie, *The Agrarian Policy of the Russian Socialist-Revolutionary Party* pp. 153–60; Spiridovitch, *Histoire du terrorisme Russe*, pp. 392–413. The major work in Russian is by V. Chernov, 'K kharakteristike maksimalizma', in *Sotsialist-Revolyutsioner*, no. 1 (1910), pp. 175–307. See also B. I. Gorev, 'Apoliticheskiya i antiparlamentskiya gruppy', in *Obshchestvennoe dvizhenie v Rossii v nachale XX-go veka* (St Petersburg, 1914) vol. iii, book V, pp. 511–23.

25. For the thinking of the Geneva group, see *Vol'nyi diskussionyi listok – izdanie gruppy sotsialistov-revolyutsionerov*, nos. 1–3, 1 May – 5 July 1905).

26. See, for example, this statement in *Vol'nyi diskussionyi listok*, no. 3 (5 July 1905), pp. 7–8: 'To resolve this task [that is, the setting up of urban communes during the forthcoming revolution] it is by no means necessary to have on hand a developed socialist conscious-ness in the mass of the urban population: it is quite sufficient to have the energetic, daring initiative of a revolutionary-socialist minority, prepared for its historic role by an understanding of the fundamental principles of workers' socialism and surrounded by the active sympathy of the masses, also prepared for revolution by their sufferings and in sympathy with the practical demands of socialism.'

27. Spiridovitch, *Histoire du terrosime Russe*, p. 395. Sokolov transferred his operations to Petersburg early in 1906 and founded an independent combat detachment in July. In August, the Maximalists were responsible for a failed attempt to kill Prime Minister P. A. Stolypin by blowing up his villa on Petersburg's Aptekarskii Island and, in October, for a major bank robbery on the Fonarnyi Alley. Soon afterwards, Sokolov founded the 'Union of SR Maximalists'. Some of the leading group were arrested in November, however, and Sokolov himself was taken on 1 December and executed the following day. In April 1907 there were more arrests, effectively destroying the Maximalists' Combat Organisation. There were still workers calling themselves Maximalists in Petersburg, however, as late as 1910.

28. For a more detailed history of the Moscow Opposition, see Chernov, 'K kharakteristike maksimalizma', pp. 203–28 and Hildermeier, *Die Sozialrevolutionäre Partei*, pp. 131–3. The judgement on the calibre of its leadership is Chernov's.

29. The Opposition accused the committee of 'bossing about' and of being a clique of rich and well-connected persons, indifferent to the needs of the worker membership (Chernov, 'K kharakteristike maksimalizma', p. 204).

30. The outlawing of private as opposed to state expropriations was a decision of the second party council in October 1906 and was ratified by the second 'extraordinary' congress in February 1907 (*Protokoly 1907*, p. 148). The Opposition had in fact been allocated a seat at the first party congress but the delegate had been forced to hide from the police and consequently missed all but the last session of the proceedings.

31. For the text, see *Platforma*, Archive 333. Relations between the Central Committee and the Opposition worsened further, owing to a quarrel over the sum of 45 000 roubles, allegedly defrauded from the Opposition by the Moscow *oblast* organisation. The Opposition version of events can be found in two MSS in Archive 333, the former dated 29 May 1906. For the Central Committee's account, see Chernov, 'K kharakteristike maksimalizma', pp. 223 ff.

32. Chernov, 'K kharakteristike maksimalizma', p. 220. The Maximalists first gained control of the Rogozh *raion*, then of the Executive Committee itself.

33. Ibid., pp. 215–16.

34. Ibid., pp. 225–8. For other (scanty) information on the Moscow PSR, see Archive 333.

35. Hildermeier lists eighteen affected organisations, namely Stavropol', Ryazan', Belostok, Pinsk, Grodno, Bryansk, Minsk, Vil'no, Vitebsk, Dvinsk, Ekaterinoslav, Chernigov, Kiev, Khar'kov, Vologda, Pskov, Arkhangel'sk and, of course, Moscow. There is also some evidence of Maximalist activity in Petersburg (see chapter 5 of the present work).

36. See the section on the North-West *oblast'* in chapter 6 of the present study.

37. The Bezhetsa factory (Bryansk) organisation is an example of this last-mentioned course. See p. 155.

38. Chernov, 'K kharakteristike maksimalizma', pp. 175–84.

39. The phrase is Chernov's.

40. See chapter 6 of this study.

41. For the psychology of such workers, see Mikhail Ivanovich, 'Anarkhizm v Rossii', in *Sotsialist-Revolyutsioner*, no. 3 (1911), pp. 75–94.

42. See above p. 144.

43. Spiridovitch, *Histoire du terrorisme Russe*, p. 233.

44. 'Statistika terroristicheskikh aktov', in *Pamyatnaya knizhka sotsialista-revolyutsionera*, second issue (Paris, 1914). See also 'Political and Economic Terror in the Tactics of the Russian Socialist-Revolutionary Party before 1914', in W. J. Mommsen and G. Hirschfeld, *Social Protest, Violence and Terror in Nineteenth and Twentieth Century Europe* (London, 1982).

45. 'Ustav organizatsii boevykh druzhin pri Spb. komitete PSR', in *Trud*, no. 5, p. 9.

46. *Rapport 1907*, pp. 58–9.

47. For Petersburg terror see ch. 5 note 75 below; for the Saratov incident: 'K grazhdanam g. Saratova', archive 521/II
48. *RR*, no. 76, p. 21.
49. See n. 30 above.
50. For details see: *Materialy III-go soveta partii*, Archive 679.
51. See ch. 6, section entitled SRs in the Mal′tsev Industrial District (Bryansk) below.

5 The Socialist-Revolutionaries in Petersburg – A Case Study

1. Rashin, *Formirovanie*, p. 353, Table 100 and p. 354. Bater, *St. Petersburg – Industrialization and Change*, pp. 309–10. The average annual growth was 50 000. During the slump years (c. 1901–4) the figure dropped to nearer 40 000 but then picked up rapidly: there was an increase of 107 000 in 1913 alone.
2. Rashin, *Formirovanie*, p. 514. See also S. A. Smith, 'The Russian Revolution and the Factories of Petrograd, February 1917 to June 1918', PhD thesis, University of Birmingham, p. 24.
3. For industrial population figures see: Rashin, *Formirovanie*, pp. 196, 354; Smith, 'The Russian Revolution and the Factories of Petrograd', p. 14; D. Lane, *The Roots of Russian Communism*, p. 63; Bater, *St. Petersburg – Industrialization and Change*, p. 213.
4. Rashin, *Formirovanie*, p. 361; M. F. Desjeans, 'The Common Experience of the Russian Working Class – The Case of St. Petersburg, 1892–1904', pp. 52, 55; S. H. Semanov, *Peterburgskie rabochie nakanune pervoi russkoi revolyutsii*, p. 40. According to the 1910 census, about 10 per cent of members of the peasant estate intended to 'work in the fields during the summer, but this of course would include non-factory workers' (Bater, *St. Petersburg – Industrialization and Change*, p. 255).
5. Bater, *St. Petersburg – Industrialization and Change*, p. 257.
6. E. E. Kruze, *Polozhenie rabochego klassa Rossii v 1900–1914 godakh* (Leningrad, 1976), p. 67.
7. See above, p. 13.
8. For a detailed study of the Petersburg metalworking industry before 1914, see: Heather Hogan, 'Labour and Management in Conflict: The St. Petersburg Metal-Working Industry 1900–1914', PhD thesis, University of Michigan, 1981.
9. In 1897, 44 per cent of textile workers in Petersburg were literate, compared with 73 per cent of metalworkers (Rashin, *Formirovanie*, p. 591).
10. Semanov, *Peterburgskie rabochie*, p. 44 (5.3 per cent of metal workers were juveniles, as were 23 per cent of workers in the clothing and shoe industry.)
11. For the history of populism in Petersburg see the following: R. Pipes, *Social Democracy and the St. Petersburg Labour Movement, 1885–1897* (Cambridge, MA, 1963), pp. 13–15, 88–9, 113–14; Franco Venturi, *Roots of Revolution, passim*, pp. 507–58; R. E. Zelnik, *Labor and*

   Society in Tsarist Russia: The Factory Workers of St. Petersburg (1855–1870) (Stanford, CA, 1971).

12. *RR*, no. 33 (October 1903), p. 20; *RR*, no. 36 (November 1903), p. 15. See also Hildermeier, *Die Sozialrevolutionäre Partei*, pp. 257–8.

13. *RR*, no. 36 (November 1903), p. 15. Two attacks on the Petersburg SRs were published in subsequent issues of *Iskra* (nos 41 and 42). In the former it was alleged that ties with the workers were 'insignificant' (p. 5).

14. M. Mitel'man, V. Glebov and A. Ul'yanskii, *Istoriya Putilovskogo Zavoda, 1801–1917* (Moscow, 1961), here p. 164. A similar reaction was recorded at the Nevskii Shipbuilding Plant the following year, after an SR had assassinated the Grand Duke Sergei. See *Za Nevskoi Zastavoi – zapiska rabochego Aleksaya Buzinova*, p. 59.

15. M. Bortnik, 'V 1901–04gg na Peterburgskom trubochnom zavode', in *Krasnaya Letopis'*, 1 (1929), pp. 182 ff.

16. See below p. 83.

17. See 'Appeal of the Council of the St. Petersburg Workers' Union PSR to the Petersburg Workers', *Trud*, no. 1–2 (September 1906), pp. 15–16.

18. The biographies of Bitsenko-Kameristaya and Loiko-Kvashnina are taken from *Politicheskaya katorga i ssylka: bibliograficheskii spravochnik chlenov obshchestva politkatorzhan i ssyl'no-poselentsev* (Moscow, 1934, afterwards PKS). See Appendix for further details on this source. The biography of Bulgakov is in *Znamya Truda*, no. 28–9, p. 23.

19. Uneasy relations are clearly hinted at in a retrospective article in *Trud*, no. 1–2 (September 1906), pp. 15–16.

20. See 'Manifest Peterburgskogo rabochego soyuza PSR', in *RR*, no. 62 (March 1905), p. 1; *Trud*, no. 1–2 (September 1906), pp. 15–16.

21. The best treatment of the subject in English to date is by W. Sablinsky, *The Road to Bloody Sunday – Father Gapon and the Petersburg Massacre of 1905*, (Princeton, 1977). See also the two-part article by Gerald D. Surh, 'Petersburg's First Mass Labor Organisation – The Assembly of Russian Workers and Father Gapon', in *Russian Review*, vol. 40, no. 3 (July 1981), pp. 241–63; no. 4 (October 1981), pp. 412–41. Surh's article confirms the impression that there was very little direct contact between the Gapon movement and the PSR.

22. See Sablinsky, *The Road to Bloody Sunday*, pp. 185–93.

23. *RR*, no. 58 (January 1905), pp. 9, 22.

24. For the significance of this meeting see Surh, 'Petersburg's First Mass Labor Organisation', p. 425.

25. *RR*, no. 60 (March 1905), p. 17.

26. A good account of the period is given by the Menshevik, D. Kol'tsov, 'Rabochiie v 1905g', in *Obshchestvennoe dvizhenie v Rossii v nachale XX go veka* (Petersburg, 1914).

27. Buzinov, *Za Nevskoi Zastavoi*.

28. Ibid., p. 52.

29. Ibid., p. 59.

30. *'Obukhovtsy' – istoriya zavoda 'Bol'shevik' (byvshego obukhovskogo staleliteinogo zavoda)* (2nd edn, Leningrad, 1965), here pp. 180 ff.

31. Mitelman *et al. Istoriya Putilovskogo Zavoda*, p. 219.
32. See the obituary of Ivan Stepanovich in *Trud*, no. 10 (March 1907), p. 7, where it is said that an SR organisation was formed there in October 1905.
33. Unfortunately, there is no opportunity to compare arms spending by the SRs in Petersburg with that of the Social Democrats. However, SD evidence is available for Moscow (see D. Lane, *The Roots of Russian Communism*, pp. 106–7. Of a total income of 25 523 r. received between December 1904 and July 1905 (7 months), the SRs in Petersburg spent 9729 r. (51 per cent of expenditure on arms). The Social Democrats in Moscow spent 13 220 r. (17 per cent) on arms out of a total income of 57 416 r. between March and October 1905 (7 months). The comparison may, however, be a misleading one. See Lane, p. 78. (The SR information is in *RR*. See pp. 34–7 above.)
34. *Iskra*, no. 100 (May 1905), p. 4; no. 107 (June 1905), p. 5; 'Za Narvskoi Zastavoi letom 1905 goda', *Krasnaya Letopis*', no. 2 (1926), p. 166; U. A. Shuster, 'Peterburgskie rabochie v gody pervoi russkoi revolyutsii (1905–7gg)', in *Istoriya rabochikh Leningrada* (hereafter *IRL*; Leningrad, 1972), p. 282.
35. Buzinov, *Za Nevskoi Zastavoi*, pp. 63–4, 79.
36. See, for example, 'Preddverie revolyutsii', *RR* no. 8 (January 1905), pp. 1–3; 'Boevoi moment', no. 59 (February 1905), pp. 1–4; summary of proclamation: 'Otvet tsarya rabochemu narodu', *ibid*, p. 21.
37. The full story can be found in M. Futrell, *Northern Underground – Episodes of Russian Revolutionary Transport and Communications through Scandinavia and Finland, 1863–1917* (London, 1963), pp. 66–85. The SRs paid for the weapons with money collected by Breshkovskaya during a successful fund-raising tour of the USA during 1904. See Hildermeier, *Die Sozialrevolutionäre Partei*, p. 144. n. 10.
38. See above, pp. 35–7.
39. Buzinov, *Za Nevskoi Zastavoi*, pp. 66–70.
40. *RR*, no. 76 (September 1905), p. 28.
41. The titles of fifty-seven proclamations issued by the Petersburg SRs between January and September 1905 are listed in *RR*.
42. These remarks are based on the evidence of PKS.
43. Lane, *The Roots of Russian Communism*, p. 74.
44. Sample assembled from information in PKS.
45. Lane, *The Roots of Russian Communism*, pp. 85–6; Anne D. Morgan, 'The St. Petersburg Soviet of Workers' Deputies – A Study of Labour Organisation in the 1905 Revolution', Ph.D thesis, University of Indiana, 1979, pp. 109–11.
46. For Bryukkel, Khachko, Piskarev and Sokolev, see Morgan, 'The St. Petersburg Soviet of Workers' Deputies'. For Feit and Avksent'ev see Hildermeier, *Die Sozialrevolutionäre Partei*, pp. 404, 406. For the remainder, see PKS. It is also known that a deputy at the Artur' Koppel factory (Moskovskii *raion*) was an SR and that there was a second SR deputy at the Putilov Plant.
47. Cited by Spiridovitch, *Historie du terrorisme Russe*, pp. 268–9. For further comment on SR policy (though not on the Petersburg

organisation's implementation of it), see O. Anweiler, *The Soviets – The Russian Workers, Peasants and Soldiers' Councils, 1905–1921* (New York, 1974), pp. 91–6; for alleged intervention by Chernov, see L. D. Trotsky, *1905* (New York, 1972), p. 220.

48. *Istoriya soveta rabochikh deputatov goroda Sankt Peterburga* (Petersburg, 1906), p. 150.
49. Morgan, 'The St. Petersburg Soviet of Workers' Deputies'; V. M. Chernov, *Pered burei – vospominaniia* (New York, 1953).
50. *RR*, no. 73 (August 1905), p. 27.
51. Chernov, *Pered burei*.
52. This policy would presumably have begun to gain acceptance as the month progressed and the workers in a number of enterprises drifted back to work, reluctant to renew industrial action.
53. *Izvestiya soveta rabochikh deputatov goroda Sankt Peterburga*, no. 5 (3 November); no. 6 (5 November); no. 7 (7 November).
54. Buzinov, *Za Nevskoi Zastavoi*, pp. 94–101.
55. Morgan, 'The St. Petersburg Soviet of Workers' Deputies', p. 307; Mitel'man *et al.*, *Istoriya Putilovskogo Zavoda*, pp. 252–6.
56. Spiridovitch, *Historie du terrorisme Russe*, pp. 270–1. (The author recalls that A. F. Kerenskii was among those arrested in one of the December raids.)
57. U. A. Shuster, *IRL*, p. 292.
58. D. Lane, *The Roots of Russian Communism*, p. 92.
59. State factories led the way in locking out their workers, Shuster, *IRL*, p. 292.
60. See 'Deyatel'nost' S. Peterburgskogo obshchestva dlya sodeistviya uluchsheniyu i razvitiyu fabrichno-zavodskoi promyshlennosti', in *Trud*, no. 11 (March 1907), pp. 5–8.
61. D. Antoshkin, *Professional'noe dvizhenie v Rossii – posobie dlya samoobrazovaniya i kursov po professional'nomu dvizheniyu* (3rd edn; Moscow, 1925), pp. 149–50.
62. Shuster, *Petersburgskie rabochie v 1905–07gg*, p. 206. Eleven of the largest enterprises closed, including the Obukhov, Nevskii and Baltic factories and the workshops of the Warsaw Railway.
63. *Ibid.*, pp. 208–9. By May, 15 776 were unemployed in Petersburg itself, 30 000 including the suburbs. SR estimates vary from 8000–10 000 but may include only the permanently unemployed within the city boundary. See *Trud, passim* and A. Levin, *The Second Duma: A Study of the Social Democratic Party and the Constitutional Experiment* (Yale, 1940).
64. Shuster, *IRL*, p. 303. Of 330 individuals surveyed, 29 per cent lost work through production cut-backs, 34 per cent for involvement in political strikes, 15 per cent for their political convictions and/or revolutionary activity, and 7.5 per cent for differences with the administration. A survey of the Town district revealed similar findings (Shuster, *Peterburgskie rabochie v 1905–07gg*, p. 207).
65. See, for example, a report from the Rechkin Wagon Works in *Rech'*, no. 23 (17 March 1906), p. 4. Also Mitel'man *et al.*, *Istoriya Putilovskogo*, p. 272.

66. *Rech'* no. 9 (12 January 1907), p. 4; Bater, *St. Petersburg: Industrialization and Change*, pp. 510–11.
67. There were half a dozen such projects, the most significant being the construction of earthworks at Galernyi Harbour. See Levin, *The Second Duma; Trud*, no. 14, p. 6; Shuster, *Peterburgskie rabochie v 1905–07gg*, p. 224. The elections to the 'Council for the Unemployed' took place during March and April 1906 and included factory representatives. In addition to the town council there were eight *raion* councils. Most of the councils were dominated by the Social Democrats (Shuster, p. 221; *Trud*, no. 14, p. 6).
68. In any case, 1500 workers had been removed from the public works schemes by the end of 1907 (Levin, *The Second Duma*, p. 366). According to Soviet sources, assistance from the city Duma more or less ceased from October 1906 (Shuster, *IRL*, p. 323).
69. Of the SRs in PKS who joined the party before 1907, 13 (17 per cent) were finally taken out of circulation during 1906. The situation got considerably worse in 1907, when 23 (nearly 30 per cent) were arrested.
70. *Trud*, no. 1–2 (September 1906), p. 17.
71. *Trud*, no. 10 (March 1907), p. 7.
72. There are references to disruption in a number of district reports. In *Trud*, for example, no. 4, p. 7 (Kolpino), no. 1–2 (Kolomenskii), no. 8, p. 14 (Moskovskii and Narvskii).
73. *Trud*, no. 5, p. 7. Five new workers' circles and 7 students circles were formed at that time.
74. Groups at the Nevskii and Aleksandrovskii factories, for example, remained more or less intact during this period (*Trud*, no. 1–2, p. 21; *Trud*, no. 4, p. 15), and the Moskovskii *raion* organisation seems to have survived the summer. Even after the arrest of the *intelligenty*, worker-members generally managed to keep things ticking over until replacement organisors were found.
75. Reactionary groups and societies began to form in the spring of 1905 or even earlier. By far the most significant of them was 'The Union of the Russian People', which was not founded until November. By the close of the year, there may have been well over 2000 workers formed into URP 'black-hundred' detachments in Petersburg (there were said to be 300 armed men at the Putilov factory alone). Of course there were many more sympathisers. See 'Chernaya sotnya na fabrikakh i zavodakh Peterburga v gody reaktsii', *Krasnaya Letopis*', no. 1 (1929), pp. 154–81, here p. 167; J. J. Brock, Jnr, 'The Theory and Practice of Black Hundred Politics', PhD thesis, Michigan, 1977; D. C. Rawson, 'The Union of the Russian People, 1905–1907 – a Study of the Radical Right', PhD thesis, Washington, 1971; Buzinov, *Za Nevskoi Zastavoi*; H. Rogger, 'The Formation of the Russian Right, 1900–1906', *California Slavic Studies*, 3 (1964), pp. 66–94; and H. Rogger, 'Was There a Russian Fascism? The Union of the Russian People', *Journal of Modern History*, 36 (1964), pp. 398–415.
76. Rawson, 'The Union of the Russian People', pp. 158–9, 160.
77. Mitelman *et al. Istoriya Putilovskogo Zavoda*, p. 256.

78. PKS – biography of V. N. Fedorov.
79. Buzinov, *Za Nevskoi Zastavoi*, pp. 108–14.
80. PKS – biographies of I. P. Kashin and Y. F. Romel'.
81. See the report of the Nevskii district representative to the Council of the Workers' Union, *Trud*, no. 4 (October 1906), p. 10; also Buzinov, *Za Nevskoi Zastavoi*, pp. 115–18. For more on expropriations in Petersburg see Garvi, *Zapiski Sotsial Demokrata*, pp. 57 ff.
82. *Rapport 1907*, p. 234.
83. *Trud*, no. 4 (October 1906), p. 10; *Trud*, no. 1–2 (September 1906), p. 20.
84. See below, n. 112.
85. See reference in n. 117; see also *Trud*, no. 5 (November 1906), pp. 10–12. For the location of some of the factories mentioned in this chapter, see map 1. For more information on them, see Factory List, pp. 110–13.
86. *Trud*, no. 3 (October 1906), p. 12; no. 4, p. 10.
87. *Trud*, no. 4, p. 10; no. 5, pp. 8, 12.
88. *Trud* no. 4, p. 15. The Baltic shipbuilding factory long remained an SR stronghold. A delegate to the first party conference singled out the electrical shop as having been a nest for conscious SR workers. See *Protokoly 1908*, p. 119.
89. *Trud*, no. 4, p. 10. Of these 1000 members, approximately 300 belonged to the Obukhov *podraion* (*Trud*, no. 3, p. 13) and judging from the sums in the account books) about 400–500 to the Aleksandrovskii (*Trud*, no. 4, p. 15).
90. *Trud*, no. 4, p. 14.
91. *Trud*, no. 5, p. 8.
92. *Trud*, no. 4, p. 10.
93. *Trud*, no. 4, p. 15.
94. *Trud*, no. 5, p. 12.
95. *Trud*, no. 8 (January 1907), p. 14.
96. The SDs' *okrug* organisation encompassed Kolpino, Kronshtadt, Sestroretsk, Shlissel'burg and 'Porokhovskoi' (gun-powder works). The last named was included in the SRs' Okhta *podraion*. There was an SR organisation in Kronshtadt, but it appears to have been independent of Petersburg and to have consisted only of soldiers and sailors. There were SRs in Sestroretsk (arms factory) during 1917, but there were only Maximalists there before the war. Shlissel'burg was the address of the Obukhov factory, which was part of the SRs' Nevskii *raion*.
97. *Trud*, no. 4, p. 10.
98. Almost all reports from the railways during this period were exclusively concerned with the repression. See *Trud*, no. 1–2, p. 20; no. 5, pp. 13–14.
99. *Trud*, no. 4, p. 10.
100. Ibid.
101. *Trud*, no. 5, pp. 8, 12.
102. There were others, naturally, who felt that acts of terrorism were a futile and unnecessary provocation which would only make their lives more difficult.

103. More detailed reference will be made to this later.
104. Of course this is not to argue that the SRs were the leaders in all these forms of activity. But all parties must have benefited to some extent from the results.
105. A. Levin, *The Second Duma*, pp. 19–21.
106. D. Lane, *The Roots of Russian Communism*, pp. 52–4.
107. *Trud*, no. 6, pp. 6, 7; no. 7, p. 17; U. A. Shuster, *IRL*, p. 325.
108. Lane, *The Roots of Russian Communism*, p. 53.
109. M. Perrie, *The Agrarian Policy of the Russian Socialist-Revolutionary Party*, p. 168. Some Soviet authors go to considerable lengths to show that in Petersburg many workers (the majority in fact) supported the Bolshevik line, which was to boycott the elections. See Shuster, *IRL*, pp. 218–19.
110. *Rapport 1907*, pp. 42–8.
111. 'Organizatsiya partiinoi izbiratel'noi kampanii v Peterburge', in *Partiinye Izvestiya*, no. 4 (5 January 1907). The Narva, Kazan, Spasskii and Kolomenskii precincts were still without committees in December.
112. *Trud*, no. 1–2, pp. 19–20.
113. *Trud*, no. 5, pp. 10–11.
114. *Trud*, pp. 8–9.
115. *Trud*, no. 6, p. 13.
116. Leaflets had been issued by the Petersburg and Railway *raiony* by Christmas. There were electoral circles and factory commissions in the Town district, and literature was distributed in Kolpino. The Nevskii district did not have special electoral machinery of its own, but campaigning went on nevertheless.
117. *Sotsialdemokrat*, no. 5, p. 7.
118. *Trud*, no. 8, p. 14; *Rus'*, no. 15 (15 January 1907), p. 3.
119. A. Mikhailov, 'Vybory vo vtoruyu Dumu v Peterburgskoi rabochei kurii,' *Otzvuki* (August 1907), p. 41. It is unclear just how frequently the fight was a 'three-cornered' one. Martov claims that on occasion the Bolsheviks did 'a deal with the SRs in order jointly to defeat the Mensheviks' (Martov to Axelrod – 10 January 1907 – *Pis'ma P. B. Aksel'roda i Yu. O. Martova*, 1924, pp. 153–5).
120. Buzinov, *Za Nevskoi Zastavoi*, pp. 125–6.
121. *Trud*, no. 8, p. 13. They are: 'Why you Must Elect the SRs', 'Where the Peoples' Money Goes', 'Black Hundreds', 'On the Party of "Peaceful Renewal"', 'How the Government Helps the Starving Peasants', 'Tsarist Power and Popular Government', 'Appeal of the Central Committee to the Citizens'. The text of some can be found in Archive 431.
122. See, for example, 'Tekushchii Moment', no. 1–2, p. 1; 'K kharakteristike nashei pozitsii v dumskom voprose', no. 5, p. 2; 'Duma i revolyutsiya', no. 6, p. 1; 'Pochemu neobkhodimo golosovat' za sotsialistov-revolyutsionerov', no. 7, p. 1.
123. Levin, *The Second Duma*.
124. *Trud*, no. 6, p. 14; no. 9, p. 12. In addition, the party's 'Military Revolutionary *Okrug* Organisation' seriously wounded an officer of the fleet on 2 February and killed an army sergeant-major on 12

February, both for 'spying'.

125. Andrei Mikhailov. See below, p. 102.

126. For a full statement of the programme, see *Protokoly 1906*.

127. See, for example, *Ko vsemu rabochemu narodu* (1905), Archive 431 and *Golos rabochikh*, no. 2 (February 1907), Archive 447.

128. *Trud*, no. 8, pp. 13, 14.

129. *Trud*, no. 9, pp. 14, 15. The SRs had made little impact on the educational establishments of Petersburg during 1905. By the end of 1906, however, they were able to boast 800 members distributed over twenty-one university faculties and institutions. This made their organisation not much smaller than that of the Social Democrats.

130. *Rus*, no. 9, p. 4; Shuster, *Peterburgskie rabochie*, p. 263. (There were also cases of policemen deciding on the age of workers purely by their appearance: 'How old are you? Then why haven't you got a beard?')

131. For example, 250 workers were dismissed from the Putilov plant on 13 January, that is 24 hours before polling – *Rus'*, no. 16, p. 5; Shuster, *IRL*, p. 327, gives the Aivaz factory as another example.

132. This happened in the case of one Pinaevskii, SR representative for the engine shops of the Aleksandrovskii factory. *Rus'*, no. 24, p. 4. At the Glebov factory the successful SR candidate was disqualified for being under age. *Rus'*, no. 15, p. 3.

133. Lane, *The Roots of Russian Communism*, p. 54 and n. 4.

134. Mikhailov, 'Vybory vo vtoruyu Dumu v Petersburgskoi rabochei kurii'. Two of the tables presented by Mikhailov are reproduced by Hildermeier, *Die Sozialrevolutionäre Partei*, pp. 299–303.

135. For example, either the Bolsheviks collapsed on the eve of the elections, or their share of the vote is suspiciously low. Without necessarily ascribing devious motives, this might simply be because Mikhailov relied principally on Menshevik *raion* officials for information. However, the theory of a collapse of the Bolshevik vote should not be ruled out. A second problem with this compilation is that one does not know how well dispersed the factories surveyed were. For example, were factories in the 50–100 worker category mainly located in the (Menshevik-dominated) Town district? Thirdly, one wonders about Mikhailov's 'non-fraction' Social Democrats, which he includes in the SD party vote. Who were these people, and might one not suspect that 'non-fraction' SRs appear in the non-party column, thus excluded from the SR vote?

136. See, for example, Lenin's assessment of the result: 'Vybory po rabochei kurii v Peterburge', *Polnoe sobranie sochinenii (PSS)*, vol. XIV, pp. 341–8.

137. Martov mentions this possibility in correspondence with Axelrod. The SR organisation was too slight 'to engage in battle on all fronts, just as our success in the major factories is only because the SRs still have not reached the less front-line (*avanpostnykh*) strata of the proletariat'. Martov, *Pis'ma*, pp. 155–8. Mikhailov's evidence may itself be misleading in this respect. If we look at factories where the SRs are known to have had organisational ties (see Table 5.4) we find that in 8 of the 69 cases for which information is available, the enterprises employed fewer than 100 workers. The explanation for the discrepancy

may be that most of the small factories were located in the Town
district, where the SRs were comparatively weak. Of the 8 factories
cited above, for example, 4 were situated in the Moscow district and
only one (the 'Svet' printing works) in the Town.

138. Diane Koenker, *Moscow Workers*, p. 205.
139. Lane, *The Roots of Russian Communism*, pp. 113–17.
140. Smith, 'The Russian Revolution and the Factories of Petrograd'.
141. *Novyi Luch*, 21 February 1907, p. 6.
142. Lenin, *PSS* (5th edn) vol. xiv, p. 345. See also *Nash Mir*, no. 1 (28 January 1907), p. 6.
143. *Proletarii*, no. 12 (25 January 1907), p. 6.
144. See, for example, the article in *Nash Mir*, no. 2 (6 February 1907), 'Zemlya i rabochie'; and Martov, *Pis'ma*, pp. 155–8. Similar comments from Maslov and Maevsky were quoted by the SRs in *Trud*, no. 9 (February 1907), p. 1. The *Nash Mir* article implied that the unemployed were particularly susceptible to SR promises of land redistribution. In fact, the unemployment problem was suddenly exacerbated during the elections themselves. On 10 January about 1500 migrants arrived at the Nikolaevskii station looking for work (there had been quite unfounded rumours of work being available after the New Year). A few days later the Narva branch of the Council of Unemployed tried to stem the incoming tide of peasants by trying to persuade them that there was no work in Petersburg. This situation must have helped the SRs' case. *Rech'*, no. 9 (January 1907), p. 4; *Rus'*, no. 17 (January 1907), p. 4.
145. Martov, *Pis'ma*, pp. 155–8.
146. Lenin, *Vybory po rabochei kurii v Peterburge* and *Bor'ba SD i SR na vyborakh v rabochei kurii v S Peterburge*, *PSS*, vol. xiv, pp. 341–53. The agreement is discussed briefly in L. Shapiro, *The Communist Party of the Soviet Union* (2nd edn; London, 1970), pp. 93–4.
147. The evidence relates to 23 factories in the Nevskii *raion*.
148. The Menshevik evidence against Lenin's argument appears in Mikhailov.
149. *Nash Mir*, no. 4 (18 February 1907), where it is alleged that a Bolshevik candidate at the pipe factory and another in one of the Nevskii *podraiony* defected to the SRs shortly before the elections. Bolshevik policies on land, partisan terror, the 'democratic' revolution and the dictatorship of the proletariat and peasantry were all seen as being close to the positions of the SRs, or at least came across as being so.
150. *Pis'ma*, pp. 155–8.
151. The SR press devoted relatively little space to the post-election debate. For their main arguments see *Trud*, no. 9 (February 1907), p. 1; and *Golos rabochikh*, January 1907, Archive 447.
152. It should be stressed that the index is only an approximate indicator of the industrial mix of 'SR' factories. By enterprises with known SR ties we mean those which at the very least received and paid for, party literature. The index is biased towards certain districts (especially Moscow and Vyborg), while Town and Vasileostrov are under-represented. To a certain extent these latter two balance each other out.

Enterprises omitted from the Town list were probably small factories or artisanal establishments. On the other hand, unknowns in Vasileostrov most likely include more large metalworking plants, for example, Siemens and Halske, Siemens-Shukkert and Wire and Nail.

153. *Fabrichno-zavodskie predpiyatiya Rossiskoi Imperii* (2nd edn; Petersburg, 1914). All information in the index is for 1914, unless specifically stated otherwise.

154. *Protokoly 1906*; see also *O tom chto trebovat' rabochim i trudovomu krest'yanstvu*, Archive 431.

155. These examples are taken from a proclamation of the Moscow SR workers' union, dated January 1905, *RR*, no. 58, p. 22.

156. Together with the students – '*A few words to the students*', November 1903, Archive 325.

157. See 'O sovete rabochikh deputatov', in *Listok Peterburgskogo Komiteta PSR*, August 1906, Archive 431.

158. 'Chego my trebuem dlya vsekh trudyashchikhsya? (raz'yasnenie programmy sotsialistov (revolyutsionerov))', *Letuchii listok*, Archive 447.

159. A survey conducted at the Baltic factory in December 1901 revealed that 46.1 per cent of the total workforce of 3917 held a *nadel: Arkhiv Istorii Truda v Rossii–vypuskaemyi ustnoi komissiei po issledovaniyu istorii truda v Rossii*, bk 1 (Petrograd, 1921), p. 80. See also n. 115 of this chapter. The Social Democrats' reaction to the SRs' success in the 1907 elections would seem to indicate that they overestimated the size and influence of the *cadre* proletariat in Petersburg.

160. For further comment see M. Perrie, *The Social Composition*.

161. Archive 447.

162. *Arkhiv Istorii Truda*, pp. 66–85.

163. Ibid., p. 82. Skilled jobs were defined as those requiring greater mental agility (*lovkost'*).

164. Financial accounts with shop contributions are available for a number of enterprises outside Petersburg, namely the Admiralty shipyard in Sevastopol' (six accounts), the Bezhetsa armaments plant outside Bryansk and the Izhevsk and Votkinsk factories in the Urals. Between sixteen and eighteen shops are represented at Sevastopol' and ten, thirteen and seven respectively at the others. So far as the 'skilled' departments are concerned, comparatively small donations from pattern workers were recorded in the Izhevsk, Bezhetsa and Sevastopol' factories. In addition the instrument shop was well-represented. Turning to the departments which were regarded as the least specialised, it is notable that over a six-month (not consecutive) spread of accounts, some of the largest total contributions at Sevastopol' came from unskilled sections such as the boiler houses, foundry, carpentry, rigging and shipbuilding shops. Of course the social composition of the PSR in Sevastopol' may have been different from that of Petersburg.

165. Rashin, *Formirovanie*.

166. *Arkhiv Istorii Truda*, p. 82.

167. Ibid., pp. 65–6 whence these figures were extrapolated.

168. In addition to the afore-mentioned sources, recourse was made in compiling this composite to Kabo, *Ocherki rabochego byta*. (Among the workers researched by Kabo in the mid-1920s were seven Moscow metalworkers.)

169. For an account see *Trud*, no. 9, p. 1. The SRs alleged that the Mensheviks resorted to 'shameless and improper tricks' in order to counter the SR speakers.

170. See chapter 7, below.

171. *Professional'nye soyuzy* (proclamation dated June 1905), Archive 436. The Petersburg committee advised that 'now is not the time to organise workers' unions' because conditions necessary to their success (such as free press and free assembly) were lacking.

172. There is, so far as I know, no extant record of the party's change of mind on the subject, but their decision probably coincided with the promulgation of the October manifesto. (This would account for SR participation in the Soviet.) The first full official statement of the SR party's position on the function and objective of the trade unions did not appear until July 1907, though a theoretical statement had already appeared in *Trud*, 'K voprosu o professional'nykh soyuzakh', *Trud*, no. 11, p. 1. In the Kolomenskii *raion*, *Trud* was criticised for not including enough material on the professional and cooperative movement (ibid., p. 17). The above quotation is taken from Hildermeier, *Die Sozialrevolutionäre Partie*, p. 187.

173. G. Swain, 'Political Developments Within the Organized Working Class: Petersburg 1906–14', PhD thesis, London, 1979; Here p. 20. The discussions were held at the Semyannikov, Obukhov and Koppel factories in November 1905 – see F. A. Semenov ('Bulkin'), *Istoriya Peterburgskogo soyuza metallistov (1906–14)* (Leningrad, 1924), p. 128. The SRs were very strong in the union cells of particular factories (for example, the Pipe works). However, generally speaking SR members tended to be passive or even indifferent to union proceedings, which helps account for the fact that the SDs were always able to retain overall control. (I. V. Golubev, 'Vospominaniya o Peterburgskom professional'nom soyuze metallistov (1907–08gg)', in *Krasnaya letopis'* no. 8 (1923), p. 234, contains the reference to the Pipe factory.)

174. B. Ivanov, *Professional'noe dvizhenie rabochikh khlebo-pekarno-konditerskogo proizvodstva Petrograda i gubernii s 1903–17gg* (Moscow, 1920). See especially pp. 53–75.

175. For instance, windows were broken, bread stores attacked and flour supplies set on fire (Ivanov, 1920, pp. 64–5).

176. G. Shidlovskii, 'Peterburgskii komitet bol'shevikov v kontse 1913 goda i v nachale 1914 goda', *KL*, no. 2 (1926), pp. 119–39; here p. 122.

177. Hildermeier, *Die Sozialrevolutionäre Partei*, p. 186.

178. 'O konferentsiakh Peterburgskogo uzla vserossiiskogo zhelenzno-dorozhnogo soyuza' *Trud*, no. 9, p. 8.

179. See, for example, the report in *Trud*, no. 5, p. 13.

180. Income in March 1907 amounted to over 2400r.: *Chugunka-organ oblastnogo i mestnykh komitetov S. Peterburgskogo uzla vserossiiskogo zheleznodorozhnogo soyuza*, no. 1 (April 1907), Archive 658.

181. The 'United SDs' boycotted the Warsaw line cell of the ARRU, as did some personnel from the Moscow–Vindav line (*Trud*, no. 9, p. 8).

182. A leaflet issued in the name of the Nikolaevskii railway, probably in the autumn of 1907, urged railway workers to 'put their quarrels aside' (*ostav'te raspri*) because the 'enemy' made no distinction between SDs and SRs – Archive 329.

183. 'Zapiska Solomona' (member of the Petersburg Committee): *Polozhenie del' v Peterburgskom organizatsii k sent. '08g* – Archive 430 (on which much of this section is based).

184. In March 1907 the SRs considered themselves to be 'rather strong' in 21 trade unions (*Trud*, no. 11, p. 15). A Soviet source cites information from the Central Bureau to the effect that in 1907 the SRs predominated in 9 out of 36 trade unions representing 16 per cent of the total unionised workforce. By 1909, it is claimed, the SDs had won over the textile, gold and silver and tobacco unions from the SRs. I have discovered no information to support the assertion that the SRs had ever controlled the textile workers' union, however. V. A. Nardova, 'Proletariat stolitsy v gody reaktsii', *IRL* (1972), p. 371.

185. The SRs' short-lived trade union paper includes reports from a wide variety of unions, including those of the printers, bakers, stevedores, electro-technical workers, wallpaper factory workers, blacksmiths, bootmakers, shoemakers, draymen, laundry workers, floor-polishers, night-watchmen, yard-keepers, apprentice seamstresses and tailors – *Professional'noe dvizhenie: obzor deyatel'nosti rabochikh soyuzov v Rossii i za grantisei*, no. 1 (Petersburg, 1 May 1907), p. 18.

186. Swain, 'Political Developments Within the Organized Working Class', p. 254.

187. V. Krasil'nikov, 'Za Moskovskoi Zastavoi v 1908–11gg. (iz vospominanii)', *KL*, no. 9 (1924), p. 115. The name of the delegate was Andrei Pashkov. The Bolsheviks also sent a representative to this congress.

188. *PKS* – biography of N. G. Korolev. An official history records that in 1913 'a minority were for the *narodnik* party'. One of the founding members of the union, N. M. Nekrasov (a Kostroma-born peasant) was also an SR, though he later switched to the Bolsheviks – *Sbornik materialov po istorii soyuza stroitelei* (Leningrad, 1926).

189. *Protokoly V-go soveta partii (stenograficheskii otchet)*, p. 8, Archive 792.

190. *Protokoly pervoi obshchepartiinoi konferentsii PSR* (August 1908), p. 30. A 'boycotting attitude' was noted among the best-organised SR workers in the major industries, especially among workers in the metallurgical industry. Many thought union work was useless, some had left in disgust because of the 'corruption' (*razvrashchenie*).

191. An interesting case is cited by 'A. Voronov' (Lebedev) in an article in the party journal *Znamya Truda (ZT)*. In December 1907 elections were held for the executive of the metalworkers' union in Petersburg. The Central Committee undertook a campaign but SR workers failed to turn up to the meetings. Nevertheless, and in the face of an effective campaign by the Social Democrats, eight SRs were elected as against nine SDs. However only a month later, three members of the SR

fraction were already absenting themselves from meetings and they were generally unable to carry out union tasks. Voronov believed that such instances were common in the PSR (and he had personal experience of the Petersburg organisation) *ZT*, no. 16, pp. 5–8.

192. See PKS, biographies of F. D. Avdeev, M. F. Boitsov, A. S. Krylov, M. Yu. Lipik, N. E. Travkin, I. F. Zakharov, N. F. Zoroastrova-Skripnik, N. I. Protopopov for SRs converting to Maximalism and that of N. P. Petrov for evidence of a Maximalist circle in 1904.

193. 'Chto takoe "Maksimalizm?"', *Trud*, no. 8, pp. 2–6.

194. *Trud*, no. 11, p. 17.

195. There is no evidence of a special interest in factory socialisation, for example.

196. *Trud*, no. 11, p. 15.

197. Buzinov, *Za Nevskoi Zastavoi*, pp. 115–25.

198. *Trud*, no. 11, p. 15.

199. *Materialy tret'ego*, Archive 679 (See note 205 below).

200. Ibid.

201. *Rezolyutsii vynesenniya na sobranii gorodskogo raiona PSR ob otnoshenii k tretei gosudarstvennoi Dume* – Archive 447.

202. 'Bezrabotitsa i fabrichno-zavodskii terror', *Trud*, no. 19, pp. 5–6 and 'K voprosu o fabrichnom terrore', *Trud*, no. 17, pp. 7–9, Archive 472.

203. *Trud*, no. 20, p. 14.

204. Protokoly 1908, p. 130.

205. See *Materialy tret'ego soveta partii* (8–11 July 1907), Petersburg report, Archive 679. The delegate failed to give a precise date for this figure, but claimed that membership had dropped to about 4000 by July. Hildermeier, *Die Sozialrevolutionäre Partei*, p. 259 n. 205, cites a letter from the Petersburg organisation to A. A. Argunov (dated 13 September 1907) as evidence of a membership of 6000 in the autumn. In our opinion, the bulk of the evidence points to maximum growth being reached sometime between January and March 1907, with a continual decline thereafter. In May 1907 there were 5991 Bolsheviks and 2800 Mensheviks in Petersburg according to the official Soviet party history (*Ocherki istorii Leningradskoi organizatsii KPSS*, p. 156).

206. *Materialy tret'ego soveta partii*, Archive 679.

207. *Trud*, no. 16, p. 12 estimated unemployment at 10000 in July 1907. The same article provides details of the situation in a number of individual factories. For more information, see *Trud, passim*.

208. The committee's own income fell considerably after the summer of 1907. In August it amounted to only 321r. but recovered somewhat thereafter. In September 1908 however, of an income of 362r., 300r. had been contributed by the Central Committee! See the accounts in Archive 430, 431.

209. See the report in *Protokoly 1908*, pp. 27–32.

210. For the history of the party between 1908 and 1914 see C. J. Rice, 'The Socialist-Revolutionary Party and the Urban Working Class in Russia, 1902–1914', pp. 275–85.

6 Five Organisational Profiles

1. For background on Baku and the Caucasus region see the following works: R. G. Suny, *The Baku Commune 1917–1918 – Class and Nationality in the Russian Revolution* (Princeton, 1972); and 'A Journeyman for the Revolution: Stalin and the Labour Movement in Baku, June 1907–May 1908', in *Soviet Studies*, 23, no. 3 (1972), pp. 373–94; G. A. Arutyunov, *Rabochee dvizhenie v Zakavkaz'e v period novogo revolyutsionnogo pod"ema, 1910–1914gg* (Moscow and Baku, 1963); Filipp Makharadze, *Ocherki revolyutsionnogo dvizheniya v Zakavkaz'e* (Tiflis, 1927).

2. Arutyunov, *Rabochee dvizhenie v Zakavkaz'e*, pp. 34, 56; Suny, *The Baku Commune*, p. 7.

3. Suny, *The Baku Commune*, p. 4.

4. Suny, *The Baku Commune*, pp. 6, 50; 'A Journeyman for the Revolution', pp. 375–6; Lane, *Roots of Russian Communism*, p. 177.

5. Lane, *Roots of Russian Communism*, p. 176.

6. The following table is based on information in B. Ya. Stel'nik, 'Ar'ergardnye boi Bakinskogo proletariat v 1907 godu', in *Azerbaidzhan v gody pervoi russkoi revolyutsii (sbornik statei)* (Baku, 1966).

7. Suny, *The Baku Commune*, p. 10; 'A Journeyman for the Revolution', p. 376 (92 per cent of oil workers were not native to Baku.)

8. Suny, *The Baku Commune*, pp. 10–12, 14–16. Lane, *Roots of Russian Communism*, p. 178.

9. Suny, 'A Journeyman for the Revolution', p. 377.

10. Suny, *The Baku Commune*, p. 6; A. N. Guliev, *Bakinskii proletariat v gody novogo revolyutsionnogo pod"ema* (Baku, 1963), pp. 18–21.

11. Guliev, *Bakinskii proletariat*, p. 34.

12. Ibid., pp. 292–3.

13. Ibid., pp. 30, 33.

14. Guliev, *Bakinskii proletariat*; Suny, *The Baku Commune*, p. 13.

15. Lane, *Roots of Russian Communism*, p. 178. Suny, 'A Journeyman for the Revolution', p. 376 quotes a figure of 89.1 per cent for illiterate Azerbaijanis.

16. A. M. Stopani, *Neftepromyshlennyi rabochii i ego byudzhet*, (Moscow, 1924), pp. 124–5.

17. The most important archival document on the early history of the PSR is: *K dokladu Sakina/Materialy po 3-mu zakavkaznomu oblastnomu s"ezdu PSR 25–30 Mart 1907g*, Archive 628. On the 1904 strike, see also: *RR*, no. 66 (May 1905), p. 14.

18. *RR*, no. 66, p. 14.

19. *RR*, no. 51, p. 24; no. 71, p. 24; no. 75, p. 20.

20. *PI*, no. 9 (May 1907), p. 12; *K dokladu Sakina*, Archive 628.

21. *PI*, no. 9, p. 12; Hildermeier, *Die Sozialrevolutionäre Partei* p. 248 and n. 59. The Dashnaktsutyun was formed in Tiflis in 1890 to promote minority Armenian interests, especially in Turkey. Like the SRs the Dashnaks favoured individual terrorism, but did not adopt a Socialist programme until 1907 (Suny, *The Baku Commune*, pp. 21–24).

22. *Materialy*, Archive 628.
23. *K dokladu Sakina*; *PI*, no. 9, p. 12; *Protokoly 1908*, pp. 32, 34.
24. *Materialy*, Archive 628; *Protokoly 1908*, p. 32.
25. See below pp. 138–9.
26. *PI*, no. 9, p. 12. A MS from Baku, dated September 1907 (Archive 553/I) cites membership figures of around 1825–1925 SRs (625 Armenians), compared with 1800 SDs (1200 Bolshevik, 600 Menshe vik). Suny, however, ('A Journeyman for the Revolution', p. 376), offers a figure of 2500 SDs. For the Armenian defectors to the PSR, see below pp. 138–9.
27. Stel'nik, 'Ar'ergardnye boi', p. 97.
28. Various documents in Archive 551, 553/I.
29. The Baku reporter to the third Caucasus Congress of the PSR in March 1907 mentions the existence of a 'young group of Tatars' (that is, Azerbaijanis): *K dokladu Sakina*, Archive 628. The existence of '*Ittifag*' is mentioned by Stel'nik, 'Ar'ergardnye boi', p. 97 and is confirmed by archival sources: *Dve Stachki*, 15 September 1906, Archive 553/I.
30. *PI*, no. 9, p. 12; *K dokladu Sakina*, Archive 628.
31. *ZT*, no. 5 (September 1907), p. 13; *Protokoly 1908*, p. 32; *PI*, no. 7 (March 1907), pp. 14–15.
32. Arutyunov, *Rabochie dvizhenie v Zakavkaz'e*, here p. 165. Also Suny, 'Labor and Liquidators – Revolution and the 'Reaction' in Baku, May 1908–April 1912', in *Slavic Review*, no. 34 (1975), p. 320 and *ZT*, no. 19 (July 1909), p. 17.
33. See below, p. 135.
34. Quoted by Suny, *The Baku Commune*, pp. 45–6.
35. *ZT*, no. 17 (April 1909), p. 15; *ZT*, no. 19 (July 1909), p. 17. The SDs experienced a parallel decline in membership. Bolshevik numbers, for example, were estimated at 300 (maximum) for the end of 1909 (Arutyunov, *Rabochee dvizhenie v Zakavkaz'e*, p. 74).
36. For this episode see *Dve Stachki*, 15 September 1906, Archive 553/I. Also Suny, *The Baku Commune*, p. 47.
37. P. N. Valuev, *Bol'sheviki azerbaidzhana v pervoi russkoi revolyutsii* (Baku, 1963), p. 229; *Protokoly 1908*, p. 32; *Ko vsem bakinskim rabochim*, 28 Nov 1906, Archive 553/I.
38. See below, p. 138.
39. *Protokoly 1908*, p. 32.
40. For the background, see Suny, *The Baku Commune*, pp. 43–6; for a Soviet (Stalinist) account, see P. N. Valuev, *Soveshchatel'naya kampaniya 1907–8gg. v Baku* (IMEL, 1946).
41. For a statement of the SR position, see the (1908) leaflet *Tovarishchi*, Archive 553/I; also, 'K voprosu o soveshchanii', in *Izvestiya bakinskoi organizatsii PSR*, no. 1 (18 April 1908), pp. 2–3.
42. *Protokoly 1908*, p. 32.
43. Suny, 'A Journeyman for the Revolution', p. 389 gives a figure of 19 000 votes for the Bolshevik position and only 8000 for the original Menshevik position.
44. Suny, *The Baku Commune*, p. 44.

45. Ibid., p. 49.
46. The Baku representative at the third Caucasus congress contradicts this, claiming that 'we' [that is, the SRs] formed the oil union and that 'the entire business is in our hands': *K dokladu Sakina*, Archive 628.
47. Arutyunov, *Rabochee Dvizhenie v zakavkaz'e*, p. 165; Stel'nik, 'Ar'ergardnye boi bakinskogo proletariat', p. 95.
48. The following information is drawn predominantly from the (Bolshevik-controlled) newspaper of the oil-workers' union, *Gudok*.
49. *Gudok*, no. 10 (16 December 1907), p. 5; no. 13 (6 January 1908), pp. 5–7.
50. *Gudok*, no. 16 (27 January 1908), pp. 4–5.
51. Ibid.
52. *Izvestiya bakinskoi organizatsii PSR*, no. 1 (April 1908), pp. 3–4 (Archive 553/I), *Gudok*, no. 25 (30 March 1908), p. 4.
53. *Gudok*, no. 49 (17 January 1909), p. 6, *ZT*, no. 19, p. 18.
54. *ZT*, no. 19, p. 18; *ZT*, no. 31, p. 25.
55. Stel'nik, 'Ar'ergardnye boi', p. 95.
56. Quoted in Guliev, *Bakinskii proletariat*, p. 49.
57. Biographical details in PKS.
58. Information on the strike is derived from 'Sredi moryakov' in *Molot-izdanie Bakinskoi organizatsii partii sotsialistov-revolyutsionerov*, no. 2 (September 1907), and 'Morskaya zabastovka Kaspiinskoi flotii v 1907g', in *Morskaya Volna – organ bezpartiin. profess. soyuza moryakov kaspiisk. Torg. flota*, no. 7 (10 September 1909), pp. 3 ff., Archive 553/I.
59. PKS.
60. See the leaflet dated 25 April 1907 in Archive 553/I.
61. *ZT*, no. 27, p. 28; no. 26, p. 23.
62. *ZT*, no. 27, p. 28.
63. On the later history of the union see *Morskaya Volna*, no. 7, pp. 3–11, 21–22 (Archive 553/I).
64. See n. 21 above.
65. *Otchet Armyanskoi organizatskii partii SR* – Archive 551.
66. This profile is based on: *ZT*, no. 26 (February 1910), p. 23; no. 45, p. 23; *Protokoly 1908*, p. 33.
67. *Protokoly 1908*, p. 33. One of the more skilled (and loyal) SRs was Grigorii Erem'yan, a fitter and son of a mining engineer. Born in Shushe in 1889, Erem'yan completed four classes of grammar school before being expelled for participating in disturbances. During 1903–4 he was a member of the Dashnaktsutyun party in his home town, before moving to Baku. In 1907 he joined the PSR and was involved in agitational, combat and trade union work as well as contributing to the party press. After being subjected to several arrests, Erem'yan was finally removed from the scene for distributing leaflets in 1914 (PKS).
68. *ZT*, no. 26, p. 23. The Caucasus *obkom* donated a total of 300r. to the Armenian literature fund between July 1908 and July 1909, the majority of which would presumably have been allocated to Baku (*ZT*, no. 26, p. 26). There were smaller Armenian centres in Erivan, Tiflis, Aleksandropol and Batum.

69. *Protokoly 1908*, p. 33.
70. *Pamyatnaya Knizhka* attributes only one killing to a fighting detachment operating in Baku – the 'execution' of a provocateur named Petrov on 28 August 1905. There are four other killings listed for other places in the Caucasus *oblast'* before 1910. See *Pamyatnaya Knizhka*, vol. II. The SRs were also held responsible for a 'series of terrorist acts' during the seamen's strike of March–April 1907 (Stel'nik, 'Ar'ergardnye boi', p. 104). Our impression is that terror in Baku was organised on an *ad hoc* basis, and that it was not given an especially high profile.
71. *Protokoly 1908*, p. 36.
72. Criminal activity of this type wreaked even greater havoc among SRs in the neighbouring North Caucasus *oblast'*. See *Protokoly 1908*, p. 37. In 1907 alone there had been 1732 recorded robberies in Transcaucasia and 1328 other 'terrorist' acts (Suny, *The Baku Commune*, p. 45).
73. *ZT*, no. 19 (July 1909), p. 17; *Morskiya Volny-izdanie ispolnitel'nogo komiteta Bakinskoi organizatsii partii SR*, no. 1 (February 1910), pp. 15–17. The archive contains a notice warning local SRs that someone had recently sent a letter demanding 400r. for political prisoners, using an old party stamp as 'authorisation' – *Zayavlenie* (Baku committee, undated), Archive 553/I.
74. The reference to the Armenian Detachments is in *ZT*, no. 5, p. 14.
75. For archival information on the Armenian organisation, see the following: 'Otchet Armyanskoi organizatsii partii SR', in *Sovremennik* no. 2 (May 1909), p. 12, Archive 551; Proclamation, dated 28 November 1909; 'Otchet o zasedaniyakh ispolnitel'nogo komiteta', in *Morskiya Volny* no. 1, p. 15, Archive 551. *ZT*, no. 45, p. 23. Two Armenians were among the Baku delegation to the sixth (Caucasus) *oblast'* Congress in October 1909.
76. Although Bryansk was, strictly speaking, included in the North-West *oblast'* it was, in almost all respects, quite distinct from other parts of the region. As such it will be treated separately in this study.
77. *Protokoly 6-go oblastnogo s"ezda severo-zapadnoi oblastnoi organizatsii*, PSR (12 October 1906), Archive 426.
78. Ezra Mendelsohn, *Class Struggle in the Pale: the Formative Years of the Jewish Workers' Movement in Tsarist Russia* (Cambridge, 1970), p. 3. (Most of the following introductory remarks are based on this source.)
79. Mendelsohn, *Class Struggle in the Pale*, p. 5. In Minsk the proportion was 52 per cent, in Dvinsk 44 per cent, in Vitebsk 52 per cent and in Gomel' 55 per cent.
80. Ibid.
81. Population of figures are for 1910 and are taken from T. S. Fedor, *Patterns of Urban Growth*, Appendix I.
82. Mendelsohn, *Class Struggle in the Pale*, p. 25, n. 1.
83. Ibid., p. 6 and n. 4.
84. Ibid., p. 21.
85. Ibid., p. 21. For artisanal conditions, see the discussion on pp. 7–26.
86. See the article 'Ob osobennostyakh raboty v severo-zapadnom krae', in *PI*, no. 8 (April 1907), pp. 12–13.

87. F. M. Watters, 'The Peasant and the Village Commune', in *The Peasant in Nineteenth-Century Russia* (Stanford, CA, 1968), pp. 146–7. See also Hildermeier, *Die Sozialrevolutionäre Partei*, p. 238.

88. Some Jews evidently did respond from purely altruistic motives: '"*Zemlya i volya*! – in Jewish this sounds so strange", one young Jew said to me. "What is the land to me, to us Jews? But in the name of the common ideal of justice I too will fight for the land"'. Jews did actually conduct propaganda work in the countryside for the PSR ('Ob osobennostyakh', p. 12).

89. See 'Iz pisem sev-zap. O.K. k mestnym komitetam' (dated variously from November 1906 to January 1907), in *PI*, no. 5 (February 1907), pp. 7–8 and 'Iz otcheta Sev. Zapadnogo Obl. Komiteta' (presented to North-West *oblast'* congress in February 1907), *PI*, no. 7 (March 1907), pp. 14–15. The financial account quoted earlier is to be found on p. 13.

90. In the summer of 1906 for example 'the entire body of progressive teachers' was arrested at a congress in Minsk ('Ob osobennostyakh', p. 13).

91. Ibid. Many had first belonged to the Bund youth organisations *Malyi Bund* and *Nadezhda*.

92. *PI*, no. 8 (April 1907), p. 13. The rival parties included the Bund, Social Democrats, Social Zionists, Jewish Socialists and the Polish Socialist party.

93. See chapter 3 of this study.

94. *RR*, no. 31 (August 1904), p. 23.

95. Mendelsohn, *Class Struggle in the Pale*, pp. 131 ff.

96. 'Ob osobennostyakh', p. 12.

97. 'Statistika terroristicheskikh aktov' (*Pamyatnaya knizhka sotsialista-revolyutsionera*).

98. See M. D. Zakgeim in PKS; also *Pamyatnaya knizhka*; and Spiridovitch, *Histoire du terrorisme Russe*, pp. 396, 405.

99. See the article 'Anarkhizm v Rossii', in *Sotsialist-Revolyutsioner*, no. 3 (1911), pp. 75–94.

100. 'Anarkhizm v Rossii', pp. 82–3; 'Koe-chto o "Maksimalistakh"', *PI*, no. 8, pp. 3–5. The exception was Dvinsk, which was apparently free of Maximalism at least.

101. 'Koe-chto o "Maksimalistakh"', p. 4.

102. Ibid.

103. *Protokoly 6-go oblastnogo s"ezda*, Archive 426. The previous intolerance of SR organisations was in fact blamed for earlier problems with the Maximalists ('Koe-chto', p. 4).

104. *Protokoly 7-go ocherednogo s"ezda severo-zapadnoi oblasti partii SR*, Archive 426.

105. 'Ob osobennostyakh', p. 12; 'Iz pisem sev-zap. O.K.', p. 8.

106. The following statistics refer to the period around October 1906–February 1907. They are taken from these sources: Dvinsk – *Rapport 1907*, p. 122; Vitebsk – *Otchet k oblastnomu s"ezdu* (12 February 1907), Archive 426; Gomel' – MS (October 1906) Archive 426; *Rapport 1907*, p. 134; for the remainder see the various reports in Archive 426 quoted below. It should be emphasised that these figures should be

taken as rough (and optimistic) approximations. However, they do at least indicate the relative strengths of the various organisations in the region.

107. *Otchet k oblastnomu s"ezdu* (Archive 426).
108. Hildermeier, *Die Sozialrevolutionäre Partei*, p. 327, citing document in Archive 483.
109. Both the information above and that which follows is taken from the following reports in Archive 426: *Otvety Minskogo komiteta PSR* (February 1907); *Otchet k oblastnomu s"ezdu* (Vitebsk); *Otvety pinskogo komiteta* (February 1907); *otvety* ... (Novozybkov, February 1907); *Otchet smolenskogo komiteta* (February 1907); MS: *Dvinskaya org-tsiya* (October 1906) and MSS for Gomel', Belostok, Vil'no (October 1906). See also *Rapport 1907*, pp. 120–41.
110. *Rossiya: Polnoe geograficheskoe opisanie* vol. ix, p. 573.
111. 'Ob osobennostyakh', p. 12.
112. See n. 109 above.
113. *Vtoroi Sovet PSR* (October 1906), Archive 489.
114. Minsk: *Otvety na zaprosy Ts.K*; Dvinsk: 6 January 1907; Vil'no: *Otvety, PI*, no. 5, pp. 8–9; Minsk: *Rapport 1907*, p. 136.
115. See n. 109 above.
116. *Protokoly 7-go ocherednogo*, Archive 426.
117. Ibid.
118. *Otchet Vitebskoi organisatsii* (Autumn 1907?), Archive 426.
119. *Doklad o polozhenii i deyatel'nosti Dvinskogo Komiteta PSR* (19 November 1907), Archive 426.
120. Background information is taken from the following: Brokgaus-Efron (ed.), *Entsiklopedicheskii slovar'*, 1900, vol. viii, pp. 815–18; vol. xxxvi, pp. 508–9; *Entsiklopedicheskii slovar' Russkogo Bibliograficheskogo Instituta Granat, Moscow 1910–1948* vol. vii, cols 34–5; vol. xviii, col. 120; O. Yu. Shmidt (ed.), *Bol'shaya Sovetskaya entsiklopedia* (1st edn), Moscow, 1926–48, vol. vii, cols. 743–53; vol. xxxvii, col. 828.
121. M. Balabanov, 'Promyshlennost' v 1904–7gg', in *Obshchestvennoe dvizhenie v Rossii*, vol. iv, pt. 1, p. 114.
122. *RR*, no. 38 (December 1903), p. 15; no. 37 (December 1903), p. 24; no. 42 (March 1904), p. 21.
123. *RR*, no. 69 (June 1905), p. 19.
124. *RR*, no. 70 (July 1905), p. 18.
125. *RR*, no. 74 (September 1905), p. 16. See also *Izveshchenie o Demonstratsii*, Archive 321.
126. Archive 321. Unfortunately no record seems to have survived of the organisation's activities during the last quarter of 1905.
127. *Politicheskaya katorga i ssylka*.
128. See, 'Severo-zapadnaya oblast' – ob osobennostyakh raboty v sev-zap. krae', in *PI*, no. 8 (April 1907), p. 12.
129. MS, Bryansk report (October 1906), Archive 426; *Rapport 1907*, pp. 129–30.
130. *PI*, no. 8, p. 12.
131. Ibid.

132.   *PI*, no. 8, p. 13.
133.   Hildermeier, *Die Sozialrevolutionäre Partei*, p. 138.
134.   'Koe-chto o "maksimalistakh" (pis'mo iz Smolenska)', in *PI*, no. 8, pp. 3–5 (here p. 4).
135.   See archive reference in Hildermeier, *Die Sozialrevolutionäre Partei*, p. 139 n. 54.
136.   For an expression of this argument see V. Chernov, 'K kharakteristike Maksimalizma', in *Sotsialist-Revolyutsioner*, no. 1 (1910), pp. 178–9.
137.   Balabanov, 'Promyshlennost' v 1904–7gg', p. 114.
138.   *PI*, no. 8, p. 4.
139.   In Bryansk, the Anarchists allegedly ceased work when their leader was killed after an unsuccessful expropriation (in the summer of 1907). By that time the Maximalists too were said to be weak (see report in *Trud*, no. 17 (October 1907), p. 14, Archive 472. In Bezhetsa, however, a (Maximalist?) group, practising economic terror and private expropriations was causing the local SRs concern as late as December 1907, but there were 'almost no' Anarchist and Maximalists at the Raditsa factory (for source of reference see n. 22).
140.   *Protokoly konferentsii predstavitelei Bezhetskogo, Bryanskogo Paravoznoi Raditsy i Privokzal'noi Slobody – rabochikh soyuzov PSR* (23 December 1907), Archive 426.
141.   *9e Yanvarya; k rabochim i krest'yanam*, Archive 321. The outcome of the elections here is unknown.
142.   *Ko vsem Bryanskim rabochim* (May 1907), Archive 321; see also comments of Bryansk delegate at seventh *oblast'* congress – *Protokoly 7-go ocherednogo s"ezda severo-zapadnoi oblasti partii SR* (July 1907), Archive 426.
143.   *Zasedanie kollektiva Bryanskoi organizatsii SR* (24 June 1907), Archive 321.
144.   *Trud*, no. 17, pp. 14–15, Archive 472.
145.   See MS from Bryansk dated 7.10.07, Archive 426.
146.   *Protokoly konferentsii* (23 December 1907), Archive 426.
147.   The last archival record of any of the Bryansk organisations occurs in March 1908, when the Raditsa workers' union issued a proclamation calling for the factory to be saved from closure (Archive 321). See also *Protokoly 1908*, p. 54.
148.   *Rossiya: Polnoe geograficheskoe opisanie*, vol. xiv, p. 176; *Bol'shaya sovetskaya entsiklopedia*, vol. l, pp. 545–7.
149.   *Rossiya*, vol. xiv, p. 176.
150.   Rashin, *Formirovanie*, p. 356.
151.   Before 1894, goods to the value of 13m. roubles had passed annually through Sevastopol'; after 1894 this figure dropped to 2.5m. roubles *per annum* (*Rossiya*, vol xiv, p. 176).
152.   Brokgauz and Efron, *Entsiklopedicheskii slovar'*, vol. lvii, pp. 293–4.
153.   Information on the early history of the party is drawn from two archival documents: *Delegate's report to the second party congress* (Sevastopol'), Archive 488; and *Kratkii ocherk rabochei organizatsii Sevastopol's-kogo Komiteta PSR so Noyabrii 1905g do fevralya 1907 goda*, Archive 488.

154. 45 000 leaflets were distributed between November 1905 and February 1906.
155. For details see below p. 163.
156. Delegate's report, Archive 488.
157. For the above see: *Delegate's report; Kratkii ocherk*; and *Answers to questions put by the orgbureau at the time of the* (second) *party congress*, all in Archive 488. For a résumé see, *Rapport 1907*, pp. 165–8.
158. *Kratkii ocherk*, Answers to questions ... (no. 3).
159. *Kratkii ocherk*.
160. The accounts were located in the 'Workers' Organisation' sections of Archive 488 and Archive 792. Abbreviated accounts (with interruptions) exist for the period 15 December 1905 to 30 May 1906. The complete accounts for October to December 1906 and March to July 1907 form the basis of Table 28, p. 331.
161. These (highly approximate) estimates are based on an average individual donation of 20 kopeks per month (the membership contribution demanded by the Kiev SR organisation before 1905). Calculations made on that basis turned out to be fairly reliable in the (admittedly few) cases where they could be tested for the 1905–7 period (at the Nevskii shipbuilding and Aleksandrovskii mechanical factories in Petersburg for example and the Bezhetsa engineering works in Bryansk).
162. See table 5.7 in my study of St. Petersburg, chapter 5 p. 119
163. The Sevastopol' detachment probably relied more than most on the participation of soldiers and sailors. Workers were also involved, however, though we have no breakdown of numbers.
164. *Delegate's report*, Archive 488.
165. See 'Statistika terroristicheskikh aktov', in *Pamyatnaya Knizhka*.
166. The full details are in Spiridovitch, *Histoire du terrorisme Russe*, pp. 367–9.
167. 'Statistika terroristicheskikh aktov'.
168. *Izveshchenie vnov organizovannoi boevoi druzhiny* (1907), Archive 488; 'Statistika terroristicheskikh aktov'.
169. *Izveshchenie po povodu otkolovshikhsya druzhinnikov* (June 1907), Archive 488; *Rabochii listok*, no. 1 (11 August 1907), Archive 488.
170. *Otchety Sevastopol'skogo Komiteta PSR*, Archive 488.
171. *Sevastopol'skaya Gorodskaya Konferentsiya* (May 1907); see also MS (Sevastopol' Committee), both in Archive 488.
172. MS Archive 488; Hildermeier, *Die Sozialrevolutionäre Partei*, p. 275 and n. 21.
173. *Provokatorskii manifest' i nashi zadachi* (June 1907), Archive 488.
174. The full story is told in Hildermeier, *Die Sozialrevolutionäre Partei*, pp. 171–2.
175. *Protokoly pyatogo soveta partii (stenograficheskii otchet)*, session 2, p. 8, Archive 792.
176. The SRs took 54 of the 77 seats in the town duma: *Delo Naroda*, no. 110 (26 July 1917), p. 4.
177. Radkey, *Agrarian Foes of Bolshevism*, p. 243, n. 14.
178. *Rapport 1907*, p. 142. For the boundaries and other details, see Map 6.

179.   Portal, R., 'The Industrialization of Russia', p. 806; Lenin, V. I., *The Development of Capitalism in Russia*, (London, 1977), pp. 490–3.
180.   Portal, 'The Industrialization of Russia', pp. 829–31, 858.
181.   Figures for 1910: T. S. Fedor, *Patterns of Urban Growth*.
182.   Portal, 'The Industrialization of Russia', p. 829 gives a figure of 105 factories, 13 of which were state-owned. My own calculations suggest that this is an underestimate and that the number of enterprises was closer to 150.
183.   R. E. Zelnik, 'The Peasant and the Factory', in W. S. Vucinich (ed.), *The Peasant in Nineteenth Century Russia*, pp. 160–1.
184.   Some details of the post-reform arrangements can be found in the essays by F. S. Gorovoi, N. D. Alenchikova and Ya. B. Rabinovich, in *Iz istorii rabochego klassa Urala (sbornik statei)* (Perm', 1961).
185.   Portal, 'The Industrialization of Russia', p. 830.
186.   The following description of the Izhevsk factory is based on A. A. Aleksandrov, 'Sostav i polozhenie rabochikh na Izhevskom i Votkinskom zavodakh (1894–1904gg)' in *Iz istorii rabochego klassa Urala (sbornik statei)* (Perm', 1961), pp. 252–61.
187.   F. S. Gorovoi, 'Vliyanie reformy 1861 goda na formirovanie rabochego klassa Urala', in *Iz istorii*, p. 165.
188.   See, for example, 'Rabochaya li partiya sotsialisty-revolyutsionery?' in *Bor'ba* (Motovilikha), no. 1 (April 10 1907), Archive 478, p. 12; *Bor'ba* (Motovilikha), no. 3 (15 May 1907), pp. 1–2; no. 4 (9 June 1907), pp. 1, 2. At the same time as emphasising the virtues of its land programme, the third *oblast'* congress of the PSR adopted a resolution in favour of including factory socialisation in the minimum programme of the party. This was a response to the 'special position' of the Urals population, being at the same time factory workers and peasant land-holders, and to the decline of private industry in particular and industry in general.
189.   There was a joint SR–SD group in Ufa in 1899, for example. See: *1905 – Revolyutsionnye sobytiya 1905g.v.g. Ufe i Ural'skikh zavodakh*, p. 17 (Ufa, 1925).
190.   See *Programma Ural'skogo soyuza Sotsial'-Demokratov i sotsialistov-revolyutsionerov*, in Archive 474, which contains eighteen flysheets, published by the Union between 1901 and 1903.
191.   See below, pp. 173–4, 174–5.
192.   For the SR role in the 'Alapaev republic' of 1905 see *ZT*, no. 10–11 (February–March 1908), p. 23.
193.   The voting went 8 votes to 5 and a minority resolution was also published: 'Postanovleniya III s"ezda Oblastnoi Ural'skoi organizatsii PSR', *PI*, no. 1 (October 1906), pp. 22–3.
194.   The SRs took 60 per cent of the vote at Izhevsk and won 1000 votes at Katav-Ivanovsk. In Ufa the party took 7 seats in the workers' curia and had one elector. They had two representatives in Perm' and only one in Vyatka. In Ekaterinburg the SDs won an outright victory. This information has been assembled from a variety of archival documents.
195.   Of twenty-three Urals activists surveyed in PKS, ten were arrested between June and November 1907.

196. See below, p. 170.
197. *Protokoly 1908*, p. 136.
198. *Protokoly 1909*, Archive 792, session 3, pp. 2 ff.
199. *Rapport 1910*, p. 18; *Rapport 1914*, p. 12.
200. Archive 478.
201. *Otchet Permskogo komiteta PSR s vesnoi 1906 g. do vesnoi 1907 g.*, Archive 478.
202. See below.
203. *Protokoly 1909*, Archive 792, session 3, p. 2.
204. See accounts in *Bor'ba*, no. 2 (May 1907), Archive 478.
205. *Bor'ba*, no. 2. See also *ZT*, no. 7 (October 1907), p. 14.
206. The following is based on information in *ZT*, no. 7, p. 14, and a report on Nadezhdin rail factory in *ZT*, no. 8 (December 1907), p. 15. According to an early Soviet source, L'bov first linked up with a group of Maximalists from Petersburg who had arrived in Perm' early in 1906. They split in the summer of 1907 and L'bov began to act independently again. Apparently, some of the terrorists from these gangs were tried by military courts in 1909. See A. Beloborodov, 'Iz istorii partizanskogo dvizheniya na Urale (1906–09 gg)', in *Krasnaya Letopis'*, no. 1 (1926), pp. 92 ff.
207. *Protokoly 1909*, Archive 792, session 3, p. 2.
208. Ibid.
209. *Iz otcheta Ekaterinburgskogo okruzhn. kom. Ural'noi organizatsii PSR* (February–October 1906), Archive 480.
210. *ZT*, no. 7 (October 1907), p. 14.
211. *Rossiya*, vol. v, p. 557.
212. *Rapport 1907*, pp. 143–8; *Otvety* (second congress), Vyatka, Archive 486.
213. Report to fourth *oblast'* congress in *ZT*, no. 7, p. 14.
214. *Protokoly 1909*, Archive 792, session 3, p. 2.
215. See biography of S. N. Krasnoperov in PKS. Krasnoperov was the son of a priest and a fitter at the factory. Having attended student circles in Vyatka from 1902 to 1904, at the age of seventeen he joined the Izhevsk PSR, where he remained until his arrest in 1907.
216. *Izhevskaya zavodskaya organizatsiya* in *PI*, no. 10 (September 1907), p. 15; *Rapport 1907*, p. 145; biography of F. I. Shipitsyn in PKS. Shipitsyn, a former SD became a member of the Izhevsk SR committee in August 1906, at the age of thirty-three, and was an elector to the second Duma.
217. Assistance mainly in the form of personnel support. For example, E. A. Deryabina-Kondorskaya, a teacher from Vyatka province conducted agitation and propaganda at Izhevsk in 1907 having previously worked in Vyatka town. Likewise P. P. Suvorova-Varaksina (PKS).
218. See *oblast'* report dated 30 October 1907 in Archive 486.
219. Accounts for Izhevsk (and Votkinsk, see n 221 below) in Archive 548.
220. *Protokoly 1908*, p. 39; *Protokoly 1909*, Archive 792, session 3, p. 2; D. I. Gorbunov was an SR on the Izhevsk committee in 1908–9 (aged seventeen) and a member of the Votkinsk group (PKS).
221. *Rossiya*, vol. v, p. 524.

222. *Rapport 1907*, p. 145.
223. *Oblast'* report (30 October 1907), Archive 486.
224. *Protokoly 1909*.
225. *Rossiya*, vol. v, pp. 458–60.
226. *1905–Revolyutsionnye Sobytiya 1905g.*, p. 8; *Statistika terroristiches-kikh aktov*. Sokolovskii was killed (?) by a worker, Bubetov.
227. See the biography of P. P. Myl'nikov, an SR joiner in the railway workshops (PKS).
228. Ufa workers' union accounts for 1906 can be found in *Sotsialist': organ Ufimskogo rabochego Soyuza*, no. 1 (January 1907), Archive 682.
229. *Rapport 1907*, p. 146. *Otvety* (second congress), Archive 486; 'Smert'tovarishcha' (notice in *Sotsialist'*), Archive 682.
230. Urals *oblast'* report (30 October 1907), Archive 486.
231. *Protokoly 1908*, p. 39.
232. *Protokoly 1909*, Archive 792.
233. *1905 Revolyutsionnye sobytiya 1905 g.*, pp. 19–34.
234. For information on the Zlatoust organisation during this period, see the financial accounts in Archive 480 and *Doklad Zlatoustavshego delegata na II-m partiinom s"ezde*, Archive 480; and *Rapport 1907*, p. 146.
235. *Doklad Zlatoustavshego* and accounts, Archive 480; *Satkinskaya rabochaya organizatsiya* (September 1906–June 1907), also Archive 480.
236. *ZT*, no. 7 (October 1907), p. 14; Zlatoust committee (Summer 1907?), Archive 480.
237. *Protokoly 1908*, pp. 39, 40. The Zlatoust armed detachment continued to be active – two provocateurs were killed in 1908 and a police inspector in December 1907. See also the biography of S. I. Perevalov (PKS), a fitter at the Zlatoust factory and a member of the committee from 1905–8. In February the police arrested him after discovering two bombs in his possession.
238. *Protokol Zlatoustovskoi okruzhskoi konferentsii* (19 November 1908), Archive 480.
239. *Protokoly 1909*, Archive 792, session 3, pt 2.

7 The SRs and the Trade Union Movement

1. P. P. Maslov, 'Narodnicheskie Partii', in *ODR*, vol iii, bk 5, p. 98. One pamphlet was devoted to worker disturbances in Rostov, the other to unemployment.
2. In the sense that it was Gershuni who founded the Minsk 'Workers' Party for the Political Liberation of Russia' in 1898. Like Lebedev, the Moscow activists, I. I. Fundaminskii, V. V. Rudnev and V. M. Zenzinov were all in their early or mid-twenties in 1905 and comparatively inexperienced in revolutionary affairs.
3. See the discussion in *Protokoly 1906*, pp. 316–25; supplement, pp. 17–40.

4. The debate on these issues is recounted in chapter 2 of the present study.
5. *Protokoly 1906*, p. 338.
6. *Protokoly 1907*, p. 13.
7. Ibid., p. 134.
8. Ibid., p. 172.
9. Third Council resolutions in *Pamyatnaya Knizhka*, p. 20.
10. *Protokoly 1908*, p. 78.
11. Ibid., p. 75.
12. Ibid., pp. 75–6.
13. Ibid., pp. 231–5.
14. *Izveshchenie pyatogo Soveta PSR* (May 1909), p. 18.
15. *Protokoly 1909*, 22nd session, p. 1, Archive 792.
16. For the precursors and early history of the Russian trade union movement see D. Antoshkin, *Professional'noe Dvizhenie v Rossii* (3rd edn.), pp. 40–70; S. Ainzaft, *Pervyi etap professional'nogo dvizheniya v Rossii (1905–07gg)* (Moscow, 1924), pp. 5–41; V. Grinevich, *Professional'noe dvizhenie rabochikh v Rossii* (3rd edn.; Moscow, 1923), pp. 3–20; and for police socialist unions, see J. Schneiderman, *Sergei Zubatov and Revolutionary Marxism*.
17. Antoshkin, *Professional'noe dvizhenie*, p. 89.
18. Ibid., pp. 106–7.
19. Antoshkin, *Professional'noe dvizhenie*, pp. 146–55; Ainzaft, *Pervyi etap professional'nogo dvizheniya v Rossii*, pp. 57–65; Grinevich, *Professional'noe dvizhenie*, pp. 58–62.
20. See the discussion in Ainzaft, pp. 65 ff.; Grinevich, pp. 70–6.
21. Elwood, *Social Democracy in the Underground*, pp. 190ff.
22. For the post-1907 history of the unions, see the relevant chapters in Antoshkin, *Professional'noe Dvizhenie v Rossii*. By 1910 there were only 35 000 registered trade union members throughout Russia. Between 1906 and 1910, 497 unions were officially closed and there were 604 cases of unions being refused registration (Antoshkin, pp. 140–4).
23. V. Bonnell, 'Radical Politics and Organised Labour in Pre-Revolutionary Moscow, 1905–1914', *JSH*, XII, 1 (1978), pp. 289ff.; also Bonnell, 'The Politics of Labour', *passim*.
24. Chapter 5, p. 81.
25. Maslov, 'Narodnicheskie Partii', p. 109.
26. *PI*, no. 4 (January 1907), pp. 2–9 (Chernov uses the pseudonym 'Gardenin').
27. 'Konferentsiya po voprosam prof. dvizheniya', *Trud*, no. 9 (February 1907), p. 14.
28. *Trud*, no. 11 (March 1907), pp. 1–3.
29. 'K zakonoproektu S-r gruppy o professional'nykh soyuzakh', in *Trud*, no. 13 (April 1907), pp. 5–6. These proposals were chiefly intended to have an agitational significance. They advocated trade unions for every category of worker, to be formed without any formal requirement for registration; freedom to combine and amalgamate trade unions; trade union control over private assets and funds, criminal and

financial immunity in the course of normal union activities; union representation on factory inspectorates, sanitary commissions, and so on, and prosecution of anyone or any organisation infringing union rights. For the full text, see 'Po povodu proekta zakona o professional'nykh soyuzakh sostavlennogo rabochei komissiei dumskoi gruppy sotsialistov-revolyutsionnerov', in *Volya i Zemlya*, no. 1 (April 1907), pp. 5–6, Archive 743.

30. *ZT*, no. 2 (July 1907), pp. 1–4. The third party council met between 8 and 11 July 1907 (*Materialy*, Archive 679).

31. See, for example: *Vpered*, no. 2 (Perm', October 1907), Archive 478; *Bor'ba*, no. 2 (Motovilikha, May 1907), Archive 478; *Rabochii listok*, no. 1 (Sevastopol', August 1907), Archive 488; *Izvestiya Ukrainskogo oblastnogo komiteta PSR*, no. 1 (June 1907), Archive 482; *Trud*, no. 17 (Petersburg, October 1907), Archive 472.

32. See below.

33. *Izveshchenie pyatogo Soveta PSR*, pp. 16–17.

34. 'Nasha pozitsiya v professional'nom dvizhenii', *ZT*, no. 2 (July 1907), pp. 1–4.

35. In English in the original.

36. There is no specific indication that Chernov was thinking of the Russian Social Democrats as such. The position outlined here is close to that adopted by the German Social Democrats at the Stuttgart Congress of the Socialist International in August 1907. See G. D. H. Cole, *A History of Socialist Thought*, vol III, pt. 1 (London 1970), p. 72. For the complex, sometimes bemusing history of the Russian Social-Democratic factions' approach to the trade union movement, see the following: Grinevich, *Professional'noe dvizhenie*, pp. 173–83; Antoshkin, *Professional'noe dvizhenie*, pp. 139–45; Bonnell, 'The Politics of Labour', pp. 194–5; Swain, *Russian Social Democracy and the Legal Labour Movement*, Introduction.

37. The following presentation of the SR position is based on: V. M. Chernov, in *Znamya Truda* (see n. 35 above); third and fourth party council resolutions (*Pamyatnaya Knizhka*, I, pp. 30–36); 'Professional'nye soyuzy i partiya sotsialistov-revolyutsionerov', *Trud*, no. 17 (October 1907), pp. 3–6; 'K voprosu o professional'nykh soyuzakh', *Trud*, no. 11 (March 1907), pp. 1–3; Yu. Gardenin (Chernov), 'III s"ezd vseross. zh. D. Soyuza', *PI*, no. 4 (January 1907), pp. 2–9; 'Politicheskii indifferentizm i neitral'nost professional'nykh soyuzov', *Professional'noe dvizhenie: obzor deyatel'nosti rabochikh soyuzov v Rossii i za granitsei-Petersburg*, no. 1 (May 1907), pp. 2–5.

38. 'Politicheskii indifferentizm' (*Professional'noe dvizhenie*), p. 3.

39. Ibid.

40. Third Party Council resolutions, *Pamyatnaya Knizhka*, I, p. 34. This phrase was standard to trade unions formed during the 1905–7 period.

41. 'Gardenin' (Chernov), *PI*, no. 4 (January 1907), p. 4.

42. *ZT*, no. 2 (July 1907), p. 1; *Trud*, no. 17 (October 1907), p. 5.

43. *PI*, no. 4 (January 1907), p. 5.

44. *Trud*, no. 11 (March 1907), pp. 3–5.

45. *Trud*, no. 13 (April 1907), p. 6.

46. Third Council resolutions, p. 33; *ZT*, no. 2 (July 1907), p. 3.
47. 'Politicheskii indifferentizm', p. 3.
48. *ZT*, no. 2, p. 3.
49. Kautsky allegedly advocated neutrality under existing Russian conditions in a letter to Social Democrats in Baku ('Politicheskii indifferentizm', p. 5). The authority of the International is claimed in the article: 'Rossiiskaya Sotsial-demokratiya i professional'nye soyuzy', in *ZT*, no. 8 (December 1907), pp. 9–10, here p. 10; and in *Trud*, no. 17 (October 1907), p. 5.
50. 'Politicheskii indifferentizm', p. 5.
51. Third Council resolutions, p. 33.
52. *ZT*, no. 2 (July 1907), pp. 3–4, 'S"ezd professional'nykh soyuzakh i tsentral'noe buro', *ZT*, no. 8 (December 1907), pp. 6–9, here pp. 8–9.
53. Some Bolsheviks advocated fully-political trade unions which would officially adopt the programme of the RSDLP. The political platform was a much broader concept, however, as will be revealed in due course.
54. H. F. Reichman, 'Russian Railwaymen in the Revolution of 1905', PhD thesis, California/Berkeley, 1977, p. 328.
55. 'S vserossiiskoi konferentsii pechatnikov (doklad po voprosu ob otnoshenii professional'nykh soyuzov k partiyam predstavitelya PSR)', in *Professional'noe dvizhenie*, no. 1 (May 1907), pp. 10–13, here p. 12.
56. *Ustav ARRU* (reprinted by the Ryazan'–Urals railway branch), Archive 329.
57. See Grinevich, *Professional'noe dvizhenie*, p. 172.
58. See n. 55, above.
59. Grinevich, *Professional'noe dvizhenie*, p. 173.
60. Ibid.
61. For the early history of the ARRU and the Russian railway industry in general see Reichman, 'Russian Railwaymen', and W. Sablinsky, 'The All-Russian Railroad Union and the Beginning of the General Strike in October 1905', in A. I. Rabinowitch, *Revolution and Politics in Russia. Essays in Memory of B. I. Nicolaevsky* (Bloomington, Ind., 1972).
62. See the Petersburg section of this study, chapter 5 pp. 122–3.
63. One-third of railway workers in Belorussia, for example, were peasants who maintained economic ties with the countryside (Reichman 'Russian Railwaymen', p. 33).
64. *PI*, no. 4 (January 1907), p. 2.
65. See, for example: *Tochka zreniya tsentral'nogo byuro vserossiiskogo zheleznodorozhnogo soyuza na predstoyashchuyu vseobshchuyu zheleznodorozhnuyu zabastovku* (Petersburg, August 1906), Archive 329. and: *K vsem zheleznodorozhnikam (postanovlenie konferentsii predstavitelei zheleznykh dorog, sozvannoi dlya resheniya voprosa o vseobshchei zabastovke v svyazi s rospuskom gosudarstvennoi dumy*, Archive 658. The participation of railwaymen was to be conditional on a mass rising of workers and peasants.
66. See below, p. 189.
67. *PI*, no. 4, p. 2.

68. Odd copies of the journals are to be found in Archives 329 and 658.
69. 'Zheleznodorozhnyi professional'nyi soyuz i politicheskaya platforma', in *Lokomotiv*, no. 5 (Petersburg, May 1907), Archive 329.
70. See the MS signed by Pereverzev and dated 30.10.1908 which asked for 800r. in order to re-start publication of the journal, *Zheleznodorozhnyi Soyuz*, which ran out of funds after five numbers. See also a typed (and undated) letter to the Central Committee of the PSR from agents of the ARRU (both documents in Archive 329).
71. 'Zametka o sovremennom sostoyanii vserossiiskogo zheleznodorozh-nogo soyuza', in *ZT*, no. 13/14, pp. 22–3.
72. 'Novyi pod"em', *ZT*, no. 53 (April 1914), pp. 1–2.
73. Reichman, 'Russian Railwaymen', p. 452.
74. *PI*, no. 4 (January 1907), p. 8.
75. 'O konferentsiyakh Peterburgskogo uzla vserossiiskogo-zheleznodor-ozhnogo soyuza', in *Trud*, no. 9 (February 1907), pp. 8–10, here p. 10 (even here the voting was close).
76. *Otchet o konferentsii Moskovsko-Yaroslavsko-Arkhangel'skoi Zhel-dor.*, Archive 658.
77. *PI*, no. 4, p. 2.
78. The relevant documents are the following: typed report of the Central Bureau, ARRU (May 1906); *Proekt vremennogo soglasheniya vseros-siiskogo zheleznodorozhnogo soyuza s sotsialisticheskimi partiyami o vzaimnykh otnosheniyakh soyuza i partii pri rabote ikh sredi zhelezno-dorozhnykh rabochikh i sluzhashchikh*, Archive 329. (A conference had discussed these subjects in April 1906.)
79. M. Dmitriev (see n. 69 above).
80. *PI*, no. 4 (January 1907), p. 6.
81. Chernov, whether intentionally or not, was apparently telling only half the story. While Moscow metalworkers were urged by their union to vote for Social Democrats, the Union of Weaving and Knitting workers supported the PSR. See Bonnell, 'The Politics of Labour', p. 175. (Bonnell cites *Professional'nye Vestnik* as her source.)
82. *ZT*, no. 6 (September 1907), p. 15. See also: *Protokoly zanyatii konferentsii rabotnikov po professional'nomu dvizheniyu Tavriches-kogo Soyuza PSR* (5–7 August 1907), Archive 596.
83. This approach accords with that adopted by the Bolsheviks at their London congress in 1907. See Elwood, *Social Democracy in the Underground*, pp. 194ff.
84. *ZT*, no. 8 (December 1907), p. 8.
85. Ibid.
86. This union was of some strategic importance but its membership was comparatively small and its activities limited. For material on the union see 'O volzhskoi sudokhodnoi organizatsii PS-R', in *PI*, no. 8 (April 1907), pp. 8–9, and documents in Archive 177.
87. See the relevant chapters of this study. Also Heather Hogan, 'Labour and Management in Conflict', PhD thesis, University of Michigan, 1981, p. 338.
88. See Engelstein, *Moscow 1905*; Bonnell 'The Politics of Labor'; MS of Summer 1907 in Archive 333. (The SRs claimed to have a lot of

sympathisers in the Moscow print-workers' union at this time.)

89. These are the phrases used in the MS fragment *Istoriya professional'-nogo dvizheniya v Rossii* in Archive 638/II.

90. 'Massovaya bor'ba i professional'noe dvizhenie', in *Rabochii Listok*, no. 2 (October 1907), Archive 488.

91. For Baku see the relevant section of this study; for Khar'kov: Archive 792; Kiev: *ZT*, no. 16 (March 1909), p. 6; Caucasus; *Sovremennik* no. 4 (September 1909), p. 1, Archive 551.

92. Lebedev, 'Rabochaya organizatsiya (Zametka propagandista)', in *ZT*, no. 16 (March 1909), pp. 5–8.

93. 'Ekonomicheskaya bor'ba v podpol'e', in *ZT*, no. 18 (May 1909), pp. 3–7.

Epilogue

1. These reforms facilitated the withdrawal of individual peasants and their families from the commune, with the intention of creating a class of independent, prosperous and, hopefully, conservative landholders from among the peasant masses. They represented a direct challenge to the policies of the PSR and had a fair measure of success before 1914. See Perrie, *The Agrarian Policy*, pp. 182–4; Hildermeier, *Die Sozialrevolutionäre Partei*, pp. 348–54.

2. The Fighting Organisation was effectively finished by the Azef affair. The last recorded terrorist incidents occurred in 1911. (See *Pamyatnaya knizhka*, 2nd issue, p. 17; Hildermeier, *Die Sozialrevolutionäre Partei*, p. 387.)

3. The 'Paris Group of SRs', led by Ya.L. Yudelevskii and V. K. Agafonov and responsible for issuing the journal *Revolyutsionnaya Mysl'* (1908–9). Their policy and tactical recommendations were virtually identical to those of classical Maximalism but, unlike that movement, 'neo-Maximalism' never acquired a noteworthy following. See Hildermeier, *Die Sozialrevolutionäre Partei* pp. 324–7.

4. For the history of the *Pochintsy* see Hildermeier, *Die Sozial-revolutionäre Partei* pp. 327–8, 325–40. For their platform and thinking, see especially *Pochin: izd. Gruppy Sotsialistov-Revolyutsionerov. Pod. red. N.D. Avksent'eva, I. Bunakova [Fundaminskii], V. Voronova [B.N. Lebedev] i S. Nechetnogo [S.N. Sletov]*, no. 1 (Paris, June 1912), Archive 672. Also: N. D. Avksent'ev, 'Boikot ili uchastie v vyborakh', *ZT*, no. 35 (April 1911), pp. 7–9; B. Voronov (Lebedev), 'Professional'nye soyuzy i zabastovochnoe dvizhenie', in *ZT*, no. 45 (September 1912), pp. 9–11. For the reponse of their opponents see especially, N. I. Rakitnikov, 'Partiya i "legal'nye vozmozhnosti"', in *ZT*, no. 36 (June 1911), pp. 1–3; 'Vybirat'-li v Dume?', *ZT*, no. 36, pp. 14–18; 'Novoe techenie sotsial'no-revolyutsionnoi mysli', *ZT*, no. 45 (September 1912), pp. 1–6; 'V chem-zhe raznoglasiya?', *ZT*, no. 52 (November 1913), pp. 4–7.

5. For evidence of SR strength in Russia's urban centres during the first half of 1917 see William G. Rosenberg, 'The Russian Municipal Duma

Elections of 1917 – A Preliminary Computation of Returns', in *Soviet Studies*, 21 (1969), no. 2, pp. 131–63.

Conclusion

1. A. Pospelov and S. Postinikov, 'Po povodu statei tt. starogo rabotnika i Al. Klyueva', in *ZT* no. 32 (November 1910), pp. 11–15 (here p. 14).
2. For more on the propaganda output of urban organisations see Eiter, 'Organizational Growth and Revolutionary Tactics', pp. 85–7.
3. Johnson, *Peasant and Proletarian*, p. 159.
4. Weber, *Peasants into Frenchmen*, pp. 278–85.
5. See McKay, *Pioneers for Profit*, p. 262.
6. Radkey, *The Agrarian Foes of Bolshevism*, p. 53. See also Lane, *The Roots of Russian Communism*, p. 42.
7. Koenker, *Moscow Workers*, p, 358.
8. Engelstein, 'Moscow in the 1905 revolution: A Study in Class Conflict and Political Organization', PhD thesis, Stanford CA, 1976. (See Engelstein in bibliography.)
9. 'Tekstil'shchiki v revolyutsii 1905–07gg', in *Proletariat v revolyutsii 1905–07gg* (Moscow and Leningrad, 1930).
10. Koenker, *Moscow Workers*, p. 205.
11. See above, p. 107.
12. See, for example, B. V. Levanov, *Iz istorii bor'by bol'shevistskoi partii protiv eserov v gody pervoi russkoi revolyutsii*, p. 106; and K. V. Gusev, *Partiya eserov – ot melkoburzhuaznogo revolyutsion-arizma k kontrrevolyutsii*, p. 52.
13. William G. Rosenberg, 'The Russian Municipal Duma elections of 1917', p. 144, ('SR strength in the European provincial capitals appears especially impressive ...').
14. It should be emphasised here that there is no intention to imply in what follows, either that support for the PSR was drawn exclusively from the ranks of migrant workers, or that support can be explained solely in terms of workers' connections with the land or the peasant community.
15. Joan M. Nelson, *Migrants, Urban Poverty and Instability in Developing Nations* (Cambridge, MA, 1969); here p. 7.
16. Haimson, 'The Problem of Social Stability in Urban Russia, 1905–1917'.
17. Daniel Brower, 'Labor Violence in Russia in the Late Nineteenth Century', *Slavic Review*, no 41, 3(1982) pp. 417–32; here p. 418.
18. Robert C. Fried, 'Urbanization and Italian Politics', in *Journal of Politics*, 29, no. 3 (1967), pp. 505–34; here p. 527.
19. See above, chapter 5.
20. Olga Crisp, 'Labour and Industrialization in Russia', p. 378.
21. Johnson, *Peasant and Proletarian*, p. 158.
22. See for example, Wayne A. Cornelius, *Politics and the Migrant Poor in Mexico City* (Stanford, 1975).

23. Bonnell, 'Radical Politics and Organized Labour', p. 283.
24. Alejandro Portes, 'Political Primitivsim, Differential Socialization and Lower-Class Leftist Radicalism', *American Sociological Review* vol. 36 (1971), pp. 820–35; here p. 832. On the influence of the local environment, see the chapter on political culture in David Mandel, *The Petrograd Workers and the Fall of the Old Regime* (London: Macmillan, 1983).
25. Koenker, *Moscow Workers*, pp. 187, 191.
26. Fried, quoted Nelson, *Access to Power*, p. 119.
27. Koenker, *Moscow Workers*, p. 192.
28. E. Kabo, *Ocherki rabochego byta*, pp. 35–9, 47–54, 54–63, 93–98, 103–11.
29. R. E. Zelnik, 'Russian Bebels: An Introduction to the Memoirs of Semen Kanatchikov and Matvei Fisher', in *Russian Review*, vol. 35, no. 3, pp. 249–90; no. 4 (1976) pp. 417–47; here p. 424. (Extracts from the Kanatchikov memoir can also be found in V. E. Bonnell (ed.), *The Russian Worker. Life and Labor under the Tsarist Regime*, pp. 36–71).

Bibliography

I Archive Sources

Narodnicheskoe dvizhenie (Populist Movement) archive, International Institute for Social History, Amsterdam. Folder numbers: 26, 45, 52, 83, 86, 87a, b, 114, 154, 164, 177, 197, 208, 238, 321, 325, 329, 332, 333, 334, 335, 374, 403, 426, 427, 430, 431, 436, 439, 442, 443, 444, 445, 446, 447, 458, 472, 474, 478, 480, 482, 486, 488, 489, 512, 521/I, II, 525, 544, 548, 550, 551, 553/I, II, 557, 561, 596, 600, 628, 635/II, 636, 653, 658, 672, 676, 679, 682, 694, 743, 757, 758, 759, 762, 792, 818, 876, 936.

II Newspapers and Journals of the PSR

Byulleten' Tsentral'nogo Komiteta Partii Sotsialistov-Revolyutsionerov no. 1 (March 1906)

Delo Naroda – organ partii SR: ezhednevaya politicheskaya i literaturnaya gazeta (March 1917–1919)

Partiinyya Izvestiya – Izd. Tsentral'nogo Komiteta Partii Sotsialistov-Revolyutsionerov (October 1906–May 1907)

Pochin – Izd. Gruppy sotsialistov-revolyutsionerov, no. 1 (June 1912)

Professional'noe Dvizhenie: obzor deyatel'nosti rabochikh soyuzov v Rossii i za granitsei (Petersburg, 1 May 1907)

Rabochii – Izd. Partii Sotsialistov-Revolyutsionerov, no. 1 (November 1911); no. 2 (March 1912)

Revolyutsionnaya Rossiya – Izd. Soyuza Sotsialistov-Revolyutsionerov/Partii Sotsialistov-Revolyutsionerov (1900–October 1905).

Sotsialist-Revolyutsioner – Trekhmesyachnoe literaturno-politicheskoe obozrenie (May 1910–March 1912)

Trud – Rabochaya gazeta Izd. Petersburgskogo Komiteta Partii Sotsialistov-Revolyutsionerov (September 1906–March 1908)

Vestnik Russkoi Revolyutsii – Sotsial'no-politicheskoe obozrenie (July 1901–March 1905)

Zavety – literaturno-politicheskii zhurnal (April 1912–1914)

Znamya Truda – Tsentral'nyi organ Partii Sotsialistov-Revolyutsionerov (June 1907–April 1914)

III Other Newspapers and Journals

Iskra – RSDLP (1900–5)

Izvestiya soveta rabochikh deputatov goroda Sankt Peterburga (1905)

Krasnaya letopis'

258

Luch' – rabochaya gazeta (1912–14)
Nash Ekho (Petersburg, 1906–07)
Nash Mir (Petersburg, 1907)
Novyi Luch' (Petersburg, 1907)
Pravda (Vienna, 1908–12)
Proletarii (1906–09)
Rech' (1906–17; selected issues, 1906–7)
Rus' (1906–9; selected issues, 1906–7)
Sotsialdemokrat – RSDLP (Petersburg, 1906)
Vol'nyi diskussionyi listok – izdanie gruppy sotsialistov-revolyutsionerov (1905)

IV Documents relating to the PSR

Izveshchenie pyatogo soveta PSR (May 1909)
Protokoly pervogo s"ezda Partii Sotsialistov-Revolyutsionerov (n.p., 1906)
Protokoly vtorogo (ekstrennogo) s"ezda Partii Sotsialistov-revolyutsionerov (Petersburg, 1907)
Protokoly pervoi obshchepartiinoi konferentsii PSR (London, 1908)
Protokoly pyatogo soveta PSR (n.p, 1909) Archive 792
Rapport du Parti Socialiste Revolutionnaire de Russie au Congrès Socialiste International d'Amsterdam (Paris, 1904)
Rapport du Parti Socialiste-Revolutionnaire de Russie au Congrès Socialiste International de Stuttgart (Ghent, 1907)
Russie: Rapport du Parti Socialiste-Revolutionnaire, in: *De 1907 à 1910. Rapport sur le mouvement ouvrier et socialiste soumis par les partis affilés au Congrès Socialiste International de Copenhague* (28 Août au 3 Sept 1910) (Brussels, 1910)
Russie: Rapport du Parti Socialiste-Revolutionnaire au Congrès Socialiste International de Vienne (1914)
'Statistika terroristicheskikh aktov', in *Pamyatnaya knizhka sotsialista-revolyutsionera*, issue 2 (Paris, 1914)

V Other Documents and Related Materials

Arkhiv Istorii Truda v Rossii, vypuskaemyi ustnoi komissiei po issledovaniyu istorii truda v Rossii, bk 1 (Petrograd, 1921)
Ocherki rabochego byta – opyt monograficheskogo-issledovaniya domashnego rabochego byta, ed. E. O. Kabo (Moscow, 1928)
Politicheskaya katorga i ssylka: bibliograficheskii spravochnik chlenov obshchestva politkatorzhan i ssyl'no-poselentsev (2nd edn, Moscow, 1934)
Polnoe sobranie zakonov Rossiiskoi Imperii (3rd series, 1882–1916)

VI Unpublished Theses and Dissertations

Blakely, Allison, 'The Socialist Revolutionary Party, 1901–07: The Populist Response to the Industrialization of Russia', PhD, California, Berkeley, 1971.

260 Bibliography

Bonnell, V. E., 'The Politics of Labor in Pre-revolutionary Russia: Moscow Workers' Organizations 1905–1914' PhD, Harvard, 1975.

Brock, J., 'The Theory and Practice of Black Hundred Politics', PhD, University of Michigan, 1977.

Desjeans, M. F., 'The Common Experience of the Russian Working Class: The Case of St. Petersburg, 1892–1904', PhD, Duke University, 1979.

Eiter, R. H., 'Organisational Growth and Revolutionary Tactics: Unity and Discord in the Socialist-Revolutionary Party, 1901–7', PhD, Pittsburg, 1978.

Engelstein, Laura, 'Moscow in the 1905 Revolution: A Study in Class Conflict and Political Organisation', PhD Stanford, 1976.

Flenley, P., 'Workers' Organizations in the Russian Metal Industry', PhD, Birmingham, 1983.

Gollan, D. E., 'Bolshevik Party Organisation in Russia, 1907–1912', MA, Australian National University, 1967.

Hogan, Heather, 'Labour and Management in Conflict: The St. Petersburg Metal-Working Industry, 1900–1914', PhD, University of Michigan, 1981.

Loizou, M., 'The Development of the Agrarian Programme of the Russian Social-Democratic Labour Party', MPhil, Birmingham, 1982.

Morgan, Anne D., 'The St. Petersburg Soviet of Workers' Deputies: A Study of Labor Organisation in the 1905 Revolution', PhD, Indiana, 1979.

Perrie, M. P., 'The Social Composition and Structure of the Socialist-Revolutionary Party and its activity among the Russian Peasantry', MA, Birmingham, 1971.

Rawson, D. C., 'The Union of Russian People, 1905–1907: A Study of the Radical Right', PhD, Washington, 1971.

Reichman, H. F., 'Russian Railwaymen in the Revolution of 1905', PhD California, Berkley, 1977.

Rowland, Richard H., 'Urban In-migration in Late Nineteenth Century Russia', PhD, Columbia, 1971.

Smith, S. A., 'The Russian Revolution and the Factories of Petrograd, February 1917 to June 1918', PhD, Birmingham, 1980.

Swain, G. A., 'Political Developments within the Organized Working Class: Petersburg 1906–14', PhD, London, 1979.

Tilly, Louise, 'The Working Class of Milan, 1881–1911', PhD, Toronto, 1974.

VII Secondary works

Ainzaft, S., *Pervyi etap professional'nogo dvizheniya v Rossii (1905–7gg)* (Moscow, 1924)

Aleksandrov, A. A., 'Sostav i polozhenie rabochikh na Izhevskom i Votkinskom zavodakh (1894–1904gg)', in *Iz istorii rabochego klassa Urala (sbornik statei)* (Perm', 1961)

Anderson, Barbara A., *Internal Migration during Modernization in Late Nineteenth Century Russia* (Princeton, NJ, 1980)

Antoshkin, D., *Professional'noe dvizhenie v Rossii – posobie dlya samoobrazovaniya i kursov po professional'nomu dvizheniyu* (3rd. edn, Moscow, 1925)

Anweiler, O., *The Soviets – The Russian Workers, Peasants and Soldiers' Councils, 1905–1921* (New York, 1974)

Argunov, A. A., 'Iz proshlogo partii sotsialistov-revolyustionerov', in *Byloe*, no. 10/22 (October, 1907)

Arutyunov, G. A., *Rabochee dvizhenie v zakavkaz'e period novogo revolyutsionnogo pod"ema 1910–1914gg* (Moscow and Baku, 1963)

Avrich, P., *The Russian Anarchists* (Princeton, 1967)

Baker, Pauline H., *Urbanization and Political Change: The Politics of Lagos, 1917–67* (California, 1974)

Balabanov, M., 'Promyshlennost' 1904–7gg', in *Obshchestvennoe dvizhenie v Rossii v nachale XX–go veka* (St. Petersburg, 1914)

Baron, S. H., *Plekhanov: The Father of Russian Marxism* (London, 1963)

Bater, James, *St. Petersburg – Industrialization and Change* (London: Arnold, 1976)

Bater, James, 'Transience, Residential Persistence and Mobility in Moscow and St. Petersburg, 1900–14', *Slavic Review*, 39, no. 2 (June, 1980), pp. 239–55

Billington, James H., *Mikhailovsky and Russian Populism* (New York: OUP, 1958)

Black, C. E. (ed.), *The Transformation of Russian Society* (Cambridge, MA, 1960)

Blackwell, W. L., *The Beginnings of Russian Industrialization 1800–1860* (Princeton, 1968)

Blackwell, W. L., *The Industrialization of Russia: an Historical Perspective* (2nd edn, Arlington Heights, 1982)

Bonnell, V. E., 'Radical Politics and Organized Labor in Pre-revolutionary Moscow 1905–1914', *Journal of Social History*, no. 2 (1978), pp. 282–300

Bonnell, V. E., *Roots of Rebellion: Workers' Politics and Organizations in St. Petersburg and Moscow, 1900–1914* (University of California Press, 1983)

Bonnell, V. E. (ed.), *The Russian Worker. Life and Labour under the Tsarist Regime* (University of California Press, 1983)

Bradley, Joseph, *Muzhik and Muscovite. Urbanization in Late Imperial Russia* (University of California Press, 1985)

Bortnik, M., 'V 1901–1904gg na Peterburgskom trubochnom zavode', *Krasnaya Letopis'*, 1(1929), pp. 182–213

Brower, Daniel D., 'Labor Violence in Russia in the Late Nineteenth Century', *Slavic Review*, no. 41, 3 (1982), pp. 417–32

Brusyanin, V., 'Chernaya sotnya na fabrikakh i zavodakh Peterburga v gody reaktsii', *Krasnaya Letopis'*, 1(1929), pp. 154–81

Buiko, A., *Put' rabochego – zapiski starogo bol'shevika* (Moscow, 1934)

Buzinov, A., *Za Nevskoi Zastavoi – zapiski rabochego Alekseya Buzinova* (Moscow and Leningrad, 1930)

B-skii, A., 'Peterburgskaya gorodskaya zhelezno-dorozhnaya organizatsiya RSDRP v 1906–1908gg (soyuz tramvaishchikov)', *Krasnaya Letopis'*, 6(1926), pp. 103–12

Carr, E. H., *The Bolshevik Revolution, 1917–23*, vol. II, *The Economic Order* (London: Macmillan, 1952)

Chernov, V. M., *Pered burei – vospominaniia* (New York, 1953)

Chernov, V. M., 'K kharakteristike maksimalizma', *Sotsialist-Revolyutsioner*, no. 1(1910), pp. 175–307

Cole, G. D. H., *A History of Socialist Thought*, vol. III. (London, 1970)

Cornelius, Wayne A., *Politics and the Migrant Poor in Mexico City* (Stanford, 1975)

Crisp, Olga, *Studies in the Russian Economy before 1914* (London: Macmillan, 1976)

Crisp, Olga, 'Labour and Industrialization in Russia', *Cambridge Economic History of Europe*, vol. VII (Cambridge, 1978), pp. 308–416

Druzhinin, N. K. (ed.), *Usloviya byta rabochikh v dorevolyutsionnoi Rossii (po dannym byudzhetnykh obsledovanii)* (Moscow, 1958)

Efimov, A., 'Iz istorii partiinogo kollektiva na Petrogradskom zavode "Staryi Parviainen", 1915–16', *Krasnaya Letopis'*, 3(1926) pp. 41–2

Elwood, R. C., *Russian Social Democracy in the Underground. A Study of the RSDRP in the Ukraine 1907–1914* (Assen, 1974)

Engelstein, Laura, *Moscow, 1905. Working Class Organisation and Political Conflict* (Stanford, CA, 1982)

Falkus, M., *The Industrialization of Russia, 1700–1914* (London: Macmillan, 1972)

Fedor, T. S., *Patterns of Urban Growth in the Russian Empire during the Nineteenth Century* (Chicago, 1975)

Fried, Robert C., 'Urbanization and Italian Politics', *Journal of Politics*, 29, no. 3 (1967)

Futrell, M., *Northern Underground – Episodes of Russian Revolutionary Transport and Communications through Scandinavia and Finland, 1863–1917* (London, 1963)

Galai, Shmuel, *The Liberation Movement in Russia 1900–1905* (Cambridge University Press, 1973)

Garvi, P. A., *Zapiski Sotsial Demokrata (1906–1921)* (Newtonville, MA, 1982)

Gerschenkron, A., 'Agrarian Policies and Industrialization: Russia, 1861–1917', *Cambridge Economic History of Europe*, vol. VI (Cambridge, 1966), pp. 706–800

Gerschenkron, A., *Economic Backwardness in Historical Perspective* (Cambridge, MA, 1962)

Gerschenkron, A., *Europe in the Russian Mirror* (Cambridge, MA, 1970)

Gerschenkron, A., 'Problems and Patterns of Russian Economic Development', in C. E. Black (ed.), *The Transformation of Russian Society* (Cambridge, MA, 1960)

Ginev, V. N., *Agrarnyi vopros i melkoburzhuaznye partii v Rossii v 1917g* (Leningrad, 1977)

Glicksman, Jerzy G., 'The Russian Urban Worker', in C. E. Black (ed.), *The Transformation of Russian Society* (Cambridge, MA, 1960)

Goldsmith, R. W., 'The Economic Growth of Tsarist Russia, 1860–1913', *Economic Development and Cultural Change*, 9(1961), pp. 441–75

Golubev, I. V., 'Vospominaniya o Peterburgskom professional'nom soyuze metallistov (1907–8gg), *Krasnaya Letopis'*, 8(1923), pp. 234–7

Gordeev-Bitner, M., 'Boevaya druzhina v 1905g. za Nevskoi zastavoi', *Krasnaya Letopis'*, 5(1926), pp. 101–9

Gorev, B. I., 'Apoliticheskiya i antiparlamentskiya gruppy', *Obshchestvennoe dvizhenie v Rossii v nachale XX-go veka* (St. Petersburg, 1914)

Gorovoi, F. S., 'Vliyanie reformy 1861 goda na formirovanie rabochego klassa

Urala', *Iz istorii rabochego klassa Urala (sbornik statei)* (Perm', 1961), pp. 156–65

Gregory, P., 'Economic Growth and Structural Change in Tsarist Russia: A Case of Modern Economic Growth?', *Soviet Studies*, vol. 23, no. 3(1972), pp. 418–35

Grinevich, V., *Professional'noe dvizhenie rabochikh v Rossii* (3rd. edn, Moscow, 1923)

Guliev, A. N., *Bakinskii proletariat v gody novogo revolyutsionnogo pod"ema* (Baku, 1963)

Gusev, K. V., *Partiya eserov: ot melkoburzhuaznogo revolyutsionarizma k kontrrevolyutsii* (Moscow, 1975)

Haimson, Leopold, *The Russian Marxists and the Origins of Bolshevism* (Cambridge, MA, 1955)

Haimson, Leopold, 'The Problem of Social Stability in Urban Russia, 1905–17', in *Slavic Review*, no. 23 (1964), pp. 619–642; no. 24 (1965) pp. 1–22

Hamm, Michael F (ed.) *The City in Russian History* (University of Kentucky, 1976)

Hanagan, Michael P., *The Logic of Solidarity – Artisans and Industrial Workers in Three French Towns: 1871–1914* (1980)

Hasegawa, Tsuoshi, *The February Revolution: Petrograd, 1917* (Washington, 1981)

Healy, A. E., *The Russian Autocracy in Crisis 1905–1907* (Hamden, Conn., 1976)

Hildermeier, Manfred, *Die Sozialrevolutionäre Partei Russlands: Agrarsozialismus und Modernisierung im Zarenreich (1900–1914)* (Böhalu, Cologne and Vienna, 1978)

Hildermeier, Manfred, 'The Terrorist Strategies of the Socialist-Revolutionary Party in Russia, 1900–1914', in W. J. Mommsen and G. Hirschfeld, *Social Protest, Violence and Terror in Nineteenth and Twentieth Century Europe* (London, 1982) pp. 80–7

Hildermeier, Manfred, 'Neo-populism and Modernization: The Debate on Theory and Tactics in the Socialist-Revolutionary Party, 1905–1914', *Russian Review*, vol. 34, no. 4 (1975), pp. 453–76

Hosking, G., *The Russian Constitutional Experiment: Government and Duma 1907–1914* (London, 1973)

Hussain, Athar, and Tribe, Keith, *Marxism and the Agrarian Question*, vol. II, *Russian Marxism and the Peasantry, 1861–1930* (London, 1982)

Ibragimov, Z., *Soyuz neftepromyshlennykh rabochikh v period Stolypinskoi reaktsii* (IMEL, 1946)

Ionescu, G., and E. Gellner (eds), *Populism – Its Meanings and Characteristics* (London, 1969)

Ivanov, B., *Professional'noe dvizhenie rabochikh khlebo-pekarno-konditerskogo proizvodstva Petrograda i gubernii s 1903–17gg* (Moscow, 1920)

Iz istorii rabochego klassa Urala (sbornik statei) (Perm', 1961)

Johnson, R. E., *Peasant and Proletarian – The Working Class of Moscow in the Late Nineteenth Century* (New Brunswick/Rutgers, 1979)

Keep, J. H. L., *The Rise of Social Democracy in Russia* (Oxford, 1963)

Khromov, P. A., *Ekonomika Rossii perioda promyshlennogo kapitalizma* (Moscow, 1963)

Khromov, P. A., *Ekonomicheskaya istoriya SSSR perioda promyshlennogo i monopolisticheskogo kapitalizma v Rossii* (Moscow, 1982)

Koenker, Diane, *Moscow Workers in the 1917 Revolution* (Princeton, 1981)

Koenker, Diane, 'The Evolution of Party Consciousness in 1917 – The Case of the Moscow Workers', *Soviet Studies*, xxx (January, 1978), pp. 38–62

Krasil'nikov, V., 'Za Moskovskoi zastavoi v 1908–11gg.', *Krasnaya Letopis'*, 9(1924), pp. 115–18.

Kruze, E. E., *Polozhenie rabochego klassa Rossii v 1900–1914 godakh* (Leningrad, 1976)

Kruze, E. E., 'Rabochie Peterburga v gody novogo revolyutsionnogo pod"ema, in *Istoriya rabochikh Leningrada* (Leningrad, 1972)

Kruze, E. E., and D. G. Kutsentov, 'Naselenie Peterburga' in: *Ocherki Istorii Leningrada*, vol. III (Akademiya Nauk SSSR, 1956)

Lane, David, *The Roots of Russian Communism. A Social and Historical Study of Russian Social Democracy, 1898–1907* (Assen, 1969)

Laverychev, V. Ya., *Tsarizm i rabochii vopros v Rossii (1861–1917 gody)* (Moscow, 1972)

Lenin, V. I., *Polnoe sobranic sochinenii*, 5th edn, vols. 12, 14 (Moscow, 1962)

Lenin, V. I., *The Development of Capitalism in Russia* (London, 1977)

Levanov, B. V., *Iz istorii bor'by bol'shevistskoi partii protiv eserov v gody pervoi russkoi revolyutsii* (Leningrad, 1974)

Levin, A., *The Second Duma: A Study of the Social Democratic Party and the Constitutional Experiment* (Yale, 1940)

Lyashchenko, P. I., *History of the National Economy of Russia to the 1917 Revolution* (New York, 1949; 2nd end, 1970)

McKay, J. P., *Pioneers for Profit: Foreign Entrepreneurship and Russian Industrialisation, 1885–1913* (Chicago, 1970)

Makharadze, Filipp, *Ocherki revolyutsionnogo dvizheniya v Zakavkaz'e* (Tiflis, 1927)

Mandel, David, *The Petrograd Workers and the Fall of the Old Regime* (London: Macmillan, 1983)

Maslov, P. P., 'Narodnicheskie partii', *Obshchestvennoe dvizhenie v Rossii v nachale XX-go veka* (St. Petersburg, 1914), vol. III, bk 5

Mendel, A. P., *Dilemmas of Progress in Tsarist Russia: Legal Marxism and Legal Populism* (Cambridge, MA, 1961)

Mendelsohn, Ezra, *Class Struggle in the Pale: The Formation Years of the Jewish Workers' Movement in Tsarist Russia* (Cambridge, 1970)

Mikhailov, A., 'Vybory vo vtoruyu Dumu v Peterburgskoi rabochei kurii', *Otzvuki* (August, 1907), pp. 41–53

Mitel'man, M., V. Glebov and A. Ul'yanskii, *Istoriya Putilovskogo zavoda, 1801–1917gg.* (4th edn, Moscow, 1961)

Mommsen, W. J. and G. Hirschfeld, *Social Protest, Violence and Terror in Nineteenth and Twentieth Century Europe* (London, 1982)

Munting, R., 'Outside Earnings in the Russian Peasant Farm – the Case of Tula Province 1900–1917', *Journal of Peasant Studies*, 3(1976), pp. 428–47

Nardova, V. A., 'Proletariat stolitsy v gody reaktsii', in *Istoriya rabochikh Leningrada* (1972)

Nelson, Joan M., *Access to Power: Politics and the Urban Poor in Developing Nations* (Princeton, 1979)

Nelson, Joan M., *Migrants, Urban Poverty and Instability in Developing Nations* (Cambridge, MA, 1969)

Nove, A., *An Economic History of the USSR* (London, 1979)

Obshchestvennoe dvizhenie v Rossii v nachale XX-go veka. Pod redaktsii L. Martova, P. Maslova i A. Potresova (Petersburg, 1914)

'*Obukhovtsy' – istoriya zavoda 'Bol'shevik' (byvshego obukhovskogo staleliteinogo zavoda)* (2nd edn, Leningrad, 1965)

Ocherkii istorii Leningradskoi organizatsii KPSS, vol. I (Leningrad, 1980)

Ocherki istorii Leningrada (Akademiya Nauk, SSSR, 1956)

Perrie, M. P., *The Agrarian Policy of the Russian Socialist-Revolutionary Party from its Origins through the Revolution of 1905–1907* (Cambridge, 1976)

Perrie, M. P., 'Political and Economic Terror in the Tactics of the Russian Socialist-Revolutionary Party before 1914', in W. J. Mommsen and G. Hirschfeld, *Social Protest, Violence and Terror in Nineteenth and Twentieth Century Europe* (London, 1982)

Perrie, M. P. (ed.), *Protokoly pervogo s"ezda Partii Sotsialistov-Revolyutsionerov. Dobavlenie k protokolam pervogo s"ezda Partii Sotsialistov-revolyutsionerov, December 1905–January 1906* (New York: Kraus-Thompson, Millwood House, 1983)

Peshekhonov, A. F., *Pochemu my togda ushli* (Petrograd, 1918)

Pipes, R., *Social Democracy and the St. Peterburg Labor Movement, 1885–1897* (Cambridge, MA, 1963)

Pipes, R., 'Narodnichestvo: A Semantic Inquiry', *Slavic Review*, 23, no. 3 (1964), pp. 441–58

Pis'ma P. B. Aksel'roda i Yu. O. Martova (Berlin, 1924)

Pogozhev, A. V., *Uchet chislennosti i sostava rabochikh v Rossii (materialy po statistike truda)* (Petersburg, 1906)

Pomper, P., *The Russian Revolutionary Intelligentsia* (New York, 1970)

Pomper, P., *Peter Lavrov and the Russian Revolutionary Movement* (Chicago and London, 1972)

Portal, R., 'The Industrialization of Russia' in: *Cambridge Economic History of Europe*, vol. VI (Cambridge, 1966), pp. 801–72

Portes, Alejandro, 'Political Primitivism, Differential Socialization and Lower-Class Leftist Radicalism', *American Sociological Review*, vol. 36 (1971), pp. 820–35

Pospielovsky, D., *Russian Trade Unionism – Experiment or Provocation* (London, 1971)

Rabinowitch, A., *The Bolsheviks Come to Power* (New York, 1976)

'The All-Russian Railroad Union and the Beginning of the General Strike in October 1905' in *Revolution and Politics in Russia. Essays in Memory of B. I. Nicolaevsky* (Bloomington, Ind., 1972).

Radkey, O. H., *The Agrarian Foes of Bolshevism: Promise and Default of the Russian Socialist-Revolutionaries, February to October 1917* (New York, 1958)

Rashin, A. G., *Formirovanie rabochego klassa Rossii* (Moscow, 1958)

Revolyutsionnye sobytiya 1905g v Ufe i Ural'skikh zavodakh (Ufa, 1925)

Rice, C. J. (ed.), *Protokoly Vtorogo (Ekstrennago) S"ezda Partii Sotsialistov-Revolyutsionerov (Proceedings of the Second (Extraordinary) Congress of the Socialist-Revolutionary Party)*, New York: Kraus International Publications, 1986

Robinson, G. T., *Rural Russia under the Old Regime* (New York, 1949)

Rogger, H., *Russia in the Age of Modernisation and Revolution 1881–1917* (London: Longman, 1983)

Rogger, H., 'The Formation of the Russian Right 1900–1906', *California Slavic Studies* 3(1964), pp. 66–94

Rogger, H., 'Was there a Russian Fascism? The Union of the Russian People', *Journal of Modern History*, 36(1964), pp. 398–415

Rosenberg, William G., 'The Russian Municipal Duma Elections of 1917 – A Preliminary Computation of Returns', *Soviet Studies*, vol. xxi (1969), no. 2, pp. 131–63

Rowland, Richard H., 'Urban In-migration in Late Nineteenth-Century Russia' in Hamm, Michael F. (ed.), *The City in Russian History* (University of Kentucky, 1976), pp. 115–25

Rymkevich, A. M., 'Iz minuvshikh dnei (iz vospominanii naborshchika)', *Krasnaya Letopis'*, 9(1924), pp. 119–24

Sablinsky, W., *The Road to Bloody Sunday – Father Gapon and the Petersburg Massacre of 1905* (Princeton, 1977)

Sablinsky, W., 'The All-Russian Railroad Union and the Beginning of the General Strike in October 1905', in A. Rabinowitch, *Revolution and Politics in Russia. Essays in memory of B. I. Nicolaevsky* (Bloomington, 1972)

Savinkov, B., *Memoirs of a Terrorist* (New York, 1931)

Sbornik materialov po istorii soyuza stroitelei (Leningrad, 1926)

Schapiro, L., *The Communist Party of the Soviet Union* (2nd edn, London, 1970)

Schneiderman, J., *Sergei Zubatov and Revolutionary Marxism. The Struggle for the Working Class in Tsarist Russia* (Ithaca and London, 1976)

Schwarz, S. M., *The Russian Revolution of 1905. The Workers' Movement and the Formation of Bolshevism and Menshevism* (Chicago and London, 1967)

Second Congress of the Russian Social Democratic Labour Party (London, 1978)

Semanov, S. H., *Peterburgskie rabochie nakanune pervoi russkoi revolyutsii* (Moscow: Akademiya Nauk SSSR, 1966)

Semenov, F. A., ('Bulkin'), *Istoriya Peterburskogo soyuza metallistov 1906–1914* (Leningrad, 1924)

Shanin, T., *The Awkward Class. Political Sociology of the Peasantry in a Developing Society: Russia 1910–1925* (Oxford, 1972)

Shatilov, T., 'Peterburgskie kozhevniki v 1905–07gg', *Krasnaya Letopis'*, 5(1930), pp. 65–84

Shidlovskii, G., 'Peterburgskii komitet bol'shevikov v kontse 1913 goda i v nachale 1914 goda', *Krasnaya Letopis'*, 3(1926), pp. 119–39

Shuster, U. A., *Peterburgskie rabochie v 1905–1907gg* (Moscow, 1976)

Shuster, U. A., 'Peterburgskie rabochie v gody pervoi russkoi revolyutsii (1905–7gg)', in *Istoriya rabochikh Leningrada* (Leningrad, 1972)

Sletov, S., 'Ocherki po istorii PSR', *Sotsialist-Revolyutsioner*, no. 4 (1912), pp. 1–101

Spiridovich, A., *Partiya Sotsialistov-Revolyutsionerov i ee predshestvenniki 1886–1916* (Petrograd, 1918)

Spiridovitch, A., *Histoire du terrorisme Russe 1886–1917* (Paris, 1930)

Stel'nik, B. Ya., 'Ar'ergardnye boi Bakinskogo proletariata v 1907 godu,' *Azerbaidzhan v pervoi russkoi revolyutsii (sbornik statei)* (Baku, 1966)

Stepanov, A. N., 'Kritika V. I. Leninym programmy i taktiki eserov v period novogo revolyutsionnogo pod"ema (1910–1914gg)', in *Bolsheviki v bor'be protiv melkoburzhuaznykh partii v Rossii* (Moscow, 1969)

Stopani, A. M., *Neftepromyshlennyi rabochii i ego byudzhet* (Moscow, 1924)

Suny, R. G., *The Baku Commune 1917–1918: Class and Nationality in the Russian Revolution* (Princeton, 1972)

Suny, R. G., 'A Journeyman for the Revolution: Stalin and the Labour Movement in Baku, June 1907–May 1908', *Soviet Studies*, xxiii, no. 3 (1972), pp. 373–94

Suny, R. G., 'Labor and Liquidators – Revolution and the Reaction in Baku, May 1908–April 1912', *Slavic Review*, no. 34 (1975), pp. 319–40

Surh, Gerald D., 'Petersburg's First Mass Labor Organisation – The Assembly of Russian Workers and Father Gapon', *Russian Review*, vol. 40, no. 3, pp. 241–63; no. 4, pp. 412–41 (1981)

Swain, G., *Russian Social Democracy in the Legal Labour Movement, 1906–14* (London, 1983)

Tarasov, V., 'Bol'shevistskaya organizatsiya i Sestroretskie rabochie v 1905g.', *Krasnaya Letopis'*, 1 (1926), pp. 105–43

Thompson, E. P., *The Making of the English Working Class* (London, 1970)

Tilly, C. L., and R. Tilly, *The Rebellious Century (1830–1930)* (London, 1975)

Trotsky, L. D., *1905* (New York, 1972)

Tugan-Baranovskii, M., *Russkaya fabrika v proshlom i nastoyashchem*, vol. i (3rd. edn; Petersburg, 1907)

Valuev, P. N., *Bol'sheviki azerbaidzhana v pervoi russkoi revolyutsii* (Baku, 1963)

Valuev, P. N., *Soveshchatel'naya kampaniya 1907–8gg. v Baku* (IMEL, 1946)

Venturi, F., *Roots of Revolution. A History of the Populist and Socialist Movements in Nineteenth Century Russia* (New York, 1966)

Vishnyak, Mark V., *Dan' proshlomu* (New York, 1954)

Voitinskii, V. S., *Peterburgskii sovet bezrabotnykh, 1906–7* (New York, 1969)

Von Laue, T. H., *Sergie Witte and the Industrialization of Russia* (New York and London, 1963)

Von Laue, T. H., 'Russian Peasants in the Factory, 1892–1904', *Journal of Economic History*, 21(1961), pp. 61–80

Von Laue, T. H., 'Russian Labor between Field and Factory', *California Slavic Studies*, 3(1964), pp. 33–65

Vucinich, W. S. (ed.), *The Peasant in Nineteenth Century Russia* (Stanford, CA, 1968)

Walicki, A., *A History of Russian Thought from the Enlightenment to Marxism* (Stanford, CA, 1979)

Walicki, A., *The Controversy over Capitalism: Studies in the Social Philosophy of the Populists* (Oxford, 1969)

Watters, Francis M., 'The Peasant and the Village Commune', in *The Peasant in Nineteenth Century Russia* (Stanford, CA, 1968)

Weber, Eugen, *Peasants into Frenchmen – the Modernization of Rural France, 1870–1914* (London, 1977)

White, James D., 'The Sormovo-Nikolaev zemlyachestvo in the February Revolution', *Soviet Studies*, XXXI, no. 4 (1979), pp. 475–502

Wildman, A. K., *The Making of a Workers' Revolution – Russian Social Democracy, 1891–1903* (Chicago and London, 1967)

Wortman, R., *The Crisis of Russian Populism* (Cambridge, 1967)

Yakovlev, N., 'Aprel'sko-Maiskie Dni 1912 goda v Peterburge', *Krasnaya Letopis'*, 3(1925), pp. 224–48

Zaikin, F., 'Iz zhizn' pekarei', *Krasnaya Letopis'*, 8(1923), pp. 237–40

Zelnik, R. E., *Labor and Society in Tsarist Russia: the Factory Workers of St. Petersburg (1855–1870)* (Stanford, CA, 1971)

Zelnik, R. E., 'The Peasant and the Factory', in *The Peasant in Nineteenth Century Russia* (Stanford, CA, 1968)

Zelnik, R. E., 'Russian Bebels: An Introduction to the Memoirs of Semen Kanatchikov and Matvei Fisher', *Russian Review*, vol. 3 (1976), no. 3, pp. 249–90; no. 4, pp. 417–47.

Zenzinov, V. M. *Perezhitoe* (New York, 1953)

Index